TOUR OF DUTY

Action in WWII, Korea & Vietnam

By CSM Glenn H. Towe [Ret'd]

7-31-06

TO: Ashley Short

Dear Ashley

Thank you for your care for Marian at Adams Place while she was there. She always looked forward to seeing you.

Love & God Bless

Glenn H Towe

TOUR OF DUTY

Library of Congress Control Number: 2004098928
ISBN 0-9640096-7-6

First Edition
Printed in Canada

Published by
Woodstock Books
Plainville, CT

Dedication

To my wife, Marian McGuffin Towe, and my two children, Kevin Lee Towe and Glenda Rachel Towe Dina.

Acknowledgments

I wish to acknowledge the individuals most responsible for the completion of this book. First and foremost are the officers, petty officers, and seamen of the US Navy; and the officers, non-commissioned officers, specialists, and soldiers of the US Army that I served with during my thirty years of active duty; and my wife of fifty-three years, Marian, and my two children, Kevin and Glenda, who have supported me in all my past endeavors and did not try to discourage me in this one; and Dr. Ed Zebrowski who felt I had an important story to tell and encouraged me to put it on paper; Major Joe Rawl, retired US Army Officer, who, after reading the manuscript, said he was waiting for an autographed copy of the book; Tom Freeman of Tom@Caberdancer.com, who used his computer skills in designing the front and back covers of this book; and lastly my parents who instilled in me the love of my family, my country, honesty, and gave me the strength to take responsibility for all my actions.

The Platoon Leader and Platoon Sergeant briefed us and we moved out along a path to establish a position where the road went through a pass near Chindong-ri, Korea. The First Platoon was moving through rock and undergrowth screening the rest of the Company as we moved along the road. I heard the machine guns and burp guns open up and I knew immediately that the First Platoon was under heavy automatic-weapons fire. The Platoon Leader, Platoon Sergeant, FO (forward observer), and a radio operator were hit with the first burst and pinned down among the rocks. The rest of the Platoon fell back on the road. The Company Commander asked me to locate the wounded and get them out.

I moved out with my squad, put them in a support position, and led two volunteers, my BAR (Browning-Automatic-Rifle) man and another rifleman to the spot where the wounded were lying. They were still drawing fire from some rocks overlooking their position. The BAR man covered me while I determined the extent of their injuries. They were all litter-patients, so I sent a runner back to bring up stretchers with a carrying party to move the wounded down. The BAR man and I continued to deliver covering fire to protect the wounded until we could extract them. I had to cut the radio off the radioman before we could move him.

We were able to get everyone off the side of the hill without any additional wounded. We did have one man collapse with heat exhaustion from carrying one of the wounded. Then our Platoon with the four squads of the First Platoon attacked the hill. I took the left flank with my squad. We overran the hill and forced the enemy to withdraw to a higher ridge, but that left us exposed to more automatic-weapons fire. We had one killed and three wounded in the attack.

I organized the remainder of the First and Second Platoons on the hill and in the process lost two more men KIA (Killed in Action) and four WIA (Wounded in Action).

I was on one knee and holding on to a small pine tree while pointing out a target to the BAR man when a long burst of machine-gun fire sprayed the ground around us, kicking dust into the BAR man's eyes and cutting down the tree I was holding. I looked for the Platoon Leader and Platoon Sergeant to see what we were going to do next. I moved back about fifty yards from the line I had established and found both of them in a deep gully. The Platoon Sergeant had been shot through the upper arm.

The Platoon Leader wanted to know what was going on up there so I told him he should get his ass out of that gully and come up with me and find out. I also told him that we had three KIAs and at least four WIAs. I informed him that we were exposed and taking casualties and couldn't stay where we were. I asked him what he wanted me to do, attack the next hill or withdraw. He said, "Just hold on, the radio is out and I've sent a runner back to the CP to bring up phone wire. Then I'll call the Company Commander."

I was standing on the bank of the gully with my M1 cradled in my arm. I brought the muzzle around and pointed it at the Lieutenant, flipped off the safety, and said, "You are the Platoon Leader and I want you to tell me now what you want me to do, not two hours from now." He then asked me if I could I get the men off the hill. I replied yes, but I don't know the location of the dead, nor do I have enough men to carry the wounded and the dead and provide covering fire as we withdraw. He told me to do the best I could and added that he would go down with the Platoon Sergeant and lead the men down.

I returned to the top of the hill and found that we hadn't suffered any further casualties. I had the right flank of the line start moving back, taking the wounded with them as they pulled back. We were in complete darkness now so I moved along the line as they peeled off and headed back with the wounded. I supervised the move and ended up on the left flank with the BAR man. We provided cover as the Platoons moved down the hill. When I reached the CP, I reported to the CO and explained why I had not recovered the KIAs. Then I sat down and cried like a baby about leaving three men on the hill.

The next morning another platoon went back up the hill and recovered the three dead men. We had one killed and two wounded from the Second Platoon. The Platoon Sergeant was evacuated and never returned to the Company. SSG Posey, the senior squad leader, said that he didn't wish to be Platoon Sergeant anymore and suggested that I should run the Platoon because in his estimation, I was the best qualified.

I again became Platoon Sergeant, the position that I had trained for so hard in Hawaii. About six months later I was awarded a Silver Star for the action that took place that afternoon.

SOME PERSONAL HISTORY

I was born in Walhalla, SC on February 20, 1926. I am the oldest of six kids, three boys and three girls. My father and mother were textile workers. He worked and played textile-league baseball in both North and South Carolina. My mother also worked in the mills in Walhalla. Their education level was about third grade. They both read everything they could get their hands on and Mama read a lot to all of us kids. That is where I got my love for books and the enjoyment of reading.

Walhalla, prior to WWII, was a small farm-to-market town located in the north western corner of the state in the foothills of the Blue Ridge Mountains. The town was settled by Germans who had immigrated to Charleston, SC in the early eighteenth century. They bought a large track of land and built the town around the farm land. The town was incorporated in 1850. The main industry consisted of two textile mills and one cotton gin. There were two blacksmith shops and three mule barns since farming was a way of life for the surrounding countryside. It was a beautiful little town with gentle rolling hills with the mountains just two miles west of town. It was located at the end of the line for the Blue Ridge Railroad. Through a switching system, the trains always backed into town.

I can remember the past better than the present, such as the house we lived in when my sister was born. I was 3 years old at the time. We lived in 11 other houses by the time I left home in January 1943. I always tell people we moved every year whether we needed to or not. We lived in Walhalla until I was 8 years old. Then we moved outside the town limits, but still in the Walhalla area. We didn't live in a house with electricity from 1934 to 1949 and no running water from 1934 to 1955.

I remember living in a one-room log cabin that had a shed on the side with a dirt floor that was used as a kitchen. There were cracks in the floor where you could see the chickens scratching for any crumbs that may have fallen through. Half of the ceiling joists had boards nailed on them that formed an area where my sister and I slept. At that time my grandmother Towe was living with us. Her bed was in one corner and dad and mama's bed was in the other corner. The other end of the cabin with the fireplace was used as a living room.

During this time my mother's sister and her husband became crippled so my mother took them in. They took the corner where my dad and mama's bed stood, so they moved their bed out in the shed on the ground. During these hard times we shared what little we had with anyone who came along. I didn't realize at that time how poor we were because we had as much as our neighbors.

My grandmother lived with us until she died in 1944. I was in the Navy at that time. Now I regret that I didn't talk to her about the past and learn more of the history of our family during the period of 1860 to my time in the thirties and forties. She described the day her father left home to go to war with the Confederate Army. I remember my Grandfather Towe who lived until 1932 and died at the age of seventy-two. My Grandfather and Grandmother Holmes both died before I was born.

The winter of 1934 was our hardest year during the great depression. I can remember my sisters crying at night because they were hungry. We lived near a corn mill where my dad helped out and got paid with some corn meal and grits. He hunted and fished, so our meat was chicken, rabbit, squirrel, possum, or birds in winter and fish, turtles, and young rabbits in summer. After that first winter we always had a large garden or farmed in a small way. No cash crops, but plenty of vegetables the year round. I remember one year before we had our large garden planted and growing, our mule died and my Dad and Mama pulled the plow and I plowed the garden.

My dad had worked somewhere and was able to buy a sack of flour for the Christmas of 1935. To have hot biscuits for breakfast in the morning for the first time in over a year was really great. Neither my father nor mother had a full-time job from the summer of 1934 to 1941. My dad got to work some on the WPA about 1937 or 38.

It was about then I started plowing with a mule or helping cut wood for neighbors. I earned 50 cents for a ten-hour day. I gave everyone I worked for a full day's work for a half-dollar. I also had rabbit traps that I checked each morning during the winter. When I caught a rabbit, I'd clean it and two times a week I'd walk about 2½ miles to town and sell my rabbits for 15 or 20 cents each. This money was used for household expenses.

When I was 14, I started helping out cutting pulpwood. Three of us worked together, two sawed with a crosscut saw and the other one trimmed with an ax. Every time I see pulpwood on a train I think of the way we had to ship it. It was cut into five-foot sticks and loaded into a steel-enclosed railroad car. Pulpwood was cut during July or August or in dead winter. The cars were loaded during the heat of summer or cold of winter. I also worked at a moonshine still and bootlegged for a neighbor. I could put a one-hundred-pound bag of sugar on my back and carry it over the top of Poor Mountain without stopping to rest.

Most of our clothing consisted of hand-me-downs. I was lucky that all of my cousins were boys a year or two older than I was so all hand-me-downs came to me.

I had my first brush with death during the summer after I turned six years old. I contracted typhoid fever and at that time the survival rate was very low for kids.

But I managed to survive. The next time I was about nine years old while trying to learn to swim in a millpond. I fell in over my head. An older boy pulled me out, caught my ankles and held me upside down until the water drained out and I started coughing. The third time was when I got my head caught between a barn and a truck as the truck was backing into the main section of the barn.

My first school was a two-room school on the "Mill Hill." That is what the cotton-mill villages were known as at that time. When a plane circled town, we were marched out into the school yard to see it fly over. I never went to a larger school than two rooms until I started high school. Due to the depression, lack of food, clothing, and moving, I failed the third grade for two years straight, so I was two years behind my peers through grammar school. The town high school and grade school ran a regular nine-month school year, while the country schools ran between planting and harvest times of the local crops.

I was small for my age and the only boy of school-age in my family. I had two younger sisters in grammar school at that time. Just about every afternoon I would fight four or five boys on the way home. Sometimes I would fight three brothers from the same family, but they never ganged up on me. It was always one on one. It seems that I was always taking up for the under dogs.

My only fight in high school was with James Satterfield, a senior. His younger brother, Sloan, would start an argument on the school bus and then his brother James would step in when we got off the bus. One morning Sloan started on Coy Hooper, a friend of mine. After we got off the bus, James slapped Coy. I said, "James, why don't you let Sloan do his own fighting or at least pick on someone your own size." He whirled around and said, "Do you want me to slap you also?" The suggestion of a slap pissed me off. If you're going to fight, I thought to myself, use your fists. I replied, "Yeah, just try and slap me." He made the mistake of drawing his arm back just like a girl and that is when I sunk a hard left into his stomach. As he bent over gasping, I caught him flush on the nose with a good right. He let out a scream crying, "You broke my nose," and ran to the boys' room. The school paper, The Echo, asked a question in the next edition, "How did one of the senior boys get a bloody nose one morning before class?" That was the only time I came to making the Echo in my two years there.

In the fourth grade we had a teacher by the name of James Mann. He was the son of the large landowner who donated the land that the school was built on. The trustees felt obligated to hire him when he finished college. I would've lost another year except for the girls in the 6th and 7th grades who really taught all the classes. The girls would bring fresh flowers for the teacher's desk and he'd throw them in the trash can and use the flower vase for a spittoon while smoking a cigar during class. My love for God, Country, and the Flag came

CSM Glenn H. Towe [Ret'd]

from those grammar-school years. Each morning we said the pledge of allegiance to the flag and had to memorize and recite a bible verse standing before the class. That is when I recited what I thought was the shortest verse in the bible and that was "Amen." The teacher didn't appreciate that as much as the class, so the next day I had to recite three verses to the class. One of my greatest honors during that period was leading the class in the Pledge of Allegiance for the entire school year.

We had a wood-burning heater in each class room. During my sixth grade, I volunteered to be the school fireman. I was given a key to the school and reported about thirty minutes early each day to build fires in the two stoves. We had a large stack of wood at the school so each afternoon after school, I cleaned the stoves and brought in the wood to start the fires in the morning. Most of the time, some of the other boys stayed to help with these chores.

I was in the 7th grade when I had my first leadership position. I was elected captain of our baseball team. I felt then and for the next few years that there was always someone more capable than me available for the position, but I was selected or appointed to the position.

When I started the seventh grade, Mrs. Hardy asked me if I would like to go to high school and my answer was yes. She drove me to the high school in Walhalla and we went to the principal's office. She told the principal that I could do the work, so he said, "Good, and if you don't keep up with the class, you'll be sent back to Zion School to finish the seventh grade." I gained back one of those years I lost in the third grade.

I remember listening to a radio at a neighbor's house in September 1939 when Germany invaded Poland and the talk was about how quickly we'd take care of Germany just as we did in WWI. Then Pearl Harbor exploded on the scene. I wanted to go into the service immediately, but the recruiters told me to come back when I turned seventeen. With the war going on I lost interest in school, so I quit in November 1942. For the next thirty years I continued to go to various schools and seminars, but when I was sixteen I felt I knew it all. My parents wanted me to continue my education, but I didn't return to school until much later.

After quitting high school, I joined the National Youth Administration (NYA). The NYA shop in Walhalla was a woodworking shop. We were trained there to use all kinds of woodworking tools. Eventually, we were placed in a defense plant or shipyard where they used wood in airplanes or wooden boats. While I was there, we made furniture, desks, tables, file cabinets, chairs, etc. for Camp Toccoa, GA. An airborne regiment trained there. Because I had two years of woodshop in high school, I was appointed a team leader.

After two months, I transferred to Columbia, SC and enrolled in electric welding and shipfitting classes. They also had a machinist course. We lived in a camp occupied by the CCCs prior to the start of the war. We had a company street with a recreation center at the upper end. The boys' barracks were on the left side and the girls' barracks and the shipfitter classrooms on the right. The mess hall was on the lower end of the street. I was appointed barracks leader and managed to miss out on KP. I had electric welding three days each week and shipfitting class the other two days.

I got to where I could run a decent vertical bead and weave before I burned my eyes. Mr. Valentine, the shipfitting instructor, asked me if I would like to take the shipfitting class only. He needed an assistant so he arranged the change.

When I turned seventeen, Mr. Valentine talked with me about going to Savannah, GA, and going to work in a shipyard. I was not due to leave there through the normal placement program for another two months. He told me that I could read a blueprint better than most of the workers there and I was just wasting my time waiting for the camp director to send me out. The conversation went something like this: "Do you know anyone in Savannah," he asked? "Yes," I replied. "I was told by my friends in Walhalla that I could get a room where they stay." "Do you have any money," he asked? "No," I answered. "Then tell the camp director that you are leaving," he said, "and catch the bus into town and hitchhike to Savannah. Stop by my home on Meeting Street in West Columbia and my mother will give you some money." I thanked him for everything and he gave me a certificate of completion for the shipfitters course. I notified the Camp Director I was leaving and recommended a man to replace me as barracks leader. I then packed my cardboard suitcase and caught the first bus to Columbia the next morning. Mrs. Valentine was kind enough to give me eighty-five cents and I was finally on my way out into the wide world and a life full of experiences that I wouldn't exchange for anything.

I arrived in Savannah about 5:00 PM. I had no trouble catching a ride. The last man dropped me off at a streetcar stop and told me to ask the conductor to put me off at Park Avenue. The streetcar did not stop at Park Avenue, so he let me off at the next street and gave me the necessary directions. I got to the boarding house at 711 West Park Avenue in time for supper. Mrs. Eve had a room I could share with another boy from Walhalla. She instructed one of the other boarders to show me the room and for me to wash my hands and face and come down for supper. She sounded just like my mother. She watched over all of us just like a mother hen.

The room was $10 a week with two meals and a sack lunch. The sack lunch consisted of two sandwiches, a peanut butter and jelly and a bologna with ketchup and mustard. My roommate lent me five dollars and told me I would need three dollars to pay a doctor for a physical. He gave me directions to the doctor's office and where to catch a bus for the South Eastern Building Corporation employment office. The complete physical amounted to a couple of questions. I felt that if you could see to find his office and walk in, you'd certainly pass.

With the physical report and completion certificate from the shipfitters school in hand, I went to the employment office. The lady at the desk asked me if I could read and write. When I answered yes, she asked me what kind of work I wanted. I said, "shipfitter" and showed her my certificate. She said that they had very few shipfitters coming from the NYA and most were welders. She

then asked me if I could go to work that afternoon on the second shift. I quickly answered yes and she gave me a slip and told me to report to the foreman on slab number 2 at 4:00 PM. In less than twenty-four hours after arriving in Savannah, GA, I was working as a third-class shipfitter. By being able to read a blueprint, I skipped shipfitters helper and apprentice.

I worked at the Southeastern Shipyard located a few miles south of Savannah on the Savannah River. We built Liberty Ships for the war effort. The workers were from the southeast mostly, South Carolina, Georgia, and Tennessee. They came out of the mountains and small towns and off the farms of America. Men and women working alongside of each other for the same wage. Most of the men were in their forties or older and the women forty or younger.

There have been many books written about the employees and their families who worked in defense plants during WWII. Savannah was no different. I would estimate the education level was lower than the third grade and my guess was that forty percent of them signed their pay checks with an X. They were hardworking poor people trying to make a living after the great depression. Most of that group of great workers would have trouble today in qualifying for manual labor, yet they accomplished feats that haven't been equaled since. They were the industrial might that manufactured the ships, the guns, and the ammunition needed to win the war. God bless each and every one of them for stepping in when their county needed them.

I reported to the foreman on slab 2 at 4:00 PM for work. He asked me if I was a welder or shipfitter. I said shipfitter and he looked a little harder at me, then looked at the slip of paper from the employment office. He said, "I see you graduated from the shipfitter school at the NYA Camp in Columbia, SC." "Yes, sir," I replied proudly. "Did they teach you anything about blueprints," he asked? "Yes, sir," I answered again. With that, he handed me a blueprint and said, "Explain this one to me." I looked at the print and told him the number, the section of the ship, the compartment, the bulkhead, and the size of the angle iron to be used.

When I finished, he said, "You are going to be my blueprint man, as of now. There are only two of us here, you and I, who know what one of those lines represents.

When you come to work each afternoon, come by the blueprint shack and pick up the prints we will need for the night. Then at the end of the shift, return the prints."

He walked with me over to the blueprint shack and introduced me to the people there and told them to let me sign for any print I asked for. I reported for work each afternoon with a roll of blueprints under my arm like I knew what I was doing. The foreman created a lot of animosity by promoting me to second-class over some of the other workers who had been there longer. A month later, he made me a first-class and that really set some of them off. I was able to take a blueprint, hammer, and punch, and lay out a bulkhead as fast as the foremen.

I remember laying out a bulkhead one day and getting a second-class shipfitter, a woman of about forty, and a welder to tack down the angle-iron beams prior to machine welding. I set the first beam in and had the welder tack it in place. Then I explained to the shipfitter that all the beams were to be tacked down like the first one, with the short side of the beam up and facing in the same direction as the one I had set in.

I went to another section and about two hours later, the foremen came over and told me to check the first bulkhead I had laid out. I went over to the lady (I gave her the benefit of the doubt in addressing her as a lady) and after looking at the angle iron, it was obvious that she had set each piece the wrong way. She had tacked the short side down instead of the long side as I had instructed.

I told her that I would get a chipper and take all her work down so that she could then lay the beams the right way. She grabbed up a chipping hammer and started for me, her eyes blazing, and I turned and ran from her like a scared rabbit. All the time she was chasing me, she was shouting at the top of her lungs, "Ain't no little snot-nosed son-of-a-bitch going to tell me how to do my job. I'll chip that little educated pea-head off them shoulders. Comes in here with a little book-learning, brown-noses the foremen, then lords it all over us poor workers who are trying to make a decent living."

I think I must have circled the slab a couple of times because that old lady could really run. Finally, the foreman cornered her and got her cooled down. He then gave instructions to someone else to correct the job she had screwed up. It wasn't so much the advantage I had in education as the fact that a seventeen-year-old kid was making more money than they were. Here were forty or fifty-year-old men and women who had been working at the same job for a year or two and a new kid comes in and in three or four months ends making the same wage or more than they were.

I'll always remember Savannah with all her beautiful parks and old buildings. While there, I rode every streetcar and city bus to the end of the line and back. I also walked through most of the streets and visited every park. It seems like every other block had a park and at that time they were magnificently maintained. I have visited Savannah quite a few times since then, but the parks now seem overgrown and not well-tended. It was during this period that I learned to appreciate parks, gardens, castles, churches, and cathedrals.

I finally quit the shipyard and returned home. After a couple of weeks there, I went to see the recruiter and he wanted a consent form signed by my parents since I was only 17. I remember what my dad said, "Are you sure this is what you want? I'll sign to get you in, but I'll never sign anything to get you out."

With those words, I departed for the United States Navy. I rode a bus to Spartanburg, SC and reported to the Naval Recruiting Station where they gave me meal tickets and sent me to the Gladstone Hotel for the night. The next morning, they put me on a bus for Camp Croft, a US Army Camp, for my physical. There, I had my first run-in with military authority. We were in a line and I unintentionally stepped over the side stripe and some one with stripes was all over me, yelling, "You dumb hick, can't you follow instructions? Let me see your papers. I'm sending you to the marines." That's when I got mad and told him, "To hell you will. I'm not a draftee. I'm seventeen-years old and if you cuss me just once more, I'll walk out of here and go back to the recruiting office in Spartanburg and tell them you refused to give me a physical." The other people in line started laughing. The corporal turned red in the face and walked away. I was sure happy I wasn't going to his unit.

THE NAVY YEARS

I could see, hear, and wave both arms, so I passed my physical with flying colors. The standard joke at draftee stations during the war was that a blind man and a man with no arms approached the doctor and the blind man said, "You can't draft me I'm blind. What could I do in the army?" The doctor told him that he could draw water from a well for the horses and the man behind him with no arms would yell when the water trough was full.

On November 18, 1943 I along with about eight other future sailors raised our right hands and were sworn into the Navy. I was still in civilian clothes, but felt very proud to be a sailor in the US Navy. That was the first of many times that I held up my right hand and said, "I do," over the next thirty years and each time I felt very proud to be a part of the US Military defending our great country.

The next morning we were loaded on a train, the Southern Railway, headed for Bainbridge, MD. We arrived in Washington, DC, about 6:00 PM and had a four-hour layover before departing. Three of us took a walking tour of Washington including the Capitol, Lincoln Memorial, and many other buildings. It was our first time in the Capitol and we took advantage of it. We finally boarded another train (Pennsylvania Railroad) and took off for Bainbridge, MD.

I arrived in Bainbridge and received my issue of clothing, learned to roll everything in sea-going fashion, so that it would fit nicely into my seabag. I learned to roll my mattress, pillow, and blankets and lash them around the seabag. I had every series of shots known to man except rabies and maybe that too. Doctors, dentists, and shots were new to me. I had seen a doctor only four times in my entire life; when I had typhoid fever, when I got my head caught between a barn and a truck, and the physicals I had in Savannah, GA and Camp Croft. I had never gone to a dentist so on my first trip, they pulled one tooth and filled about four cavities.

Our first week the company was on mess duty. We had a consolidated mess that fed about 2000 sailors. I hadn't yet learned the military rule never to volunteer for anything and when they asked if anyone knew how to peel potatoes, I raised my hand and was immediately placed in charge of the spud locker. We washed, peeled, and prepared all fruits and vegetables used in the mess. I never had any trouble with any of the men assigned to my detail. That first week also covered the Thanksgiving dinner and that morning was exceptionally busy. We had worked until 2300 hours the night before and started again at 0400 that morning. By the time we cleaned up that evening we were completely exhausted, but felt good that we had accomplished the mission assigned to us. The mess steward and mess officer came by with a personal thanks for each of us for a job well done.

I was smoking at that time and obeying the smoking lamp was not a problem. When I finally decided to quit however, it took me twenty years to break the habit. I was in good physical condition, so all the navy training was easy for me. I especially enjoyed the weapons training and shooting at the range because I had used rifles and shotguns since I was about ten. I got my first shotgun at Christmas prior to my thirteenth birthday. I remember a neighbor loaned my dad a shotgun once. It had a thirty-six-inch barrel and full choke. He said it was a duck and squirrel gun. Every time I fired that gun it knocked me down and made me feel as though I had been stomped in the mud. Still I lied and said it didn't hurt, just so my mother would let me hunt with it again.

We had to pack up in sea-going fashion and make a couple of trips around the grinder because someone talked after lights-out. I think every company that took boot training in Bainbridge did the same. Upon completion of Boot Camp, I was promoted to Seaman Second-Class and received nine days leave. I went home to show off my uniform. I am just as proud of my uniform today as I was that day sixty years ago. When I returned to Bainbridge after boot leave, I volunteered for submarine service, but was selected for gunners-mate school instead. Gunners-mate school lasted twelve weeks and because I made good grades, I was rewarded with liberty pass each weekend.

The Pennsylvania Railroad ran like a well-oiled clock so we could go north and south as far as New York City and Washington, DC.

In gunners-mate school, we learned to fieldstrip, clean, repair, and fire all weapons from the Colt .45 pistol to the 5.38-inch antiaircraft gun. This included the Thompson submachine gun, the Lewis machine gun, .30 Cal air and water-cooled machine guns, the .50 cal machine gun, along with the British 1.1 antiaircraft gun, .20mm and .40mm antiaircraft guns, and the 5.38-inch antiaircraft guns. This training proved to be invaluable to me in later years when I was a weapons instructor in the US Army.

The east coast from Washington north was a wonderful place to be stationed during WWII. The people were friendly and the girls beautiful. I spent weekends in New York, Philadelphia, Baltimore, and Wilmington, DE. Of all the places, Wilmington was my favorite. It was smaller and fewer GIs were there at any one time.

Three of us were in a bar down on East Baltimore Street one Saturday night when a fight broke out. We were seated by the door and were watching the progress of the battle. A French sailor was trying to fight his way to the door and it looked like every GI in the place took a shot at him as he made his way out. When he got to the street, he felt for his little red beret and found it was missing from his head. He appeared to be at least seven-feet tall. He looked back to the bar and saw his beret lying there. He fought his way back to the bar, jammed the beret on his head, and fought his way back to the street. He was across the street and in another bar when the Shore Patrol (MPs) arrived. I think the fight somehow got started over the red beret and it must have been a prized possession for him to go back into that bar to retrieve it and risk his life a second time.

Half the time when you went to a restaurant for a meal, or a bar for a drink, some complete stranger would pay the tab. All the YMCAs and churches had cots set up for sleeping and bathrooms with towels for a shower. You could walk down the street on Sunday and a dozen cars would stop and ask you to attend church or go to lunch with them. There were teen clubs that served coke and cookies with plenty of beautiful hostesses, who would dance with you, sit and talk, or write letters home for you. Something that surprised me was the number of men in the service that couldn't write. Postage was free so the ladies would provide stationary, write a letter home, and even mail it for you. There were plenty of bars for those who wished to drink. I corresponded with one girl I met there until 1950.

At the end of April, 1944, I graduated from Gunners-Mate School and was promoted to seaman first-class (that was the equivalent of corporal). I had a pass every night until we shipped out. That was a time to go to all the friends I had made and say my good-byes. I departed Bainbridge, MD on a troop train for San Diego, CA. We went through Chicago, Denver, Las Vegas, and Los Angeles.

It was a seven-day trip and very enjoyable for me because I had never been in that part of our great country before. At every stop, day or night, there were ladies with coffee, milk, juices, and donuts. They would also collect letters and mail them for us. Evidently, we didn't have a priority on the rail lines because we got side-tracked for all trains, including passenger and freight. We stopped in Las Vegas for about three hours and they let us off the train to look around. In 1944, Las Vegas consisted of about two blocks. It was just a small rancher's town. Since there was alcohol there, we were searched when we got back aboard. A lot of good booze was poured out, but still a lot was passed in through the windows.

We hit a snowstorm in Utah. This was most unusual for me, coming from the south. People were planting their cotton and corn back home. We finally arrived at the US Naval Receiving Station, Balboa Park, San Diego. Balboa Park was a World-Fair site back in the thirties and was a beautiful place. I got my first taste of California temperature change at that time. We arrived at Balboa Park around noon and it was a very hot day. We received liberty and we all asked why we had to wear blues, since we had changed into our white summer uniforms before leaving Bainbridge. That night around 2200 (10:00 PM), the fog rolled in like a thick curtain and a brisk wind blew in from over the Pacific

Ocean. That was when I learned why we didn't wear our summer-white uniforms in San Diego, California.

There were no fences around the base so a lot of the older sailors went and came as they pleased. I had a pass each day so I didn't have to worry about being placed on restriction. I met a girl at a service club and she invited me to her home for Sunday dinner. She told me to catch the La Jolla bus to the street where she lived. I waited over an hour for the bus and not one came by for that destination. That night I went to the service club and when I saw her, I could tell she was really mad. I said I had waited for almost two hours for the bus to La Howai and not one came by. The only buses I saw were for La Jolly. She began to giggle and told me that the J was pronounced as an H and we had a big laugh at my expense. That saved the day and I was back in her good graces.

I was transferred to Camp Elliott (US Marine Base) to wait for orders to the Pacific. I was detailed as barracks fireman in a Lady-Marine barracks. I went in and checked the coal stoves every hour. When I entered someone would yell, "man on deck." Some of them covered immediately, while others proudly paraded. I ate in their mess hall and I remember a large sign over the door as you entered. "IF YOU MUST HAVE SEX, HAVE IT WITH ANOTHER SERVICE MAN. HE IS AS CLEAN AS YOU ARE."

Three of us were in San Diego when I learned of the D Day Invasion. A kid was hawking papers on the street and one of the men bought one and we stood under a street light and read of the invasion. I felt that date, 7 June 1944, was the first major step toward ending the war.

That very day, I was transferred from Camp Elliott to the USS Wisdom Bay (Carrier Escort) for transportation to Pearl Harbor. The Wisdom Bay was loaded with F4U Corsairs (Navy and Marine Corps Fighter Planes). I slept on the hanger deck under the wing of one of the planes. The first morning out, General Quarters was sounded and they test-fired the 5.38-inch antiaircraft gun. I came up so fast that the dent in the wing where my head hit probably remained until the war was over or the plane was lost in action.

Sailing into Pearl Harbor at that time was an eye- opener. This was my first contact with the horrors of war except for news reels shown at movie theaters and news- paper articles. The USS Arizona was still sitting where she sank on December 7, 1941. The super structure had not been removed and you could see the torn metal from the bombs and explosions. I knew that very many of her crew were forever entombed in their underwater crypt as they'd been from the first day of the attack. The USS Oklahoma was lying on her side where she rolled over and sank. At that time, she still hadn't been moved.

I was transferred from the USS Windom Bay to the US Naval Receiving Station, Aiea Heights, HI. The Camp was on a hillside overlooking Pearl Harbor. It consisted of wood-frame huts with canvas covers and was more like a dust bowl than a tropical island. NOTE: When I refer to old people such as the old gunners-mate in the next paragraph, you have to remember that at the age of seventeen to twenty-one, everyone from twenty-five and up was considered to be old. As I got older, it seemed that everyone around me was getting younger. At that age, "The Old Man" was usually a lieutenant twenty-years old and up.

While I was there I had a bad case of diarrhea. About 0200, I had to run for the head (latrine) in a big hurry and when I arrived, I found all the seats were full. This being the only building in our area that had a light, everyone went there to read their books or magazines. They sat on the seats and no one offered to get up. An old gunners mate who had taken me under his wing, was in the same condition that I was, said, "I'll get us a seat in a hurry." He showed me a clever way to get a seat on the commode in an emergency. The commode was an open metal trough with two pieces of wood attached for a seat. There were usually ten or twelve seats on each trough. Water flowed in the high end and down the trough by the force of gravity. The gunners-mate stood there looking at twelve men with no one looking up. He went over to the high side of the trough and began rolling up toilet paper around his hand A couple of the men peeped around their books, but didn't look up. When he had a good ball of paper, he reached into his pocket for his Zippo lighter and lit the ball. When it was burning brightly, he dropped it into the water and it floated down the trough. It only had to singe a few hairs before everyone was off the seats cursing. He and I got a seat before any of the others began to return. No one said a word to either of us. I guess his second-class gunners-stripes discouraged them from making an issue of their singed balls.

We were given liberty into Honolulu from 0800 until 1700 hours. It was estimated at that time there were over a million men on the Island of Oahu. When I went on liberty, I could believe it. The main street downtown was wide and the flow of GIs met in the center of the street and walked with the flow of traffic. The men on the other side moved in the opposite direction. It was quicker to walk down the street than to try and ride a cab.

A couple of friends and I went to Honolulu together and we tried the bar for a drink. To go to a bar, you got into a line at least a half-block long and when you finally got to a table, you were limited to two or three drinks.

Then you were asked to leave, so that someone else could get a drink. We had one drink and gave our seats to other sailors. We went to the street where all the "cathouses" were located and looked at the lines waiting to go in, some of them a block long. We decided on a hamburger instead.

At the end of June, I was assigned to Commander Service Squadron #10 and went aboard the USS Orvetta. This was an old banana-boat that had been used as a cargo ship to carry bananas from South America to New York. They had converted the holds into living-quarters by putting four-decker bunks in the holds. It was hot and you could still smell the rotted bananas. Most of the time we carried our blankets up on deck and slept there. This was to be my home for the next year.

We were to sail for Kwajalein in the Marshall Islands on the evening of the Fourth of July. They started up the engines and one of them blew up almost immediately. It sounded as if a bomb had gone off. We were quickly herded off the ship. We didn't have to jump overboard; they let us use the gangway. Most of Pearl Harbor went on the alert and navy brass, fire engines, and ambulances came from everywhere. They thought it was a torpedo or sabotage. During the next year aboard that ship, we wished many times that it had sunk.

After about three hours, they let us back aboard. This delayed our departure for ten days. During this ten days, we were given liberty every other day. The Red Cross set up shop alongside the ship and would lend you the equivalent of a partial pay. For a seaman first-class, this was fifteen dollars. You signed a chit and then the finance officer repaid the Red Cross. My friends and I took the loan and went to the USO where we went on daily tours of Honolulu and the surrounding areas. We went to the palace, Diamond Head, the Blow Hole, and the cane and pineapple fields. We went to the Dole Packing Company where they served fresh pineapple and pineapple juice with cookies. That was when I learned for stealing a pineapple, the deck-court fine was fifty dollars. This was equal to a month's pay for a seaman or private.

Believe it or not, we never did return to check the lines at the cat houses. All the houses of prostitution had been closed by the next time I was ashore in Honolulu in April 1947. We sailed to Kwajalain in the Marshall Islands and began work on 5.38 antiaircraft ammunition and the VT fuse. This was a top-secret project and the ammo couldn't be fired over land because the Japanese might recover a dud and learn what was shooting down so many of their planes. The fuse had a sending and receiving unit. When the round passed within seventy feet of a solid object it exploded automatically.

We were broken down into three or four-man crews. When the fleet came in, we went aboard the ships and changed the fuses and batteries in the antiaircraft ammunition. I got aboard just about all the battleships, cruisers, destroyers, and aircraft carriers in the Pacific. I was also aboard the British battleships, HMS King George V, HMS Admiral Howe, and the aircraft carrier Illustrious. We were aboard each ship from 4 hours to three days according to the amount of work needed. We would report to the gunnery officer and describe how we set up and worked. He'd have a chief or petty officer get a detail of men. We worked with an assembly line. One man unscrewed the fuse and handed it to the next man who replaced the battery. Then he passed it to one of our team, where we removed the current modification number and stamped a new lot or model number. Then we replaced the fuse into the shell. The shell was filled with a yellow powder called explosive D. Each shell weighed about fifty-three pounds. The ship's crew would bring the rounds up to the work detail and return them to the ammo locker or magazine where they were stored. After working around explosive D without shirts, we all turned a yellow color. Someone just coming out from the states would ask if we were sick or something and we told them simply that is what happens when you stay in the Pacific too long.

In early August we sailed to Eniwetok in the Marshall Islands and continued to work with the fleet. The Marshall Island natives' clothing consisted of a loincloth for both men and women. Most of the women's breasts hung down like a sock about half-full of sand with usually a small child attached to the end of it. One of the chaplains went ashore with a medical team and decided that exposed breasts were bad for the morals of the enlisted men. He went to the ship's store and got Navy round-neck t-shirts and then went back to the island and gave one to each of the women. They donned the shirts and he left feeling that he had done a great service by saving the morals of the enlisted men. Two days later, he returned to the island and just stood in shock at what he saw. Each of the women still had on the t-shirts, but two round holes had been cut in the front for the breasts to hang out.

That was also my first time to observe a person with elephantiasis. There was an old man who weighed all of seventy pounds and his testicles were so large that he carried them around in a crude wheelbarrow. I'd read of this disease, but was still shocked when I saw it for the first time.

In October, we sailed again, this time for Uthliti in the Caroline Islands. Here we really got busy because the fleet began forming for the Leyte, Philippines invasion. A lot of nights, we rigged lights and worked around the clock to keep up with the demand for antiaircraft ammo. When not working aboard a ship, we worked on a barge. Here we stored ammo and worked on outdated fuses and batteries. Two civilian scientists from Johns Hopkins University in Baltimore, MD came to test the fuses. They had testing equipment that checked all aspects of the explosive system. I was assigned to work with one of the scientists. I learned to operate all the testing equipment, keep records of our test results, and completely dismantle one of the fuses. I worked with him constantly except when the fleet was in. That's when I went with one of the crews to the ships. We had a coxswain and his assistant, along with an LCVP boat (Higgins Boat) assigned to us the same as you would have a jeep or truck assigned to the unit in the army. All of us learned to handle the boat and the coxswain seldom had to drive anywhere. I could bring the boat alongside a ship, pull up to the gangway, and hold it in place while loading or discharging passengers.

For Christmas 1944, we went to a small bare island near where our barge was anchored. We were always anchored a couple of miles away from the other ships due to the amount of ammo we had aboard. The island didn't have one tree on it. We had hot dogs, beer, and cokes. I swam off the barge a lot, but that was in deep water. Around this island, the water was so clear, you could see at least a couple of hundred feet down. I spent the entire day going underwater

CSM Glenn H. Towe [Ret'd]

*2nd Class Signalman Brown, 2nd Class Gunners Mate Towe, 3rd Class Cook
Higenbotham, Joker Bar, Tsingtao, China, December 1946*

Gunners Mate Towe, center of front row.
*We were the only unit west of Pearl Harbor who serviced 5 inch/38 anit-aircraft
ammo with the VT Fuze.*
I went aboard almost every ship in the Pacific Fleet that had a 5 inch gun.
I was in the unit from June 1944, until the end of the war in the Pacific.

Gunners Mate Towe standing on the dock along side of the LSM 447.
We were tied up on the Hi Ho River in Tientsen, China, August 1946.

Seaman Towe and O. O. Langford on pass in Wilmington, Delaware. We were classmates in Gunners Mate School, Bainbridge, MD, March 1944.

The USS LSM 447 returned to the US after WWII. San Francisco Bay. This was my ship for my China Cruise 1946-47.

looking at the coral and tropical fish. It was just like swimming in a large fish tank.

The nearest I came to the actual shooting in WWII was on the evening of 11 March 1945. The USS Orvetta was at our normal anchorage spot. The USS Randolph, an aircraft carrier, was anchored next to us. I was sitting on the fantail watching a movie when I heard a plane coming in low as if in a dive. My first thought was that he was going to try landing on the Randolph, but then I figured he was going too fast as he pulled up. Then I heard the explosion on the aft part of the Randolph. The plane had bombed the Randolph and flew on over to the island and crash-landed into the radio tower. I believe he thought the tower lights belonged to another carrier and he would get two ships as he went down in glory for the Emperor.

About this time, all hell broke loose in the harbor. All the ships went to General Quarters and some trigger-happy gunners let a few rounds go at imaginary planes. They managed to get the fire out on the Randolph and after about four hours, the harbor was back to normal. I don't remember the name of the movie, but that pilot could have flown into our movie screen and killed more men than he did on the USS Randolph.

At this time the fleet was in preparation for the invasion of Okinawa. One evening, the harbor was packed with ships of all sizes and classes from battleships to minesweepers. The next morning when I went out on deck, not a warship was in sight. The fleet had sailed during the night. The fleet finance office was aboard the USS Orvetta at that time. One evening I happened to meet a friend from the finance crew. He asked me if I'd ever seen a million dollars before. I replied hell, I've never seen a thousand. We went into a large plywood shack that had been erected on the deck and they had desks stacked with money three and four feet high. He said there was over seven million dollars in the room. It was all in twenty-dollar bills or less denominations.

In March 1945, we sailed to Leyte Gulf in the Philippine Islands and continued working with the fleet ammo supply. Our first liberty in the Philippines was to the city of Tacloban. It was really torn up from the shelling and the battle that was fought there during the landing. There was a recreation area where you could get warm beer. Everywhere you looked there was a crap game with stakes from a buck up to hundreds of dollars on one roll of the dice. I think everyone felt that they were going to invade the Japanese homeland and you couldn't take it with you.

Our next move would have been somewhere in the Korean area had the war lasted another few months. One of my good friends, O. O. Langford from Charleston, SC, a man with whom I went through gunners-mate school and often had liberty in Wilmington, DE, was a crew member on another cargo boat the same as our ammunition barge. It was being towed to Okinawa when a large typhoon struck. The barge broke its towline and was lost at sea. We received word that everyone on the barge was lost. I hated to think that another good friend was gone.

Seven years later in September of 1952, I was standing in a line at the Fort Jackson, SC Finance Office to pick up a partial pay before going to Germany. I felt a tap on my shoulder. I turned around and there stood Langford. My mouth dropped open and I had trouble saying, "You really aren't Langford, are you?" He nodded and we gave each other bear hugs to beat all bear hugs. I stood there with tears streaming down my face as he told me that a Liberty Ship that was headed for the states had rescued him. They dropped him off in Long Beach, CA, where he was discharged from the Navy. After a year or so, he enlisted in the US Army and we met again in a pay line. Then came the atomic bomb on Hiroshima, followed by the one on Nagasaki. At about 2100 hours on 14 August, we received the news that Japan had agreed to surrender. The entire sky was awash in light from flares, star shells, as every weapon in the gulf must have fired. The fireworks lasted a couple of hours at least. When it was all over, I went below deck and wrote my mother I'd see her in the near future, but had no idea how long it'd be.

Then I started the long wait for transportation back to the states. We off-loaded all the ammo from the barge and about a dozen of us moved there. It was nice and comfortable. We had our own mess area and were able to round up plenty of good food and we lived like kings for about a month. We had muster each morning, then caught a bumboat to the island and spent the day and most of the night ashore. Everyone pitched in to keep the barge and especially the mess area spotless. The petty officer in charge reported to our CO each morning as to the status of the men. The CO came out to inspect only once. He was nice enough to let us know when he was coming out to look around, so we were all prepared and shipshape. That was the last time we saw him until the day we were all shipped out. He thanked us for a job well done. He had a pat on the back for each of us and a warm handshake.

In September, most of us were transferred to the US Naval Ammunition Depot #3149 on Samar Island in the Philippines. It was located back in the jungle about twenty miles from the town of Guiuan. The depot consisted of Quonset huts, a mess hall, and about twenty-two ammunition bunkers.

I had my second attack of kidney stones while there and was sent to a US Naval Hospital. Being a urology patient, I was placed in the VD Ward. There were men in there with every venereal disease known to man. There were two people I remember from there. The old navy nurse in charge of the ward and a loudmouthed Seabee from Brooklyn, NY. The nurse must have been at least fifty-years old and rough as a cob. Her language was as salty as any sailor's. She came in every morning and hollered, "Get those damned clapped-asses out of those sacks right now," and we rolled out. One morning this Seabee was running his mouth off as usual. I don't know what he said to the nurse, but I remember her answer. She whirled around and in a voice that raised the top of the hut, she said, "Son, I've been looking at those things for the last twenty years and you sure as hell don't have any thing to tie a blue ribbon on."

I don't remember hearing his voice for the rest of my stay in the hospital. I was given a jeep and assigned to check half of the ammo bunkers each morning and afternoon. The bunkers were dug into the side of a mountain and the road ran along the beech. I checked twelve of the bunkers and kept a log of the temperature and humidity. I also checked to see that no water was dripping from the ceiling. It was a nice drive down the beach and I usually spent two or three hours each morning and afternoon just to kill time. The jetty where all the food scraps from the mess were dumped into the ocean was on my route, so I would collect any candy, cookies, gum, or other goodies and give them to the kids who gathered there each day. The adults and kids all went through the garbage for any edible morsel of food. These people had been under the control of the Japanese for about three and a half years with very little food or clothing, so they were desperate for any thing to eat or wear. The mess crew each day cooked a large pot of rice to give to the Filipino workers. They came with cans, buckets, or pots for this ration. They also received any leftovers from our meal.

One evening, I was one of the last men to go through the mess line and had just sat down to eat when a disturbance took place at the entrance to the mess hall. All the Filipinos were screaming and beating two men. About a half dozen of us rushed over and stopped the commotion. One of the Filipinos kept saying something in Japanese. We held everyone there until we could get an interpreter and the Officer of the Deck (Duty Officer) to the mess. The two men they were beating were two Japanese soldiers. Upon questioning them, it was learned that a platoon of Japanese soldiers was on the mountain over the depot. The next morning an officer and a detail of men went up with the two captured soldiers and finally talked the platoon into surrendering. They thought the war was still going on and that the Japanese would return for them. They had watched the Americans move in and build the depot. They'd come down at night and steal food. They just fell in line with the Filipinos, got their ration of rice each evening, and returned to the mountains. It is well known that theft is the one thing that will lower morale quicker than anything else in a unit. We had a rash of thefts, much finger-pointing, and plenty of harsh words. You'd go into the shower and when you came out, your watch would be gone. Everything was missing, watches, rings, glasses, and anything shiny. They began shaking-down everyone leaving for the states. One afternoon, Oats, a friend of mine, and I were climbing up the side of the mountain and came upon a stump hole full of the stolen items. We went to headquarters and reported the find. The officer of the deck, Oats, and I went up with laundry bags and collected the loot. An announcement was made for anyone who had lost items to come to headquarters and identify them. The culprits were monkeys. The depot was overrun with them. If you laid down anything that was shiny, it was gone instantly.

We had a slop chute (beer garden) where you could get a warm beer and a can of peanuts. The beer was Fort Pitt, Olympia, or Iron City. When you got a beer, you put your thumb over the top and gave it a good shake. If it sprayed when you removed your thumb, you drank it. If it didn't spray, you kept getting another one until you got a good one. We also had a "ge-dunk stand" that was like a soda fountain. If they had an ice-cream machine and coke syrup, you could even get a coke or a cup of ice cream occasionally. They also had candy bars and peanuts. Most of the larger ships of the fleet had these stands and that was the first thing we looked for when we went aboard to work their ammo.

About a thousand yards back in the jungle from the south end of the ammo-dump, there was Tubabao, a small village where a lot of us ended up at night. They had a rice whiskey that would knock your head off. It was stronger than torpedo juice (190 proof alcohol used in torpedoes). They also had a kind of beer/wine mixture made from the sap of one kind of palm tree that was called "tuba" and was very powerful. One hangover from the two mixed with coke was enough for me. This is where I saw my second case of elephantiasis.

They had a small band that played for change dropped into a passed hat. There was a nineteen-year-old Castilian Spanish beauty that had a wonderful singing voice and she sang all the favorites of the day. She was tall and slender with a wonderful figure and she also spoke proper schoolhouse English. She had only one visible flaw. Elephantiasis had developed in her left arm when she was a child. It settled in from her elbow down through her arm and hand to the base of her fingers. The fingers protruding from that large hand were normal in size. I talked to her a lot and her desire was to be a school teacher and improve the lives of the Filipino children.

On November 16, 1945 I was promoted to Gunners-Mate Second-Class and transferred to the US Naval Repo Station in Samar to await transportation back to the US. I had no idea how many men were stationed there. We lived in tents and were served two meals a day. Breakfast was served from 6:00 AM until ten, then we were given two sandwiches, a peanut butter/jelly and a salami, and an apple for lunch. Then dinner was served from 3:00 PM to 8:00 PM. We usually carried a book with us and just got back in line after breakfast to wait for dinner. If you took a book the first reader would tear out pages as he read them and they were passed back. As many as twenty people were reading the book at the same time.

Around 1 December, I went aboard the USS Biscian Bay (Carrier Escort) for the trip home. They had stacked bunks four high in the hanger deck and it was crowded. There were no lockers, so we lived out of our seabags. Thankfully, the sea was kind to us on our way home with no more than an occasional ground swell the entire crossing of the Pacific Ocean. We stopped off in Pearl Harbor for fuel and supplies, but no liberty and then promptly went on to California. The food I remember consisted of fresh mashed potatoes, fresh eggs, and all the fresh milk you could drink.

We docked in Port Hynemia, Oxnard, CA to bands playing, movie stars, coffee, donuts, and cokes. It was a very warm welcome home and considerably different from my return from later wars. I received my pay and a sixty-day leave. I went out and bought a pair of tailor-made dress-blues with my gunners-mate stripes on and was ready to go home. Los Angeles was a mess to get transportation out of the city. The only thing I could get was a bus at 0010 hours 26 Dec 1945. I got a hotel room a couple of blocks from the bus station and paid the rent to Christmas Day and for my bus ticket home.

Then I started to make the most of my stay in Los Angeles for Christmas. I went to the Hollywood Canteen and met some of the movie stars who acted as hostesses to welcome returning GIs. I toured Hollywood and walked all over Los Angeles. On Christmas Eve I went out to the Hollywood Canteen and stayed there until about 9:00 PM.

I stopped in the hotel lounge when I came back and a couple there invited me to sit with them. He asked me what I was doing on Christmas Day and I replied that I didn't know. He turned to his wife and asked her if she was work-ing the next day. She answered, "No, but our rent is paid for a full week and I still have a few dollars left over from last night." Then he turned to me and said, "Come by our room tomorrow for breakfast about 1030." I thanked them and politely said no. However, they insisted by saying that was the least they could do for a sailor returning from the war and being away from home at Christmas. We sat there and talked until the bar closed, then wished each other a Merry Christmas. During this conversation, I learned he was an alcoholic and was suffering from a bad case of asthma and couldn't work. She was supporting both of them plus his alcoholism by being a prostitute. They discussed this situation freely and it didn't seem to bother them one bit.

I checked out of my room at 10:00 AM on Christmas morning and stopped by to see them for breakfast. They ordered from room service and we ate, or rather, she and I ate and he had a couple of good stiff shots of Southern Com-fort. It was misting rain with a wind blowing in off the ocean and cold as only California can get under those weather conditions. We started to listen to the football games on the radio and about 1500 hours, he said he was hungry and insisted that I stay with them for Christmas dinner.

She ordered a full dinner with turkey and all the trimmings. We ate, talked, and continued to keep track of the football scores. When I got ready to leave, she decided to go to the bus station with me. We caught a cab and rode the couple of blocks to the station. I checked my seabag through to Westminster, SC. We went into the snack bar and talked and drank coffee until it was time for me to board my bus. Before I got on the bus, she slipped a bill into my breast pocket where I carried my cigarettes and said, "On New Years, buy a beer and think of me."

She gave me a big hug and we waved as the bus pulled out. It was about an hour later that I decided to smoke and I remembered she'd put a bill in my pocket. I pulled the bill out and almost went into shock when I discovered it was a twenty. I learned a good lesson from that chance meeting: judge people by their hearts, not their looks or occupations.

At ten minutes after midnight on 26 December 1945, I started home.

The bus trip took four days and nights. I arrived home about 0900 on 30 December 1945. During the time I was away, my youngest sister was born and my grandmother had died. She was my only remaining grandparent. I spent an uneventful fifty days at home visiting friends, learning who was killed in action, how many of the girls I knew had married and other news of the day. Many of my friends and classmates were still overseas. They had entered service perhaps a year later than I did and didn't get home until late in 1946 or early 1947.

I reported to the US Naval Recruiting Station, Columbia, SC on 19 February 1946, hoping for shore duty or the Atlantic Fleet. But I had no luck and it was back to the Pacific. I boarded a train the next day for San Diego. I was routed through Chicago, so I got to see a friend, Donald Stonebreaker, from Elgin, IL. I called him when I arrived in Chicago. We had met in gunners-mate school and spent the war together. He and his father and mother came to see me at the train station. It was nice meeting his parents.

A petty officer from the Great Lakes Training Center met me at the station and gave me orders for thirty-nine new recruits that I was to escort to San Diego for boot camp. The conductor took charge and put the boots in a car with sleeping compartments and gave me a first-class berth. I had meal tickets for the forty of us. I was told to send the boots to the dining car at the end of the regular meal. They had a special menu for meal-ticket holders. I was allowed to order anything I liked along with a dinner drink or two. Traveling first-class was a pleasure, since my last train ride had been in a troop train. A petty officer met the train in San Diego and after roll call, he took charge of the thirty-nine boots and I caught a bus to Camp Elliott.

Camp Elliott had changed considerably since I left there in 1944. The Navy and Marines were now separated into two distinct sections of the camp, the US Naval Receiving Station and the US Marine Corps Training Center.

To the best of my knowledge, they are still training marines there.

I remained at Camp Elliott, CA until 15 March 1946 when I was assigned to the USS LSM 447, presently tied up at Mission Beach. The 447 was a landing-ship medium, two hundred and three feet long and thirty-one feet wide and as flat-bottomed as a table top. This was to be my home for the next sixteen months. The 447 had been on picket duty during the invasion of Okinawa. There were only two men on board who had been part of the original crew, Jim

Westcott and Jim McConoghy. Westcott left the ship before we sailed for Hawaii. McConoghy was a yeoman and he stayed aboard for the entire cruise.

I went to Los Angeles with one of the men from aboard the ship. He was going up to see a girl he had met there before going overseas in 1945. He said they were going to get married when he got out of the navy. I hope that they did and are still living happily ever after. I stopped by the hotel where I spent Christmas in 1945.

The shoeshine boy, a black man about sixty, was still shining shoes. I got into his chair and during the shine, I told him about my stay there and asked him if he remembered a couple that I had met at that time. He knew who I was talking about immediately and knew their names.

The man had died about a month after I was there and the lady had left the hotel.

The old man on the 447 was a "bang-tail", an officer who had come up through the enlisted ranks and received a direct commission. He was Andrew Jackson Horton, Jr., Lieutenant Senior-Grade (equal to captain in the other services) from Nashville, TN. He was a good skipper and stayed aboard until we decommissioned the 447. I stayed in hot water about half the cruise all of my own making. Captain Horton welcomed me aboard and said he was glad to have a school-trained gunners-mate for our coming cruise. He said, "Your duty station when we sail or dock will be on the helm." I had run the LCVP (Higgins Boat) enough so I could come alongside a ship and hold it until we were tied up or discharged passengers. But to steer a ship in and out of a port floored me. The first time we left port, I was as nervous as a pregnant cat crossing Peachtree Street in downtown Atlanta on Saturday night. During the next sixteen months I got to the point I could have brought the ship alongside a dock even without directions from the conning tower, if necessary.

In the Navy your watches were four on and eight off, (a watch was similar to guard duty, but at sea you pulled a four-hour shift except between the hours of 1600 and 2000 when you went on duty for a two-hour shift). That was called dogging the watch.

You came off duty at 1600 hours and went back on again at 2000 until 2400 hours. This was done so that you rotated times every twenty-four hours. You didn't get any time off after a watch to sleep or relax. You continued to perform your normal duties. Should you come off watch at 0400, you got two hours of sleep, then up again at 0600 for your normal morning activities, then back on duty again at 1200 hours for the 1200-1600 hour shift. Then dog the watch and back on regular watch for the 2000-2400 hour shift. It could wear you down, as you can imagine.

Here are entries from the ship's log from the time we left San Diego, CA until we returned to San Francisco. This was called the China Cruise.

Departed San Diego 0900, 27 Apr 46.
Arrived at Pearl Harbor, HI, 1000, 4 May 46.
Departed Pearl Harbor 1300, 10 May 46.
Arrived Midway Island 1000, 12 May 46.
Departed Midway Island 1600, 16 May 46.
Arrived Yokosuka, Japan, 0900, 26 May 46.
Departed Yokosuka, Japan 1300, 30 May 46.
Arrived Shanghai, China 1500, 3 Jun 46.
Departed Shanghai, China 0800, 13 Jun 46.
Arrived Taku, China 1400, 16 Jun 46.
Departed Taku, China 0900, 30 Jul 46.
Arrived Tsingtao, China 1000, 1 Aug 46.
Departed Tsingtao, China 1100, 21 Aug 46.
Arrived Taku, China 1300, 22 Aug 46.
Departed Taku, China 1600, 13 Sep 46.
Arrived Chinwangtao, China 0900, 14 Sep 46.
Departed Chinwangtao, China 1700, 14 Sep 46.
Arrived Taku, China 1600, 15 Sep 46.
Departed Taku, China 1000, 2 Oct 46.
Arrived Tsingtao, China 0900, 4 Oct 46.
Departed Tsingtao, China 1000, 14 Oct 46.
Arrived Inchon, Korea 1200, 15 Oct 46.
Departed Inchon, Korea 1000, 26 Oct 46.
Arrived Chaishuto Island 1500, 27 Oct 46.
Departed Chaishuto Island 0900, 1 Nov 46.
Arrived Kangnung, Korea 1100, 3 Nov 46.
Departed Kangnung, Korea 1600, 3 Nov 46.
Arrived Chaishuto Island 1000, 6 Nov 46.
Departed Chaishuto Island 1500, 6 Nov 46.
Arrived Inchon, Korea 1100, 8 Nov 46.
Departed Inchon, Korea 1200, 13 Nov 46.
Arrived Pusan, Korea 1600, 15 Nov 46.
Departed Pusan, Korea 0800, 17 Nov 46.
Arrived Kangkung, Korea 1600, 18 Nov 46.
Departed Kangkung, Korea 0800, 19 Nov 46.
Arrived Formosa Straits 20 Nov 46.
(Rode out a typhoon for four days.)
Departed Formosa Striates 24 Nov 46.
Arrived Inchon, Korea 1000, 25 Nov 46.
Departed Inchon, Korea 1100, 15 Dec 46.
Arrived Tsingtao, China 1300, 17 Dec 46.
Departed Tsingtao, China 0900, 21 Feb 47.

Arrived Guam, Mariana Islands 1100, 8 Feb 47.

Departed Guam, Mariana Islands 0900, 18 Mar 47.

Arrived Eniwetok, Marshall Islands 1300, 22 Mar47.

Departed Eniwetok, Marshall Islands 1000, 25 Mar 47.

Arrived Kwajalain, Marshall Islands 1400, 30 Mar 47.

Departed Kwajalain, Marshall Islands 0900, 12 Apr 47. Arrived Pearl Harbor 20 Apr 47.

Departed Pearl Harbor 1500, 1 May 47.

Arrived San Francisco 1000, 9 May 47.

NOTE: During the period 16 June 1946 to 30 July 46 and 23 August to October 2, 1946, we had the Hi Ho River run in support of the US Army Air Force and the First Marine Division. The run was about three to six hours depending on the current and tides. We usually left Taku in mid-morning, arriving in Tientsin some time after noon. Then we were unloaded and reloaded the next morning for the return trip down river. We never knew just what our turn-around time would be. Sometimes we would load from a cargo ship in the Yellow Sea and then from a warehouse at a dock along the river. On two different occasions we ran down river as a passenger ship loaded with service personal and their dependents headed back to the States by troop ship.

The oceans have fascinated me ever since I first gazed upon the Atlantic at Tybee Island, near Savannah, GA in early 1943. Since then, I have crossed the Pacific Ocean by ship five times and the Atlantic Ocean four times. No two crossings were ever the same. I have stood watch in the central Pacific when you could read a paperback book by the moonlight. On a dark night when there was no moon, the stars were so bright that it seemed that you could almost jump up and touch one. The Pacific could be so calm that you couldn't see a ripple between you and the horizon, just as if you were sailing on a mirror. I have also seen the same ocean where the waves were breaking as tall as the ship's mast. I have never seen the Atlantic completely smooth like the Pacific, but I was never on the Atlantic anywhere near the Equator. I have survived two winter storms in the north Atlantic aboard troop ships and a typhoon in the Pacific aboard a Landing-Ship Medium. I was afraid the troop ship would roll over and that the LSM would stand up on end and just slide beneath the waves and not surface again.

The trip from San Diego to Pearl Harbor was uneventful, completely routine and very dull. Also my workload was increased when the captain informed me that since I was the senior right-arm rank aboard, I would be the Master-at-Arms. At that time the deck-rank chevrons were worn on the right sleeve and all other chevrons were worn on the left sleeve. I believe that was changed in October 1948 when they changed the stripes in all the services.

The ship's crew consisted of a number of men who outranked me, a chief motor-machinist mate, first-class motor-machinist mate, first-class electrician, and a first-class pharmacist mate, all left-arm rank. The duties of the Master-at-Arms were to sound all calls, and to see that details cleaned the entire ship twice each day. This was accomplished by announcement over the PA system. "Sweepers, man your brooms, clean sweep-down fore and aft, all ladders, gangways and heads (latrines)." This was usually preceded by the proper call on the boatswain's pipe. I never mastered the boatswain's pipe so I used the PA system. The gunners mate duties were to keep all guns and ammo cleaned and ready for action.

We were armed with a twin 40mm antiaircraft gun with a Mark 14 sight. Two 20mm antiaircraft machine guns, Thompson submachine guns, .45 cal. pistols and two 22 cal. target rifles. We had a fat lazy executive officer who was supposed to be the gunnery officer. I went to him about getting a striker to assist me with the guns and to help scrape and paint the gun mounts. He looked at me, squinting his eyes, and said, "You don't need a striker, all you need is to go to work." That was all the help I got from him. I went to see the captain and told him about my problem. He sent me to the coxswain with instructions for him to give me a striker out of the deck force.

The striker was Parker from Mississippi. If you ever asked him where he came from, he would say Memphis. His nickname was Dum-Dum. Parker was a good seaman and enjoyed working with the guns. He had only one bad fault. Every time he went ashore, his drinking got him in trouble. He would come back off liberty and attempt to destroy the ship. It would take four of us to hold him down long enough to get a straitjacket on him. Then we tied him down in his bunk until he sobered up. The next day he never remembered anything that happened after his first drink the night before.

One day the Executive Officer let me know that he would get even with me for going over his head a number of times and he eventually did. I covered my rear pretty well, but not close enough. He'd sneak around looking for poker games and collect the money for the Navy Emergency Fund. He caught five of us playing ten-cent blackjack, two petty officers and three seamen. He wrote me up for gambling with enlisted men, and I received a deck court. I was sentenced to forfeit five liberties and there went my Good Conduct Medal from the Navy.

Most of my trouble in service came from speaking up when I felt that I was right. A lot of people didn't want to hear their method might be wrong. My wife told me once, if I wanted to get promoted I should play politics like most other NCOs and I replied that when I got promoted it would be from the job I did and not who I brown-nosed. I screwed up enough along the way until I reached the point feeling I had to soldier twice as hard as anyone else just to keep even.

In the military service, regardless of where you were going, there were shots to be taken. At Pearl Harbor when it came time for shots, I discovered that the pharmacist mate was an alcoholic. He asked me to come to the dispensary and assist him with the injections. The first thing we had to do was sharpen the needles. He got out two whetstones and we whetted the needlepoints, then we boiled the needles and syringes to sterilize them. All during this time, he was sipping medicinal brandy. When we lined the men up for the injections, he was shaking so badly he was unable to give a shot. He had me practice on his arm until I could get a needle in properly and then I gave all the shots to the crew.

Long had been a Chief Petty Officer at one time. We never discussed why he was busted, but I felt that it was due to his drinking. He had spent two years on Midway Island shortly after Pearl Harbor and that would drive anyone to drink. After we finished with the shots, Doc Long and I went on liberty. We caught a boat over to Pearl City and headed for the Pearl City Tavern which was one of Doc's favorite water holes from his past. That was the cheapest and quickest I ever got loaded. After two beers, I passed out and Doc long carried me back aboard ship and put me in my bunk. Then he went back ashore because he was still too sober.

We stayed in Pearl Harbor until 10 May 1946. We then sailed for Midway Island, arriving there on 14 May. Midway is the home of the gooney bird (albatross). Doc Long was an authority on them since he had spent two years there. They were a protected species, so you didn't dare bother them at any time. They might make a nest by crossing two sticks in the middle of the street and lay their eggs. You could move the nest about a foot or two each time they left the nest until you had it out of the road.

The Battle of Midway was the turning point of World War II in the Pacific. The Japanese planned to occupy the island and be close to Pearl Harbor, but the US Navy defeated their carrier task force and saved the island. We departed Midway on 16 May for Yokosuka, Japan. This was a ten-day trip. We arrived in Japan on the morning of 26 May and stayed there for four days. This was enough time to visit Yokohama and Tokyo. I also managed to visit a couple of Japanese nightclubs to sample the local beer. There was still a lot of war damage as they had just begun to clean up the rubble from the bombed buildings. Other than the sunken ships at Pearl Harbor, this was the first time I saw the devastation of war involving a large city. Down through the islands you could blow away a bamboo hut and it would be rebuilt in a day.

I went ashore the first day in port and we had one of the large Japanese beers before boarding a train for Yokohama. Before we arrived in that city, the beer began working on my kidneys and just as we arrived at the station, I made a beeline for the nearest head. The head was a large tiled room about half the size of a football field and the commodes were just holes in the floor with footprints embedded on each side. The urinal was a long tile-lined trench down the center of the room. The most shocking thing was this was a dual-sex bathroom, with both men and women using the same facilities. After the beer, I thought what the hell, when in Rome, do as the Romans do, so the same must apply for the Japanese. So I joined the masses at the public trough.

Prostitution was rampant in Japan at that time and every scam known to man was being perpetrated on the innocent American GI. It was easy to get ripped off as two members of our crew found out the second day in port. They had watch-duty the first night in port, so they received liberty about 1300 the next day. Two sailors from our ship were walking down a street in Yokosuka, just a few blocks from the Naval base, when two Japanese girls waved for them to come to the front door of this practically bombed-out building. They approached the door and the girls motioned for them to remove their shoes before coming in. They obediently removed their shoes and followed the girls inside. There was no light and the interior was very dark as they stumbled around trying to find the girls. They called and there was no answer. When they found their way back to the door, they discovered their shoes were missing. About an hour after leaving the ship, they returned walking very slowly and carefully. We had a good laugh at their expense. It could have been worse. Two sailors from our sister ship lost their pants the same way. They had to return to their ship with just their t-shirts and shorts. They were docked along side of us and had to pass at least twelve or fifteen ships on their way back. From the jeers and catcalls from all the ships, we concluded at least half of the fleet had fallen for the same setup.

On 30 May, we departed Japan for the four-day trip to China, arriving in Shanghai on the morning of 3 June. We sailed up the Yangtze River to the Wangpo River, then on to Shanghai. Shanghai was a large port-city. I got to see a lot of the city because we stayed in port for ten days.

The first thing I noticed that was different from other ports was as soon as we entered the Wangpo River, the bum-boats were there waiting for us. They would row up along side of us if we slowed down. They were begging for anything you'd throw overboard. When we docked they came along side to sell sea shells, jewelry made from beer cans, and other items. Some of the boats had been in the family for generations. One boat that came by about twice a day had a Papason (grandfather), son and his wife, and a grandchild living on this small boat. It was at most ten feet long and four feet wide. We found out that each of them had spent their entire lives on the river aboard that small boat.

The gangway watch counted the bodies of the dead Chinese who floated by each day. One day we counted about twenty. We asked a Chinese who spoke a little English why nobody attempted to recover the bodies. He said that whoever touched a dead body was then responsible for it and the custom was they had to give it a decent burial. No one wanted that responsibility, so they just let the dead bodies float on down the river and out to sea.

They were in the middle of a severe three-year famine and people were starving to death each day. Someone would suddenly drop dead on the street and a crowd would gather, but no one would dare touch the dead person because they didn't want the responsibility for burying him.

We had a jeep that had been rescued off the beach at Okinawa. The ship was not authorized a jeep, so when we were inspected we had to show papers indicating the shipping destination of the jeep. We finally put it ashore in San Francisco when the ship was ready for decommissioning.

I also got to see a lot of each port we visited by going along with Doc Long when he went for medical supplies. Doc sure believed in treating most any symptom with a shot of medicinal brandy. This usually consisted of two doses, one for the patient and one for Doc. As soon as we landed, Doc had to report to the nearest Naval Headquarters with a request for medical supplies. He always managed to find the long way through a town or city on the way to our destination.

We usually had to stop in front of some bar, so I would pull out a heavy piece of chain and run it through the steering wheel and a hole through the left front wheel and lock it. Many times I had to drive Doc back to the ship. Three of us would rent rickshaws and tell the Chinese coolies (rickshaw boys) who pulled them, "we want to see," so they pulled us along a random course all over the city. The rickshaw boys could trot all day with a full load. We got the same three boys for three consecutive days. We rode out to embassy row and viewed all the embassies. They were not as elaborate as the ones in Washington or Berlin, but still very nice. The bars and nightclubs were in full swing, but we were cautioned not to drink the water or eat the food, so all that was left were alcoholic beverages and canned American peanuts. Not a healthy diet, but it kept you going until you got back aboard the ship. We were surrounded by what looked like half the Chinese Army one day. They began loading our tank deck with wooden boxes. When they finished filling the weld deck, they covered the boxes with tarps and placed official seals on them.

After we were loaded, we cast off and headed down river to the ocean and then north for Taku, China. We arrived off shore at Taku in the early evening of June 16. We dropped anchor and remained off shore all night. Early the next morning, we started to feel our way up the Hi Ho River to Tientsin, China. This was our first river run on a small river, so the going was slow. After a few months, we cut our time in half.

When we docked in Tientsin, the Chinese Army again fell out to greet us. One General pointed to the sealed tarp and another officer jumped on the tarp and ripped a hole in it. Then the General got a fire-ax and started breaking open some of the boxes. Each of them was filled with Chinese currency. The report was that we had carried about five million dollars US to Tientsin. It was in Chinese currency at an exchange rate of about a thousand to one. We were unloaded that afternoon and everyone aboard gave a sigh of relief. I was glad I didn't know what was in those boxes while we were anchored overnight off Taku.

One of the first things we did when we arrived in Tientsin was to hire two Chinese mess boys. They did all the mess duties (KP) except cook. I think the officers and petty officers paid about two dollars a month and the seamen weren't required to contribute. This was a good arrangement as it allowed all hands to work at their assigned duties every day.

Taku was a very small village on a mud flat at the mouth of the Hi Ho River. It did not offer any activities of interest to a sailor. The marines had a small detachment there of about the size of a platoon, so the nearest liberty site was up river in Tientsin. We were lucky in that we made the run two or three times a week and as usual, we had either port or starboard duty or liberty if you were off. The marines welcomed us with open arms because we were their transportation for the first leg of their trip back home. They gave us membership cards for all of their clubs. You could get a drink and an occasional sandwich there. We were required to be back aboard ship by 2400 hours and that gave us plenty of time for any activity we might choose.

The most poplar spot for a couple of us was the American Embassy Dining Room. They served a fresh BLT with fresh milk at a table with a white tablecloth and linen napkin. The Chinese waiters were first-class. That was usually the first stop for us and if I had duty and any excuse to go ashore, I always headed for the Embassy before conducting my other business.

During this period all work in China was done by mass manpower. I watched them move a loaded boxcar once. The car was brought alongside a docked ship and bags of wheat were off-loaded from the ship to the box car. Then they moved the car about two hundred yards back along the railroad tracks to a street. Wheels with iron rims were installed under the boxcar so they could move it on the street. Then they attached ropes to the front and rear of the car and hundreds of Chinese pulled it along the street to a warehouse about a mile away. The car was unloaded and pulled back to be loaded again. They followed this procedure until the ship was unloaded. It took about three days to finish the job.

The Chinese workers were garlic eaters and on a warm morning you could almost see the fumes rising from the crowded streets. The people reeked of it. The workers never sat down for lunch. They practiced what I called the Chinese squat. They sat back on their heels with the seat of their pajama pants dragging on the ground. All they ate was a piece of rice bread and a clove of garlic. They'd peel a clove of garlic the same way we'd hull peanuts and eat it with their bread and a jug of tea.

To this day I can't stand the smell or taste of garlic.

Prostitution was legal in China, but all the houses were off-limits to US troops. The Marine Military Police and the US Navy Shore Patrol raided them frequently. Tientsin did not have a navy unit stationed there so the marines did the raiding. They'd bring most of the crew back to the ship and turn them over to the officer of the deck. Men who were drunk and disorderly had to be picked up from the MP Station. That was usually another one of my duties. When we beached or tied up in an area that didn't have shore patrols, then two petty officers were detailed to shore-patrol duty.

On 30 July we departed for an overnight trip south along the China coast to Tsingtao for repairs. The gray marine diesel engines required a lot of maintenance.

Tsingtao was a major seaport and a larger city. Liberty there was about the same as in Tientsin. There was a large US Navy contingent stationed there. The Marines were not as friendly and quite a few fights had to be broken up. The Navy operated a plush Top-Three Club there. I enjoyed the mess because they served a large T-bone with fresh salad and fries that was out of this world. They had a very nice bar and a lounge with overstuffed soft leather chairs. The only problem that occurred after sitting for a short time was that you needed help to get back on your feet. However, they didn't mind if you took a long nap while sitting there.

In Singtao there was a bar named the ABC Bar. They had a stack of country-music records about a foot high with a crank-type record player with the big horn on top. It must have been about a 1930 model. We had a young sailor aboard that was on his first cruise and had never been away from home until he joined the Navy. Each time he got liberty he went to the ABC, ordered a beer, and sat down at the table with the record player. He sipped on that one beer until closing time and cranked that player and played country music without stopping. He never ordered but the one beer and said that two made him drunk. All this time large tears would run down his face and drip off his chin.

One of the Chinese waitresses would occasionally bring a cloth over and wipe his face.

There was also a nightclub there, The Great Tsingtao Cabaret, where we went frequently. They had a good band with the "big-band sound." You could sit alone or sit with a hostess for the price of a cherry-water drink. This assured you of a dance partner of your choice. As you probably know, it was very easy to sit around over a drink and make snide remarks about other customers. Sometime these backfired and left you feeling like a fool.

We were sitting there one night when this sailor, who must have been at least seven-feet tall and thin as a pencil, came in with a Chinese girl about four-feet tall. They walked over and observed the couples dancing and listened to the band. When the band finished that set, they walked over and he spoke to the band leader who nodded back. Then the music started again with a fast version of Two O'clock Jump and again we made our comments as couples moved to the floor.

The tall sailor and his girl moved to the center of the floor and started jitterbugging. Within a few seconds all the other dancers cleared the floor and just stood there watching the couple put on an exhibition that was the best I had ever seen. He threw her around like you see in ice dancing today and they never missed a beat or repeated a movement. They must have danced for twenty or twenty-five minutes. All the people in the house were sitting with their mouths hanging open. When the music stopped, they walked out to a thundering ovation and never looked back or said a single word.

That was another lesson I learned that night: never judge dancers by their size or difference in size.

One of the scams a couple of our crew got caught in involved rickshaw boys. They would pick up two drunken sailors and run down a side street or back alley, drop the handles and let the passengers go flying out. While they were still in a daze, they quickly stripped them of all their valuables and ran away with the rickshaw. Fortunately, our crew members didn't get hurt anywhere except in their egos. The Chinese could take a watch off your wrist while shaking hands with you. They'd try to buy your watch and even count out the money with you while you watched them closely. Both of you would hold the watch and money and let go at the same time. If he started to run immediately, you had been taken. When you started to count your money, you would find one bill and many pieces of cut-up paper.

On 21 August we headed back north to Taku with several thousand cases of beer for the US Army in Peking (Beijing). Machinist-mate Faculo asked the Captain for permission to drain the fresh water tank to the drinking fountain and fill it with beer. He received a negative reply. I think every sailor stashed at least a case or two somewhere aboard. I put mine in the 20 mm Ammunition locker. I knew the executive officer would never find it because I had to take the ammunition reports to his room for signature. I was still finding beer after all the troops had left the ship and we were decommissioning her.

We continued the river run until 13 September, when we loaded supplies in Taku for a supply run to a US Marine outpost at Chinwangtao.

During this period there was a lot of unrest in north China. The communists were advancing rapidly on Peiping (Beijing). They ambushed a marine patrol and killed a number of marines. We were fired on only once during our river runs. It was a single shot by a sniper and he missed the ship. I reported the incident and one marine officer asked me if I could have been mistaken. I told him that if he'd ever pulled targets on a rifle range, he'd know when a bullet passed close to him.

Chinwangtao is where the northern section of the Great Wall of China meets the Yellow Sea. We beached early in the morning and while the Marines unloaded their supplies, we went up and walked on the great wall. That made you want to go back to your history books and find out more about the wall, when it was completed, and the length and time that work on the wall was in progress. After the tour of the wall, we pulled off the beach and arrived back in Taku the next day. We resumed our river runs until 2 October when we departed Tientsin and Taku for the last time. We returned to Tsingtao and stayed in port until 14 October when we sailed for Inchon, Korea. It was only an overnight trip from Tsingtao to Inchon, Korea.

Inchon could only be reached from the Yellow Sea by small boats or ships as the tide averaged about twenty-six feet. They had a saltwater basin with a set of locks. You sailed in at high tide, the locks were then closed and you stayed in the basin until the next high tide.

We had been in Korea about three days and almost caused an international incident. Benny Bennington, a cook third-class, had fallen in love with a Chinese girl while we were in Tsingtao and decided to take her home with him.

The aft steering compartment on the LSM was in the farthest part of the stern and nobody ever went there except during an emergency. Benny set up housekeeping there for the two of them. He carried mattresses, sheets, and blankets to the compartment and brought her aboard the night before we departed China. There was no heat in that compartment and the weather in North China and Korea was very cold at that time of the year.

The girl got seasick on the trip from China and was still sick after arriving in Korea. Benny went to Doc Long for medicine and Doc, realizing the seriousness of the situation, reported the incident to Captain Horton. The Captain went to the Army and then all of them went to the Korean officials. A group of officials, embassy personnel, medics, military police, and others took the girl off in an ambulance and Benny in an MP paddy wagon. That was the last I heard of either of them. This could have developed into a major international incident because we also had the two Chinese mess boys aboard. They stayed hidden and remained on board. They were told to tell anyone who asked that they were Koreans. The US Army occupied South Korea at that time, so we came under army control while on liberty and were policed by the US Army Military Police.

There was only one nightclub there within walking distance of the basin. You could get Korean beer and rice whiskey with something similar to lemonade for a chaser.

You could take your own beer and pay a corkage fee at the door. I met a Korean girl there and was invited to her home. I went there with her one afternoon. It was one small room in a larger house. There were no chairs, just mats to sit on, a small table, and a clay stove where she cooked her rice and fish. The heat came from a heating system under the floor and was controlled by the landlord. There was no running water and her bathroom consisted of a pitcher of water and a bowl.

She fixed a lunch of warmed-over rice, fish with soy sauce, and hot tea. That doesn't sound very appetizing, but over the years I have eaten a lot worse and seen times that kind of lunch would have kept me from being hungry. After that experience, we went to the NCO Club for a hamburger when we were hungry.

One night a group of us were at the club drinking beer and listening to a Korean band slaughter some good American music. Dum-Dum Parker stood up to go to the head. He walked straight into a wall, let out a scream, yelling at the top of his lungs, "I can't see, I'm blind." We got him back into a chair and I looked at his eyes. I saw that they were sharply crossed.

There was a US Army jeep out front with a Korean driver. He spoke some English, so I told him to take us to the US Army dispensary. His driving was atrocious and at times, I thought he was blind, too. We arrived at the dispensary and led Parker in and placed him on an examination table as instructed. The doctor came in, examined Parker's eyes and asked if he had been drinking the local whiskey. I said yes and he answered, "I thought so," as he picked up a rubber hammer. He hit Parker a resounding blow between the eyes. Dum-Dum's eyeballs went from side to side a couple of times like a pinball machine before they settled down. The doctor explained that the local whiskey sometimes acted on the optic nerve, causing the eyes to lock in a crossed position. He advised us to prevent Parker from drinking it.

The Korean's driving had not improved on the return trip to the ship. We put Parker in his bunk and went back to the club. We stayed in the basin at Inchon for ten days, then made an overnight trip to the island of Chaishuto (Koje-Do) with supplies and aviation gas for the Army.

Koje-Do was a small island just off the south coast of Korea. There was a small Army detachment stationed there.

The island was noted for its pearl divers. They were all young women and were trained from an early age for this occupation. We went down and watched them dive. I was told they were diving in water up to ninety feet in depth and could stay under water for up to three to five minutes. That may not be a fact, but I know that they stayed down a long time and this was in cold water.

There was only one bar on the island and we had to provide our own shore patrol while we were in port. I volunteered for this duty just to have something to do. I also had less trouble enforcing regulations than a lot of the other petty officers. While there, I never had any real trouble except one time when I had to load a couple of drunken sailors into a jeep and practically carry them back to the ship. We stayed in Chaisthuto (Koje-Do) until 1 November before departing for Kamgnung.

Kangnung was located on the east coast of Korea just a couple of miles south of the 38th parallel, the dividing line between North and South Korea, There was a small Army detachment and a dirt airstrip there. They flew observation missions along the 38th parallel with L19 air- craft. We beached at Kangnung and unloaded the supplies and aviation gas and then left the beach and headed back to Koje-Do. We stopped in Koje-Do only long enough to pick up four soldiers going back to Inchon.

That afternoon I oriented the soldiers regarding the ship and warned them to be careful on deck because the sea was rough and we didn't want to lose anybody overboard. There was one wise guy in the group as always. He informed me that he had spent years in the merchant marine and that he had been over the side painting the ship in worse water than this. "Don't worry about me," he kept on repeating, "I've sailed in a lot of rough storms." I passed this information along to the rest of the crew and advised them to keep an eye on him.

He got through the night okay and came to the mess the next morning for breakfast and sat at the table with Doc Long, Signalman Brown, and me. He never said a word and looked a little green around the gills. Audrey Higginbotham was the cook on duty that morning. He had observed this particular Sergeant going down to the mess so he came down, looked at me and said: "Towe, you want the usual?" All three of us answered yes. He asked the Sergeant how he wanted his eggs and the Sergeant replied over hard. Higginbotham went back up to the galley to fix breakfast for us. When he returned, he set a tray of eggs fried to perfection, with bacon and toast in front of the Sergeant and three bowls and a dozen eggs still in the shell for the three of us. As we started to break the eggs into our bowls, the Sergeant suddenly left the table in one big hurry. I was told later that he barely made the rail, but unfortunately he was on the wind side so every thing blew back over him.

NOTE: Another lesson learned: never put on an act of bravado unless you can prove that it's really the truth.

We arrived in Inchon on 13 November, off-loaded and then loaded supplies for Pusan. We stayed two nights in Pusan and then went on to Kangnung. I never thought that when I left Pusan on 15 November 1946, that in less than four years, I would be returning to the same dock and off- loading as an infantry Sergeant in the US Army and heading for combat in the Pusan Perimeter.

We beached in Kangnung and off-loaded supplies and aviation gas and remained beached overnight. The watch had to constantly check the tide and back off to keep from becoming stuck on the beach. Kangnung is almost straight across the Korean Peninsula from Inchon, yet its tide was only six feet compared to Inchon that was twenty-eight feet.

The next morning we departed Kangnung for the Formosa Straits to ride out a typhoon. I had been through a typhoon on Samar Island in the Philippines a year earlier, but never one at sea. We had a sister ship with us and during the storm I watched the other LSM ride up a wave, stand on its stern and quiver with the forward half of the ship out of the water, then slide back down the wave until it looked as if the entire ship was going under water.

Then after a breathhless moment I saw her emerge and start climbing another wave. I knew that we were doing the same thing. When we reached the top, we slammed down and I felt sure every rivet and weld in the deck was going to pop loose. We were three days in the teeth of the storm before she relented and eased off. I had spent most of the four days in the conning tower with my duty station on the wheel. It was a constant battle between engines and rudder to keep the ship headed into the storm and not get pushed broadside into a channel between waves. We had a few people with bruises and cuts, but no broken bones. After the storm abated, we headed for Inchon to patch our wounds, both body and ship, and with a prayer of thanks for our survival.

We then headed back to Inchon. About 1400 on a Sunday afternoon, we received a call from the port authority that two soldiers were adrift in the channel on an LCM and they were wondering if we'd go out and rescue them. The temperature was about 25 degrees with a twenty to thirty mile-an-hour wind. Should the two continue to drift out to sea, they'd most likely freeze to death overnight.

The old man didn't waste any time and called the senior petty officers together and said, "Let's go. If we get caught out there, we'll just sail all night and come back in the morning." We went through the docks with the tide going out. We had a two-hour window to find the LCM and tow it back in. The sea was too rough to try a rescue except in an emergency. If it happened that we were unable to get back into the basin. We'd then have to rescue the soldiers from the LCM, no matter what the danger.

We located the LCM and tried to close with it, but we couldn't get close enough to toss a hawser to them in fear of bumping them and knocking one of them overboard. I went down to try my luck with a heaving line. I missed with my first toss and as I coiled it for another attempt, the line and my gloves froze. I pulled the gloves off and beat the line on the deck to free it from the ice, so that it'd uncoil on the next toss. I hit pay dirt on the second try. They caught the line and pulled the hawser over and secured it to the LCM.

We headed back to the basin and as we went up the channel, we could see the mud flats on both sides. The dock master kept telling us to hurry because he had to close the gates to the basin. We got in with minutes to spare. There was an ambulance on the dock waiting for the soldiers. Only one of them suffered from exposure.

We only had one casualty and that was me. Doc Long said I had a slight case of frostbite of my fingers. A couple of shots of Doc Long's medicinal brandy took care of that. The next morning, he drove me to an Army medical unit in AS COM City. This was just outside of Seoul. An Army medical officer examined my hands and said they were recovering nicely and to keep them out of the cold for a few days.

We left Inchon and arrived back in Tsingtao, China on 17 December and remained there until 28 February 1947. All the rivers in North China were frozen solid, so we performed maintenance, trained, and went on liberty.

CSM Glenn H. Towe [Ret'd]

On Christmas Eve, we went to the Great Tsingtao Cabaret. It snowed all evening and got too deep for the rickshaws so we had to walk back to the ship.

On 28 February, we sailed out of Tsingtao and for me it was a final farewell to China. I was ready to head home again. I will always have fond memories of China and that early trip to Korea. The travel was priceless and you have to get down on the level of the peasants to know the country. We made the trip to Guam in the Mariana Islands in ten days and remained there until 18 March. I walked over some of the battle grounds where the Marines had fought and died to capture the island.

During this stay on Guam, the executive officer had another shot at my stripes. A group of us were at the Navy slop chute (beer garden) and our primary troublemaker had one too many as usual and was itching for a fight. He would always try to pick on someone smaller than he was or some one who also had a couple two many. Today it was Doc Long. Doc never bothered anyone. He was older than any of us and very frail from his drinking. Fireman Bochen started on Doc by knocking his beer over. He even accused him of bad-mouthing him to the Captain, among other things. He even tried to pull Doc to his feet so that he could hit him. I told Bochen to knock it off or I would escort him back to the ship. He turned around and punched me in the mouth. At that point, I proceeded to prove to him that he shouldn't sucker punch anyone. After the fight, he went back to the ship and Doc Long took me to the Naval Dispensary. The Doctor put eight stitches in my left upper lip before we went back to the ship. The next morning I heard that Bochen had gone to the executive officer with the story that I had jumped on him while he was sitting enjoying a beer and minding his own business. The executive officer had already had the yeoman, Jim McConoghy, draw up court-martial papers. The Captain called me in and said the executive officer had recommended me for court-martial for starting a fight with an enlisted man. Jim McConoghy spread the word about the court-martial and about six or seven men who were present on the beach, came to the Captain and explained the facts. Captain Horton called Bochen in and confronted him before the other men. Bochen said he was too drunk to remember just what had happened, except that I had hit him. The Captain asked if I'd like to press charges against Bochen for striking a petty officer. I declined the offer. The Captain reprimanded Bochen severely and let us all go.

This fight resulted in a couple of problems, one short lasting and one that is still with me. The first was that for about five days, I could not chew and had to suck my coffee and beer through a straw. The second one that is still with me was the cut on my lip. The lip line healed perfectly, but after I retired I wanted to grow a mustache and that's where the difficulty arose. I had the regular part at the center of my lip line, but where my lip was lacerated I had another perfect part and it looked like hell.

While I was on Guam, I also found out an interesting fact about individual habits. We had a fireman who would go ashore and buy a pound box of choco-late-covered cherries and two warm beers. He would sit down with us and when the cherries and beer were gone, he went back to the ship. That was the extent of his liberty.

Speaking of warm beer, after I returned to the states from WWII and eigh-teen months without a cold beer, it was months before I could drink a cold one without having pain in my teeth. It wasn't severe enough to stop me from sip-ping, but enough to be uncomfortable.

We departed Guam and arrived in Eniwetok, in the Marshall Islands on 27 March. We loaded cargo for Pearl Harbor and departed the next day. We were out just overnight when a generator suddenly blew. We drifted for two days before our engine-room crew could get it started.

We were very fortunate that the ocean was as calm as a swimming pool for the entire time. Finally, the generators were running again and we sailed to Kwajalain for repairs.

We remained there for about two weeks undergoing repairs before sailing again for Pearl Harbor along with LSM 454. We landed in Pearl Harbor on 20 April, unloaded our cargo, had the generators worked on again and were ready to head for San Francisco. During this time, we spent our liberties getting reac-quainted with the familiar watering holes. I had always stopped by the Alexander Young Hotel for a drink each time I was in Honolulu. It was the first and only bar I went to during my first trip to Hawaii in 1944.

We arrived in San Francisco on 9 May 1947. We had been gone only a little over a year, but had traveled more than most people did in a lifetime. We had also been to places and seen things that most Americans would never see. I'll admit that probably most Americans wouldn't want to see them, but they were very interesting to me.

It was a great feeling to sail under the Golden Gate Bridge and know that we were back in the U.S.A., undoubtedly the greatest country in the world. We entered San Francisco Bay and tied up alongside a dock in Richmond, CA. and went directly into Richmond the first night ashore. We went to a large dance hall and all the people there were Okies. We soon learned that the entire area was nothing but Okies and their descendents. They were the people who left Oklahoma during the dust bowl back in the thirties and settled in California. Our coxswain, Yodle, went to the juke box and found there was only one record that was not country western, so he played it. As soon as the record started, an Okie about the size of a professional football tackle went over and turned the record off and announced, "That kind of music ain't played in here, and if you don't like it, you can go to hell." We didn't go to hell, but we got out of there in a hurry.

We off-loaded our cargo the next day and sailed back down close to the San Francisco docks and tied up to a buoy out in the bay. We stayed there for about three weeks before we were able to tie up to a dock and get shore water and electricity. The Navy provided a boat that made scheduled runs to the ships tied to the buoys, so we used that to go ashore and back.

Some of the crew had been stationed in the bay area before and were familiar with the best places to visit. They insisted that you couldn't go to San Francisco without going to Phonochies.

Therefore, one night we all decided to go. There were five in our group and only Yodle and I hadn't been there before. Yodle was always bragging about being a lady-killer and how the women couldn't resist him. We had just come in and were standing in the entrance waiting for a table when this long lanky blond came in with a couple of friends. She looked at Yodle and winked and he went wild. The other guys told him that was a high-class woman and no ordinary sailor would ever have a chance with her. Yodle replied, "Just watch me go to work." He took off after the blonde like a dog chasing a rabbit. A few minutes later the two left together, much to our astonishment. Yodle gave us a big wink as if to say, I told you so.

The next morning we were sitting in the mess having coffee when Yodle came in and sat down at the next table without saying a word to any of us. He sat there for a couple of minutes totally silent and one of the guys who had been with us the night before said, "Yodle, did the blonde you left with last night have hair on his chest?" Yodle jumped up and I thought he was going to fight all of us right there. He yelled, "You dirty SOBs, you knew all along there were no women there." He cussed for about five minutes more before he started to laugh himself.

LESSON LEARNED: never judge a package by the wrappings.

If the other men had not told me about the place, I could have been fooled myself because the individual in question really appeared to be a beautiful blonde woman.

We had liberty every other weekend from Friday morning until Monday morning. A couple of us would hitchhike across the mountain to Reno, NV for the week end. We'd arrive Friday afternoon and leave Reno about noon on Sunday to hitchhike back to San Francisco. At that time, anyone in uniform could hitchhike anywhere about as quickly as you could ride a bus.

When we arrived in Reno, we headed for Harold's Club. As we entered, they handed us five dollars in chips and we had a free run of the entire casino. The bar had food, so you could go in and order a drink and they wouldn't charge you for the drink or the sandwiches. The nuts, chips, and all the other snacks on the bar were also free. They gave us passes for breakfast each morning in the dining room. During the next two months, I became well-acquainted with San Francisco and the surrounding area.

At that time, we had to prepare the ship for decommissioning. The senior petty officers from each section and I were the last crew members to be transferred. I was the Gunners-mate and had to supervise the unloading of all weapons and ammunition and the transportation of the same to Mare Island in Valle Jo, CA. I invoiced everything, unbolted the weapons from the deck, and made arrangements for a crane, a flatbed eighteen-wheeler and rode up on the truck carrying all the paper work. I had been transferred to Treasure Island, but remained on the LSM until I cleared all the weapons.

When I returned to San Francisco, I reported to Treasure Island to pick up my leave papers. On 3 July, I finally got my leave papers and departed San Francisco by bus. The first thing I did when I arrived home was buy a car. It was a 1937 Ford convertible that had been painted pink. One of my cousins who had just been discharged from the Navy and I had a wonderful time for the next three weeks. It was his final fling before starting college under the GI Bill.

When we see each other now we still talk about that summer and the pink convertible with a sailor in the white uniform behind the wheel. At the end of my leave, I returned to San Francisco by train. I had a four-hour delay in New Orleans, so I called one of my shipmates, Seaman First-Class Pendas. He told me he had been in the Army Paratroopers during WWII. I knew that he'd been in the Army during the war, but had no idea what he did. He was a man who would read some military history in a magazine and then include it as part of his own military background.

Doc Long ran the ship's store and when new magazines came in, I would look through them and then start a pool with bets as to how long it would be before Pendas started one of the same stories aboard ship. You'd call him on it and he'd deny he had seen the magazine, much less having read the article. He also refused to show us the scars from all the bullet wounds that he supposedly received in combat. I missed seeing Pendas by three days, but had a wonderful lunch with his sister.

I returned to Treasure Island with the intention of going for another four-year hitch in the Navy. I reported to personnel and asked about shore duty or the Atlantic Fleet and was told that my job specialty number was in great demand in the Pacific Amphibious Fleet. I was trained to be a gunners-mate on a small ship that didn't have a school-trained gunnery officer. That would mean another LSM or an even smaller LCI. I inquired about going somewhere else and re-enlisting and was informed that my records would remain with the Commander, Western Sea Frontier, for ninety days and if I re-enlisted anywhere in the world, I would be returned to Treasure Island for assignment. And if I waited over ninety days, I would lose one stripe and most likely still be sent there.

I didn't know it at the time, but they were assembling ships and crews for the atomic tests that were to be conducted in the Marshall Islands sometime later. Some of the crews stayed out there for two or three years. They gave me my separation papers on 29 August with a discharge date of 17 November and a transfer to the US Naval Reserves.

I bought another bus ticket for home and traveled a different route. I went back through Reno, stopping there for a couple of days, then up through Ogden, Utah, and on to Cheyenne, WY, in time for the rodeo. Salt Lake City, Omaha came next and St Louis, Nashville, Atlanta, followed and finally home sweet home. The trip took fifteen very enjoyable days. As you can see, I wasn't in any great hurry.

When I arrived home from my hitch in the US Navy, I knew that I needed a job, but I didn't want to try and find a job in the shipyard again. I decided that I needed more than a ninth-grade education, so I decided to go back to high school. Since I quit Walhalla High School back in 1942, they had added another year to the curriculum. That meant that I would need two more years of high school before college, but I enrolled anyway.

School was a snap. I carried five subjects and had an A average except for English, where I was rewarded for my hard work with a glorious C that was considered average. School was not much of a challenge, so after about five months I decided I'd also work while attending school.

One day while riding the school bus, I met the girl that would be my future wife and my companion for life. She was Marian McGuffin and lived with her sister on Bear Swamp Road, Walhalla, SC.

I went to the textile mill in Westminster with my father to look for a job. The foreman said he had a job that paid sixteen dollars a week before deductions. I told him that I'd never applied for my 52-20 benefits. This was a program for WWII veterans that promoted laziness. While you looked for a job, the government paid you twenty dollars a week for fifty-two weeks. I didn't join the 52-20 club even though it was enticing. Instead, I decided to go into the US Army. If I had returned home with the rest of the WWII veterans and started school then, most likely I would have gone and completed college along with so many of my friends. At this time in my life, I have no regrets as to the profession I'd chosen for my career.

One Friday morning, I walked a block up to the Star Cafe for a cup of coffee. While I was sitting there, the US Army recruiter came in and sat down with me. I had spoken with him before, so I asked him what he had open that day. He replied with a smile and said, "Just about anything you wish, my dear young man." And with a bigger smile, he added, "Exactly where do you want to go?" I snapped at it immediately, "Europe would be nice," I answered. He said, "Okay, when do you want to go?" I quickly said, "Monday." We did the simple test and he quickly gave me a bus ticket and an envelope and told me to report to Fort Jackson for a physical on the following Monday. I wasn't involved with anyone at the time, so saying my good-bys to my family and a few friends wasn't all that difficult.

MY ARMY DAYS

I reported to Fort Jackson on Monday, had my physical on Tuesday, was sworn in on Wednesday and received all my initial shots and clothing issue. I was again in the military service as a corporal in the brown-shoe US Army before I could blink my eyes. I was told I could go home and report back ready to start a refresher basic-training course on Monday.

The only unhappy incident during this entire period occurred while I was taking my physical. Some thief, who was probably in greater need than I, traded shoes with me. I had a new pair of penny-loafers and after I finished the physical, I was the proud owner of a pair of scuffed wingtips with cardboard in the soles where the leather was worn out. That didn't bother me too much because the Army had issued me a new pair of shoes.

As I reviewed my Army records in preparation for this book, I looked at all my transfers and thought I must've been the biggest foul-up in the Army. But I really felt that I was an expert as a trouble-shooter. When things were screwed up, I was sent in to get the situation straightened out. A lot of the transfers were due to my habit of volunteering. I just never learned to say no to a challenging situation.

The refresher basic course was a breeze. There were about eighty men in the company and all of them, except perhaps one or two, were combat veterans of WWII. We were of all ranks from private to master sergeant. We received the usual basic-training subjects and all the other activities of the service, including drill duty and a variety of ceremonial formations all in the first week. The second week consisted of PRI (preliminary rifle instruction) for two days and then three days on the range. We graduated on Friday and were given our leave papers along with our next assignment. My orders were for the US Army in Europe and I went home on a seven-day leave before reporting to Camp Kilmer, NJ for surface transportation to Germany.

At Kilmer I met Sergeant Hutchinson, who had been with a tank-destroyer unit in General Patton's Army. On a Thursday night we went to the NCO club for a beer and started back to the barracks. There was a boiler-room crap game in the next barracks and between us we had two dollars so we said what the hell, let's blow it. We left the game about three in the morning with over seven hundred dollars in our pockets.

As NCOs we stood the morning formation to see if we were shipping. We then checked the duty roster for any details and if your name didn't come up, you were free until the next morning or Monday morning roll call. After roll call and a check of the duty roster, Sergeant Hutchinson and I picked up week-end passes. I sent my mother a money order and Hutch and I headed for New York City. We picked up a couple of bottles, checked into two adjoining rooms in a hotel about two blocks off Time Square, and called room service for a chaser.

After a long leisurely bath and a couple of drinks, we headed out to find something to eat. We devoured two of the largest steaks in New York and we walked in the rain to Times Square where we met three girls. One of them told Hutchinson that he had splashed water on her mother's shoes. He said in a pleasantly quiet voice, come with me and I'll buy all of you new shoes. We proceeded to the nearest shoe store and sure enough, he bought each of them a pair of shoes. After that, we went to a couple of nightclubs before we put them on the subway for the trip home.

I made a date with one of the girls for the next day. I often think that I went to the exotic city of New York just to meet a girl with the plain name of Mary Smith. I dated her every night for the remainder of my stay at Camp Kilmer. I'd meet her in Grand Central Station and we'd eat, and then go to a movie or a show. Afterwards, we rode the subway and walked about four blocks to her home. We sat and talked until it was time for me to catch the subway back to Grand Central Station and a bus back to Camp Kilmer.

I left New York on the troopship USS Breckenridge for a seven-day crossing of the Atlantic to Bremerhaven, Germany. On a troop ship, there are always many details, so I decided that the best and easiest detail for a crossing would be a head count, so I volunteered. It was a good detail because we got to eat first and could go back to the galley for coffee and rolls at any time. I posted myself at the hatch going into the mess. This helped to avoid the stench when we hit rough weather for five continuous days and half the soldiers aboard were seasick.

When we arrived in Bremerhaven, we were loaded aboard a German train for an overnight trip to the US Army Replacement Depot at Marburg, Germany. Again I saw the massive destruction of war the same as it was in Japan a couple of years earlier. I stayed there for three days before being assigned to the US Forces in Austria. We boarded a train in Marberg for Munich, where we had to change trains.

The only train through the Russian Zone of Austria was the Mozart Express that originated in Munich and ran overnight to Vienna, Austria. All window blinds had to be drawn while passing through the Russian Zone. We had a five-hour layover in Munich, so I went with a couple of other men, who had been in Germany before, on a tour around the Bahnhof (railroad station). They introduced me to schnitzel, potato salad, and German beer. I still like all three items. Later, we boarded the Mozart Express for a two-hour ride to Linz, Austria.

At that time, the first three-grader went to the School of Standards located in Zel am Zee, Austria. Corporals, T5s, and privates went to "Foley's Concentration Camp." That was the troop's name for A Troop, 24th Constabulary, located at what was a German air base during the war. This was similar to basic training and strictly spit and polish. This was the only unit of my entire career where we placed our shoes and boots on top of the bed with the soles up and polished them the same as the uppers.

Our primary training was bayonet practice and riot control. We made regular raids on DP camps (displaced person barracks), to get a head count and look for men on the wanted list. Austria was the same as Germany, every wall had a mural painted on it. I learned that the painters were hired by the government to do the painting. This gave a large number of men employment when jobs were scarce and unemployment high. The four weeks in A Troop passed quickly, but the training was hard and all new to me. They checked our records and every corporal who didn't have company punishment, a court martial, a record of VD, or an IQ of 100 or more, was reassigned to Vienna Area Command in Vienna.

I was further assigned to Company A, 796 Military Police Battalion and billeted in the city of Vienna. I found out that an IQ of 134 impressed a lot of people and would get me into any school in the Army. Vienna was controlled by the four powers, the US Army, the British, the French, and the Russian Military. The city was divided into zones called Besatzungs. Each unit patrolled their own zones except for the First Besatzung, which was known as the International Zone and the controlling power changed each month.

The Russians would relieve us and when they lowered our flag, they allowed it to fall on the ground most of the time and we had to leave it there until they completed their ceremony. Company A pulled guard duty and street patrol, both walking and motorized. I guarded a chocolate factory. I had to check all people as they left the plant for stolen chocolate.

I had guard duty at the check point where the autobahn entered Vienna from the Russian Zone. We logged in every vehicle entering or leaving Vienna. This was a rough post. The day shift was ten hours and the night shift was fourteen hours with no provisions for a break. There was one post that I enjoyed and that was being guard at the (VAC) Vienna Area Command Building. You stood guard in the lobby, just outside the Commanding General's Office. There were only two drawbacks. Our Eighth Special Order was "I will stand at parade rest except when saluting or rendering other military courtesies." The other was the clock. It was a large wall clock that hung in full view. It didn't have a second hand and the minute hand only moved on the full minute. You could go to sleep or go completely nuts waiting for the minute hand to drop, especially during the midnight to 8:00 AM shift. There were four of us Corporals assigned to this duty and we had twenty-four hours off between shifts.

On September 1, 1948, I was promoted to Buck Sergeant. It was one of the most prized ranks in the Army at that time. On October 1, 1948, they changed the rank structure and dropped the buck-sergeant rank from the US Army. I continued to wear the Buck-Sergeant chevrons until I was promoted to Staff Sergeant when the Korean War began and nobody ever told me to change the chevrons back to Corporal. When I got my promotion, I was moved from VAC duty to Desk Sergeant in the Grienzing District and started Desk-Sergeant school.

During this period I also completed my high school GED. Passing this test gave me a high-school equivalency. For the next ten years, various commanders talked to me about applying to OCS and becoming an officer. This also left me open for all schools that the unit did not have another qualified NCO to attend. I always enjoyed school and you'll see that I was detailed or I volunteered for my share of them.

Company B and D pulled the same type of duties that we did in A Company. Company C had the International Patrol that consisted of a military policeman from each of the four powers. They rode in an open command car left over from WWII. The American was always the driver and they all ate in our mess hall. If the Russians got teed-off at the US for some reason, the Russian member of the patrol was then forbidden to eat in our mess. He sat at attention while the other members of the patrol ate.

My first of many encounters with the IG (Inspector General) happened there. The (CID) Criminal Investigation Division had broken up a ring of auto thieves and black marketeers. They were stealing cars from military personal and moving them to the Russian Zone for sale. One of the GIs was in our stockade waiting to be moved to Germany for court-martial. I was Sergeant of the Guard at the time and responsible for seeing that the prisoners ate.

We marched the average prisoners over to the mess as a group, but this bad guy was to be personally escorted to the mess by the Sergeant of the Guard or a Corporal of the Guard. On the way over he told me that he felt like running and he didn't think I had the guts to shoot him. I told him, you sorry SOB, any time you feel like it, take off. I unholstered my .45, slid a round into the chamber, and said I'm ready. He didn't utter another word. We entered the mess and while he ate I laid the loaded .45 on the table. After he ate, I escorted him back to his cell. I locked him in and unloaded my pistol. He said, "I believe you would have shot me if I had taken off." All I said was, you'll never know.

Later, I was called in to see the IG. His report stated that I had pulled a loaded weapon and threatened the prisoner for no reason. I told the IG exactly what had happened and I didn't wish to serve time because I let a prisoner escape. He told me he understood the situation and I should be extremely careful while guarding prisoners. I thanked him and left his office. When they were bringing this prisoner out of the stockade in chains for the trip to Germany, a loaded .45 slipped out of his belt, down his leg and out on the floor. He laughed and said I have another one in my belt.

In the 1960s, I lived next to one of the CID Agents that investigated the case. He had testified as a witness at the court-martial and told me the prisoner had received life in the US Army Prison, Fort Leavenworth, KS. We lived in an old Austrian Army Barracks. It was said that troops had lived in the barracks for over four hundred years. I would often lie in by bunk at night and think about being a soldier and living in those barracks many years ago.

There was a black trucking company located in Vienna, that had white officers and black enlisted men. Over the course of a couple of months I picked up four or five soldiers from the company for curfew violations. I gave them

Cpl Glenn H. Towe in front of the chapel at Schofield Barracks, Oahu, Hawaii, May 1950.

Company I, 5th Regimental Combat Team, Schofield Barracks, Hawaii, December 1949

a ride to the Company and turned them over to the Charge of Quarters. Each one begged not to give him a ticket or he'd never get another pass.

The First Sergeant had been in the army ten years, since 1938, and was the size of a medium tank. He stood six-foot-four and weighed about two hundred and fifty pounds. He called me one day and asked me if I could stop by and see him when I was in the area because he'd like to have a talk with me. I rode a street car over one afternoon about 4:00 PM. He thanked me for bringing his soldiers to the CQ and not giving them a ticket. Tickets counted against the entire Company and this reflected on the top-kick and Company Commander. He told me to bring them to him and he would take care of them.

He asked me to go around the corner with him to the Company Club. The Club opened at 1:00 PM each day for the enlisted men who were off duty. It had bat-wing doors and was a noisy place. He said, "Watch this," and opened the doors. They had a live band that instantly stopped playing and every one stopped talking when we entered. One girl started to talk and at least four men hissed her at once to be quiet. We finished our drinks and walked to the door. He turned and said, "Carry on." The band began playing and the talk resumed. As a Corporal, I talked with this First Sergeant for about an hour and a half. To this day I still rate him in the top-three First Sergeants I ever met. He talked of his love for the army, how he cared for his troops and the knowledge and leadership skills required of a First Sergeant. He also told me I was on the right track in taking care of all the soldiers regardless of rank or color.

One of the most comical incidents of my military career happened here. We had a large German flack tower that stood just outside my squad window. The officers were out preparing for a ceremony near the flack tower when a car came to a screeching halt and a woman jumped out with what appeared to be a tire iron in her hand. During this period, every unit in the army had a VD Lecture once each month and it was a mandatory formation for every soldier. Our VD Officer at that time was LT Morall, and it was his wife who came out of that car like a raging tigress. She chased him around that flack tower three or four times, constantly screaming at the top of her voice, "You sorry SOB, you'll never give me another dose of the clap." He kept saying, "Let me explain." He finally ran out the gate and she got back into her car and left. You can easily understand the reaction of the troops when LT Morall came into the room for his next VD lecture. The troops started laughing and he walked out. That was the last time I saw him. He was either transferred somewhere or booted out of the army.

I dated two girls while I was there, Anna and Greta. Each came from a completely different social and family background. They were both around twenty-years old and remembered when the Germans first came to Vienna. Anna was the daughter of a doctor and Greta was the daughter of a Stube (pub) owner. The doctor was conscripted into the German Army as a physician and later was a participant in the invasion of France. The other man went into the German Army as an infantryman and fought on the Russian front.

I met both of the fathers. They refused to talk about their military experiences except to say that it was too terrible to discuss. Anna was a college student and loved the finer things in life. Each time I saw her she had an itinerary for us to follow. We visited the Schonberg Castle, all the museums, art galleries, and cathedrals in the US, French, and British Zones of Vienna. Her desire was to finish college, marry an American, live in the US and get a PhD. All this was well over a poor boy's head from South Carolina. Still, I enjoyed it all and felt that maybe some of her intellectual prowess would rub off on me.

She knew all the best restaurants that had table cloths with cloth napkins and more silverware than our entire family used when I was a kid. She was not above having me doing a little black marketeering to afford these elite places. I could pay for a good meal, desert, and a glass of wine with a bar of soap or some cigarettes.

While we were at the Schonberg Castle, she told me a story that was difficult to believe. She had a remarkable knowledge of the history of Vienna and if she made up the story, it's a good one. There was an Empress with wanton ways who ruled the Empire a couple of centuries ago. She was a beauty and all the officers of the palace constantly took peeks at her every time they had a chance. When she caught one of them admiring her, she'd look him over carefully and if he caused her passions to rise, she invited him to her quarters for the night. After a night of insatiable lovemaking, she had the palace surgeon amputate his penis the next morning and preserve it in a bottle of alcohol. She did this so that the man couldn't go out and have sex with another woman and proudly say, I slept with the Empress.

Greta was happy in her environment and wanted nothing more than to marry an Austrian man and work as a barmaid in the stube (pub) until her father retired or died. The stube had been in the family for over a hundred and fifty years and she desired to keep it in the family. The only reason she dated GIs was to attend American movies at the army theaters. She had studied English in school prior to the war and used the movies to improve it. I believe she would have watched movies twenty-four hours a day if they were available.

The Grinzing District was along the Danube River and the entire area was full of vineyards. One tradition of the stube owners took place on a certain Sunday each year. They packed a picnic basket and the family walked from one vineyard to the next sampling the current wine. After visiting all the winegrowers, they returned to their choice of the current vintage, spread their tablecloth on a table and had lunch. This was a sign that he would purchase his next year's wine supply from that vineyard.

One Sunday, she invited me to go along with the family to sample the wines. She packed a separate basket for us so that we wouldn't have to stay with her father constantly. All the vineyard owners knew her from her former trips with her father, so they treated us like royalty. She taught me how to sample the wine without getting too high. The trick was to rinse your mouth with the wine, then spit it out, eat a bite of bread, and sample the next variety. We had lunch at one vineyard and the owner asked her if she was sampling for the stube and she said, no, my father is here and will do that, but sometime in the future, I plan to do the buying for our establishment. The owner gave her a hug and welcomed her back at any time.

Across the Danube River was the Russian Zone. It had a large beach next to the river that was off-limits to us. However, occasionally we managed to get over there to eye the girls, most of whom wore thongs and a skimpy bra. They really were an eyeful. Another sector along the river was a nudist beach with a wooden fence that extended about ten feet out into the river. We would swim around the fence to see who was at the nudist beach. Usually, the nudists were a lot older than the young girls with the thongs.

LESSON LEARNED: The view from the other side of the fence is not always better.

There was a Battalion of the 350th Infantry, 88th Infantry Division in the compound with us. They went down into the Austrian Zone for training twice a year that lasted for three or four months each time. During this period, we assumed their guard duty. The First Sergeant frequently met you at the barracks door as you came off a post and sent you back out for another tour. One time I stayed on duty as Desk Sergeant for sixteen hours because there wasn't anybody there to relieve me. When I returned to the Company, the First Sergeant was waiting for me to stand guard mount for a twenty-four hour tour of post guard as Corporal of the Guard.

During the period when we were pulling duty sixteen hours out of twenty-four, there was a call for volunteers for jump school to become airborne troopers. I volunteered immediately, had a physical, and promptly forgot about it. I didn't think they'd take anyone who had been in the outfit for such a short time. I felt there'd be plenty of volunteers that were close to rotation.

The Infantry came back and resumed their normal guard duties and we started to get a lot of time off. This was the period when I was really enjoying my tour in Vienna. About a week before Thanksgiving, my good-luck bubble burst. I came out on orders for jump school in Fort Benning, GA. I went to see the First Sergeant about getting off the orders, and he said emphatically, no way. You asked for it and you got it. I had put in for the transfer back in July and promptly forgot about it. I was to learn later that a shortage of personnel existed throughout the Army. When the units provided enough men for all the details that were assigned, there was no one left to train. This was most vividly exposed when the combat divisions on occupation duty in Japan were ordered into combat in Korea in July 1950.

I ate Thanksgiving Dinner with the 796th MP Battalion and that evening I boarded the Mozart for Bremerhaven to await surface transportation back to the U.S.A. This was a miserable trip. Seven of us were assigned to a section with wooden seats for eight. There were no baggage racks and each of us had a duffel bag and at least one piece of hand luggage. The train ride lasted four days with no change of trains or layovers, just four days of misery being packed in like sardines. They even issued us C rations. We were able to open the windows after we crossed the Danube River into the US Zone of Austria at Linz. Each time we stopped in a station, we'd buy bratwurst sandwiches and coke or beer from the station vendors.

We were loaded directly from the train to the USS Breckenridge. I was going to make the round trip on the same troop ship that brought me to Germany. Again I volunteered for head count for the rough voyage back to the U.S.A. We passed the Statue of Liberty and the Old Lady still looked good to me as we went up the river to Pier 91. We were bussed to Camp Kilmer for future transfer to our next duty station. The first night, SGT Fosdick, from the 796th MP, and I closed the NCO Club and decided to go into town. We were stopped by the local MPs for passes. All we had were 796th MP special passes. SGT Fosdick gave the MPs a hard time and they drove us back to our company with a ticket. The next morning the Company Commander gave us Company punishment and a seven-day restriction.

I was detailed as a guard for the dependent quarters. At this time they were trying to get all European brides, whose husbands had already returned to the states, into the country before the regulations changed. On January 1, 1949, I pulled the 4:00 PM to midnight shift. I was to make sure no males went into the quarters and that no wives left the building. There was another guard at the back door to see that no one left by the back door or stairs. One evening they loaded a bus with the wives whose husbands failed to show up. They were being sent back home. I remember one couple, a French bride who had married a black Sergeant. She spoke excellent English and was arguing about going to his home in Alabama to meet his family. He told her that they couldn't go there and she wanted to know why he hadn't told her that before they were married. I felt sorry for both of them, but that was the world we lived in at that time. They were hauling the brides out by bus loads for transportation back to their homes in Europe because their husbands were not there to pick then up. I completed my seven days of company punishment and left Camp Kilmer for South Caroline and a short leave before reporting to Fort Benning, GA. I enjoyed this leave because I was home for Christmas. This was an important day for my mother because all six of us kids were home together.

I reported to Fort Benning in early January 1949, ready to start jump school. The training was tough, but I was able to keep up with it. Again I stated an opinion and let my big mouth overload my little ass.

CSM Glenn H. Towe [Ret'd]

MG Salet and LT Griffis pin First Sergeant Chevrons on Glenn H. Towe, Company B, 6th Battalion, 2nd Training Regiment, Fort Gordon, GA, May 11, 1964.

MSG Peter Vowel. The most perfect combat soldier I ever knew. Paschal High School, Jr. ROTC, Fort Worth, Texas, May 1958.

This was our wedding picture.
Marian McGuffin and SFC Towe were married in Walhalla, SC, August 12, 1951.

Regt CO COL Sutherland and Adjutant CPT Giles presenting Silver Star to SFC Glenn H. Towe, 61st Infantry Regiment, 8th Infantry Division, Ft. Jackson, SC, June 1951.

This sand table of the 61st Infantry, 8th Infantry Division bivouac area, was made by SFC Glenn H. Towe, Hqs 4th Battalion, 61st Infantry, Ft. Jackson, SC, April 1951.

CSM Glenn H. Towe [Ret'd]

There was a friend of mine from Vienna who lived in Fayetteville, NC. He got engaged while home on leave and was planning on a June wedding after being assigned to Fort Bragg, NC for duty with the 82nd Air borne Division. Both of us were Corporals with the same MOS. Orders were posted sending him to Japan with the 11th Air Borne Division and me to Fort Bragg. We went to personnel to swap assignments. I asked a PFC about speaking with the Personnel Sergeant or the Personnel Officer. He asked why and I told him. He said, scowling, you are in the Airborne now and you'll go where you are told. A Sergeant came up and wanted to know why we were there. The PFC butted in and said, I told them to go where the orders indicated. The Sergeant told us in a very stern voice, in the Airborne you do as you are told and the PFC told you to go back to your Company. I looked at the Sergeant and said if this is the way the Airborne is run, I don't want any part of this chickenshit outfit and you'd better give me a quit slip.

That ended my Airborne training and career as a jumper. I was sent to the Military Police Company, 3rd Infantry Division at the Sand Hill area, Fort Benning, GA. We were in a training status and again short of personnel. We trained when we could get enough men together for a class. Again I screwed up, but it wasn't my mouth this time.

There was a Corporal there by the name of Bob Gillespie from Walhalla with whom I had gone to grammar school. He told me I should get a transfer to the main Post in the 3440 ASU (Army Service Unit) MP Company. I told him that we were so short of personnel that they'd never release me. On payday night, we went into Phoenix City, AL, the town that everybody called Sin City and we stayed out all night.

The next day I was falling asleep in class, so the Sergeant told me to go to the barracks before I fell out of the bleachers and broke my neck. I went back to the barracks and looked for a place to sleep. I sat down in a broom closet and immediately went to sleep. I was rudely awakened by the Company CO during his morning barracks inspection. He told me in no uncertain terms that I had better find me another home and that he didn't want any deadbeat NCOs in his company. I reported to the First Sergeant and he asked me where I'd like to go. I quickly said the Main Post MP Company. He signed a release form and I went to see Gillespie. He went with me to see the First Sergeant. Top said he'd gladly accept me, but to watch Corporal Gillespie because he might get me into trouble again. I pulled gate guard and walking patrol with a Columbus, GA policeman for a couple of weeks and after that, it was walking patrol back in Phoenix City, AL.

At that time Phoenix City was wide open. When you crossed the Thirteenth Street Bridge from Columbus to Phoenix City, the first three businesses on the right were bars with open gambling. You could see the crap tables from the street. No one was ever turned away from the bar regardless of age. Most of the waitresses were prostitutes and did their business activities in the back rooms.

On one occasion, an Indian soldier was shot by a policeman. The soldier weighed about one hundred and thirty or forty pounds and was arrested and placed in the rear seat of the police cruiser. One of the police officers was already in the rear seat. Together, the two men weighed over two hundred and twenty pounds. The story they told was that the soldier was choking the driver and the only way the officer in the rear next to the GI could stop the choking was to shoot him. Nobody was ever charged with the crime. Phoenix City was finally cleaned up in the early fifties.

The Georgia Attorney General was shot on Main Street one afternoon while making a personal investigation. One of my sisters and her husband lived in Phoenix City at that time. He was restricted to a direct route from his home to the Post and return without stopping in town in either direction. The only time I got into trouble while in the Post MPs was when I was accused of not going to the aid of another MP. We had a PFC who was also on walking patrol. He was assigned as my assistant. One Saturday afternoon, he went into a bar and caught a GI that was smaller than he was. He punched him in the ribs or stomach and demanded to see his pass. I told him that was not the way to conduct a checkup while on duty. He informed me that was the way that he operated and had never had any trouble. I said, one of these days, someone is going to make you eat that night stick. He laughed and said, that would be the day.

We went off duty at midnight. The first thing on Monday morning, I spoke to my Platoon Sergeant about the guy who was my assistant the night before and we went to see the First Sergeant. I told him my story and that I didn't want to go on patrol with that individual again. A couple of weeks later we came up on patrol together again. I asked my Platoon Sergeant about my request and was told that the First Sergeant had no other choice.

In the second or third bar we checked, he turned to me and said, watch me get that infantryman over there. It was a PFC from the 30th Infantry Regiment, 3rd Infantry Division, and in proper uniform, sipping on a beer and watching the crowd. He went over and punched the PFC in the stomach and said, let me see your pass. The PFC said, okay, I'll show you my pass, but if you punch me again with that stick I'll make you eat it. My partner punched him in the gut really hard again and said, you don't tell me anything, you hear me? I don't think the punch was very effective, but I've never seen a man move as fast as that PFC did. In a matter of seconds, he took the night stick away from my partner and checked to see what I was going to do. I didn't move so he handed me the night stick and proceeded to whip ass in a manly way. I finally said, he's had enough, now get out of here. He replaced his cap, said thanks, and swiftly left the bar.

I stopped a mounted patrol and asked them to take my partner back to the post dispensary to get patched up. I reported back to the Columbus Desk Sergeant and he said don't worry about it. This isn't the first time this sort of thing has happened.

Later, I was sent to Ma Beachees with a duce and half (2 1/2 ton) truck to haul the drunks and fighters back to camp. We usually had about three or four truck loads during the night. Every Saturday night the 3rd Infantry Division Troops and the Airborne School Troopers tried to see which group could throw the others off the Thirteenth Street Bridge into the river.

On Monday morning my Platoon Sergeant informed me that I was to see the Company Commander. It was reported that I didn't go to the defense of another MP who was in trouble. We went to the First Sergeant's office and I explained what had happened and he said okay. We went in to see the CO. He called me Sergeant, saying Sergeant Towe, this is a serious charge. He told us that PFC Southard had related to him what had happened. The First Sergeant said since PFC Southard hadn't reported to him prior to going to the CO, he would like to hear the story.

According to Southard's version of what had transpired the night before, he was merely doing his duty by asking a suspicious-looking soldier, who he felt might be AWOL, for his pass. The First Sergeant then asked Southard if I'd ever cautioned him about his night stick while we were on duty together. Southard replied in the negative. Then the First Sergeant opened his book and read to the CO dates and times that Southard had caused trouble with his night stick while on patrol. He also related that I had come to him asking not to be placed on duty with Southard.

At this time, the CO turned to Southard and asked him point blank, did you punch that soldier with your night stick? Southard admitted to touching him with the stick, but not hard. The CO said, since you like the infantry and the airborne, I am going to send you to them. He told the First Sergeant to take him to the personnel office and get him transferred with a recommendation that he never serve in an MP unit again. That's all, the CO said, you're dismissed. We saluted and got out of there. No one in the company ever mentioned this incident again.

Another incident that happened in Columbus, GA while I was there occurred on payday at the end of May. The City of Columbus decided to fill their coffers with the Fort Benning payroll. That Saturday afternoon and evening they arrested over one hundred and fifty soldiers from Fort Benning for being drunk and disorderly. I had two friends, one who didn't drink, who were picked up coming out of Jack's Playhouse. One had one beer and the other a coke.

The one who had the coke told the policeman that he didn't drink. The policeman replied that makes no difference. Your buddy had a beer and you were with him. Most everyone arrested that day told the same story.

The Provost Marshal and some officers from the 3rd Infantry Division went to the Post Commanding General. The CG went into Columbus and demanded that every one of the soldiers be released. The Mayor of Columbus refused so the CG gave him and ultimatum, turn them loose or I will put Columbus off-limits and have passenger train service to Atlanta for all shopping and recreation for all troops stationed at Fort Benning. This got the Mayor's attention at that point and he gave the order to release the troops. Columbus had tried this once before and General Patton, then a Colonel, lined his tanks up and threatened to blow Columbus off the Map.

Again I volunteered, this time for the Post Rifle Team.

But in June the MP Company was levied for an NCO for assignment to Hawaii. Since I had been there before, I again volunteered to travel. I went home to South Carolina for leave before going overseas. I crossed the country again by train. This was to be my last crossing by land transportation. Each time I had crossed, I had traveled a different route and this gave me the chance to see a lot of this great country we live in. I still enjoy traveling on the ground rather than flying. The only time I fly now is when I am short on time.

I reported to Camp Stoneman, CA to await transportation to Hawaii. I was one of three NCOs selected to fly over with the records of a troopship load of GIs headed for Hawaii and Japan. I was glad to fly to Hawaii because I had made this same crossing four times by ship. We flew over on a C46, a two-engine cargo plane with basic canvas jump seats and noisy as hell. The only thing that was better than going by ship was the time, because it was only an overnight flight. We landed and reported to the US Naval Station, Ford Island, with the records.

A Sergeant from some Army personnel office came and talked with me. He told me that I shouldn't have been shipped to Hawaii. Apparently, all US Army, Marine, Air Force, and Naval Shore Patrol were assigned to HASP (Hawaii Armed Forces Police) and they had a size restriction. I didn't meet the height requirement. I was too short. They were sending me to the Infantry. I was informed that I could make a written request through channels and maybe they'd ship me to Japan. I wanted to stay in Hawaii, so I feel that I made a great career decision at that time.

I said, what the hell, send me to the Infantry. He left saying he'd request orders and get back to me. So what do I do in the mean time? He told me to check in with the Duty Petty Officer each morning at 8:00 AM. I spent a week loafing around Hawaii and visiting old watering holes.

On my first trip into Honolulu, I headed to the Alexander Young Hotel. The bar was still done in dark mahogany with a large mirror over the bar. There were white table cloths and the service was superb, just as I expected. It was always nice and cool inside as I remembered from my visit in 1944. I also found another place that I enjoyed in the afternoon. It was a hamburger and hot-dog stand across the street from the Alexander Young Hotel.

About mid-afternoon you could sit outside with a burger and coke and watch the beautiful Hawaiian girls cross the street. They wore short skirts without any slips underneath. The sun would shine through the thin dresses and it looked as if all they had on were skimpy bathing suits. Honolulu and Hawaii had changed considerably. There were fewer military people there and none of the places were crowded, so you could move about freely.

About six days later I received a message to check with the personnel office. I did and they gave me orders to report to the 5th Regimental Combat Team. I caught a military bus and headed for Schofield Barracks. I had seen the movie "From Here to Eternity" and passed the front gate on an earlier trip through Hawaii, but I had never even considered that I would be reporting there for duty. I was assigned to Company I, 5th RCT, Schofield Barracks, Hawaii for a three-year tour of duty. The 5th RCT came from Korea when all combat units were withdrawn. Having been in Korea for a short time myself, I could understand where they were coming from.

Duty in Hawaii was about the same as it was prior to WWII. I reported to First Sergeant Daniel W. McGuire and he assigned me to the 57mm recoil-less rifle section as Squad Leader. He brought me in to see the Company Commander, Captain Kenneth L Sutherland, a WWII Infantry Company Commander and a wonderful soldier. He talked with me for a few minutes and then dismissed me.

Our rifle squads were all short at least two men per squad and we had many other personnel and equipment shortages. That is the usual situation when the army is downsizing. We didn't have a weapon, so we used two sections of small stovepipe bolted together to simulate a weapon. This brought back my US Navy boot training with wooden 1903 Springfield rifles.

Sergeant Knowlton was the Weapons Platoon Sergeant and after a couple of weeks he made me Section Sergeant. First Lieutenant Thomas W Grant was the XO. He was a WWII Infantry Officer and highly respected. I remember my first Saturday morning inspection by LT. Grant. I had really cleaned my M1 rifle for this inspection since the other men had warned me that he was hell on new men. He looked at my rifle and said, what the hell is that rope doing in your sight, Corporal, and returned my rifle. After inspection I checked the sight and there was a tiny piece of lint in the front sight. This caused me to be restricted for the weekend. Since spending a full week on pass, I hadn't planned to go anywhere except to the library anyway.

I was still wearing Buck-Sergeant chevrons and continued to wear them until I was promoted to Sergeant when the Korean War started. Nobody ever told me to remove them. Soldiering at that time was easy. We had a wonderful unit athletic program and everybody was required to participate. You signed up for a sport and were required to continue the same sport unless you could find another sport instructor that would agree to accept you in his or her group. I started playing tennis, but soon got tired of that and checked with LT. Hula's wife about swimming. I was accepted since I had qualified as an Expert Swimmer while in the Navy.

Mrs. Hula had been an Olympic diver. She was a beautiful young woman and displayed her diving talents frequently. I tried diving, but couldn't keep my feet together. I ended up just swimming laps in the Olympic-size pool.

I had been at Schofield a couple of weeks when Billy Campbell came to visit me. He was in C Company and had been in the 5th RCT in Korea. I had known him since the third grade. I was two years older than he was and he wasn't a WWII vet. I went on pass with him a couple of times. He was too rough for me. He would rather fight than eat even when he was hungry. The Blue and Gray Hotel was in Wahiawa and Campbell was after me constantly to go down with him on a Saturday night. I finally said okay and we went and paid two dollars each for a room. There were no locks on the doors and the walls were wood siding, just like in a barracks with a latrine in one end and no shower.

We went on into Honolulu and ate before starting to drink. About 1:00 AM, we caught a bus back to Wahiawa and the Blue and Gray. There was a fight in progress when we arrived there and it seemed that all the battlers knew Campbell. He joined in and they fought up and down the halls on both floors and in most of the rooms. During a slack period I took Campbell aside and said, let's get the hell out of here before you get hurt. His reply was, the fun is just starting, I'm staying. I left him there fighting and caught a ride back to Schofield. We had a Field First Sergeant, Sergeant First-Class Henry Eickhorst. Ike was a WWII Infantry Platoon Sergeant who had landed on Omaha Beach on D Day. I think at that time most every company in the army had one of these sergeants. They soldiered with the best of us and were leaders that set the example for twenty-eight days a month.

On pay day they disappeared for the next three or four days. They were never carried AWOL and when they returned, they were outstanding soldiers for the rest of the month.

I had known one like that before, Staff Sergeant Fosdick. He was the one who caused me to get company punishment in Camp Kilmer. While in Fort Benning, I visited Fosdick and suggested we go for a beer. He refused, so we went to a movie instead. He showed me his footlocker that looked like a well-stocked PX. Cigarettes, extra toilet items, and change for two movies a week for the rest of the month. He told me that on payday he usually went to Atlanta or Savannah, got a hotel room for three days, a couple of bottles, and stayed until either the whiskey or the money ran out. Then he came back to the Post and didn't take another drink or go off Post for the rest of the month.

First Sergeant Jackson of K Company, 5th RCT was that type of soldier. The following letter was sent to the Editor, Battle Stars, The Official Newsletter of the 5th RCT and published in Volume XII, Number 5, September/October 2001.

CSM Glenn H. Towe [Ret'd]

"Hugh, after 50 years it is time to reflect on experiences in the 5th RCT. Much of this reflection goes back to Schofield Barracks where the Regiment became a well-trained team that was able to withstand the rigors of combat under extreme physical conditions.

"K Company had two types who made up the team. First were experienced NCOs in combat in WWII, who in spite of often being 28-day soldiers in Schofield, were excellent models to the very young soldiers in combat. Second were the very young soldiers, many under age, whose parents offered them to the Army in order to get rid of them. As a new shave-tail assigned to K Company, I found many problems.

"The First Sergeant, Kermit Jackson, was a 28-day soldier, who after payday was AWOL in the hospital with a broken jaw. He had been hit over the head with a chair in a bar in Wahiawa. When told to investigate the incident, I found that none of the employees of the bar could remember anything. Then when the Battalion Commander called me he said, 'Don't you dare bust him, just take away some of his money.' It seems that he had a wonderful combat record at Anzio, where he won the Silver Star. Later when he was my Platoon Sergeant during the winter of 1950, he would laugh about it. It seems that by that time he had been recommended for the DSC for his actions at Waegwan and the Pentagon threw out the activities at Wahiawa.

"The underage men were problematic. One night they 'borrowed' a jeep and drove down to Hickam Field, home of the Air Force, where they shot out many of the street lights and even forced the MPs to take cover. All were court-martialed and sent to the 'brig'. When word came that we had to go to Korea, the General released them to return to their companies. In Korea they were outstanding. One man was even recommended for a battlefield commission.

"When word came that we had to go to Korea, some of those battle-hardened Platoon Sergeants went down to Honolulu and became intoxicated. On a Sunday morning as the Colonel of the 5th RCT went to the chapel with his wife, he witnessed several of these Sergeants urinating on the side of the chapel. All were busted. When we embarked for Korea, most of the K Company Platoon Sergeants were privates. Once we were in combat, it didn't take long for these experienced combat soldiers to get their stripes back. All types make up a military team. In Schofield they may have been wild, but in Korea, these same traits helped make them better soldiers."

I knew most of those Sergeants and on a few occasions was honored to have a drink with them. Shortly after my arrival in Company I, Corporal Leroy Turner, the other 57mm recoil-less rifle Squad Leader told me an easy way to make the long hikes we went on frequently. He showed me his neatly rolled shelter half on his pack. I picked his pack up and it was as light as a feather. He explained this mystery as we fixed my pack. First, we went to the commo shop and got a battery box that just fit inside the pack, then to the mess hall for a couple of number 10 tin cans. After the box was in the pack and the cans rolled in the shelter half, I was a sharp looking soldier. We carried our rifles and packs every where we went, so I was in hog heaven for a couple of days.

We fell out for PT and drill one morning when Sergeant Eickhorst said there was a change in schedule. We were going on a fifteen-mile hike. At the end of three hours we marched into a field, halted and the order was given to form for company inspection. Turner and I spread our shelter half and neatly arranged our cans as the other troops laid out the proper equipment. I saw a blur as Turner flew across his display. Before I had time to look, I had SFC Eickhorst's size eleven boot in my ass and I followed Turner head over heels.

Sergeant Eickhorst didn't let the Company Commander know what we'd done. He told us to pack up and stand guard at the entrance to the field and guide the mess truck in. He also told us to be in front of the orderly room at 7:00 PM that night. We discussed what he might do while we waited for the CO to complete the inspection. The only thing we knew for certain was that it would be rough. After lunch in the field we hiked back in, cleaned our equipment, and repacked our packs for the night. We were in front of the orderly room at seven as instructed and this time our equipment would have passed any IG inspection. Ike came out, felt of our packs and said, hand me a couple of those bricks. He put them in each of our packs.

You know where the top of Kola Kola Pass is, he asked.

Yes, Sergeant, we answered like good little soldiers. Okay, hike up there and back and I will see you here tomorrow night. We had just made our turn at the top when a jeep came up. Ike got out and asked us if our shoulders and feet were okay. We were both in good condition considering that we had an exceptionally long hike earlier that day. He rode back down and when we arrived, I was ready for that cot and hated to roll out the next morning.

I didn't bother to remove the bricks during the following days because I knew he'd put them back. The seventh day fell on a payday. Turner and I hung around all afternoon hoping that Ike would let us off the hook, since he normally took off on payday. Unfortunately, we weren't that lucky. He met us at seven, lifted our packs and we went up Kola Kola discussing the possibility of thirty days of hiking. Ike had checked on us each night somewhere around the top, not to see if we'd try to cut back before we reached the top, but to see if we were all right. That night the jeep arrived at the top just as we did. Ike got out and told the driver to take the jeep back to the motor pool and that he'd walk back with us. He picked up a brown paper bag from the jeep before it drove off. He had a bottle of good bourbon and a couple of cokes for chasers. We each had a drink and walked back to camp.

It was four and one-half miles from C Quadrangle to the top of the pass. This meant we had a nine-mile hike each night. On the walk back down, Ike talked about NCOs and their duties, the training we were doing, and why he

CSM Glenn H. Towe [Ret'd]

Kevin, Glenda, Marian and CSM Towe, Augusta, GA, 1968.

was so tough about it. He talked about Normandy and D Day and the importance for the NCO not only to know his job, but to be in the best possible shape should we have another war. He talked about endurance and explained why he hadn't turned us in to the old man. The Army needed good NCOs that could stand the heat. The seven nights were to see if we'd come back to him and ask for a break. You should learn when you screw up to take your punishment and not cry over it. We finished the bottle on the way down and the conversation with Ike was worth a week of training any day. I remember one morning I came in with my head smoking and decided that I didn't want to go to Kauhuka Range for an overnight problem. First Sergeant McGuire was out with the troops, so I knocked on the Company Commander's door and asked for a pass. Captain Sutherland told me in no uncertain terms, to get my gear and go to the field with my Platoon. I was Assistant Platoon Sergeant at that time. I thanked him, left the orderly room, and walked out the gate and across the highway to Kemoo Farms to the bar. I had another drink and made my way back to the barracks. All the Company was gone by then, so I proceeded to lie across my cot and fall asleep for about six hours.

It finally dawned on me what I'd done, so I got my pack and rifle and caught the mess truck out to the Company. When I arrived, I reported immediately to the Company Commander. I knew I would have to face him sooner or later, so why delay the meeting and live in the agony and suspense until he called for me. I reported to him exactly what I'd done. He didn't raise his voice or ask for an excuse. He talked to me like a father. He said, Towe, you have the potential for being an outstanding NCO and I don't wish to be the one to take away those stripes that you have evidently worked so hard for, but actions like this cannot go unpunished. Every one in the company knows what you did and I must make an example of you. I thought to myself, man, you'll be lucky to get out of this without going to the stockade. Then he said, you know that I cannot order you to dig a six by six as an NCO, but I can sure as hell make you a Private, then order you to dig one. What is your answer to that? I replied I'll go get a shovel. That won't be necessary, Corporal, he said, just use your entrenching tool. I saluted and said, yes, Sir.

I started digging in that hard ground. It was the dry season and the ground had cracks six inches wide and two or three feet deep. I dug for my rank and my career because I knew he had given me a break. I dug all night until about three the next afternoon. I was on my own, no one checked on me, so I knew that my survival in Item Company depended on the size hole I dug.

The Company was ready to truck back to Schofield Barracks and Captain Southerland came over to where I was still digging and said, "That looks good, Corporal. When you get it filled in, come on back to the barracks." I had dug a hole about six by six feet and about five feet deep. I filled it in and heaped it up the way I had been instructed to. I secured my pack and rifle and started the fifteen-mile hike back to camp. Some of the local people offered me a ride, but I knew that the Captain wanted me to walk, so I thanked them and kept trudging along. The CO came by and stopped to check on my general welfare and see if I had blisters on my feet to match those on my hands. He drove on out and checked the hole and on the way back he stopped and said you did a good job covering that hole and gave me a full canteen of water.

He came by again about 10:30 P.M. with another canteen of water and asked about my feet again. Then I really knew he was interested in how I was doing because he left his home and family to check on my feet. That was an example of leadership that I never forgot. Regardless of your rank, you always take care of your troops before caring for yourself. The next morning I fell out with my platoon and none of my leaders ever made a comment about the punishment I received.

I was at a reunion about forty years later and some of the men from my Platoon were laughing about the hole I had dug. At that time, they said "that old man is one tough son-of-a-bitch," and they weren't talking about the CO. From that time on, they had more respect and admiration for me and wanted to be a part of the platoon.

On Christmas Eve of 1949, Sergeant Romeo A Chalifoux asked me what I was doing for Christmas and I said I was staying in the barracks. Christmas was always a big deal at home even when there was no money for presents. I came from a very loving family and we understood that our parents were doing the best they could; now I know that the greatest thing I ever received from them was their love for each of us kids. Christmas was a tough time to be away from home and family.

He said let's go over to Kemoo's for a beer and a hamburger, then you can go to Christmas Mass with me. We walked over, ordered a beer and burger and sat talking until about 11:30 and then walked back to the Chapel for the Christmas Mass. I had never attended a Christmas Mass before, so it was a new experience for me. After the Mass we returned to the barracks and I went up to my Platoon section and to bed.

The next morning at chow I learned that Sergeant Chalifoux had been arrested for fondling a PFC in another platoon. The Judge Advocate General (JAG) wanted me to testify against the Sergeant and I refused; I stood by my story. They questioned me four or five times about a great variety of activities, such as had I ever been on pass with Sergeant Chalifoux, and had I ever spent the night in a hotel when he was there, and so forth. All my answers were the same. I still feel that the PFC cooked up the story to get even with Sergeant Chalifoux for giving him extra details. In the end, Sergeant Chalifoux was sentenced to prison with a dishonorable discharge. During this period, the US Army was still reducing forces and the following example probably changed my career decision a number of times. Just about all of our officers, except regulars, received pink slips. This was notification that they would be removed from the officer ranks by reduction in force. They were to leave the Officer Corps by the first of October 1950.

Included in this group were Captain Sutherniand, LT. Grant, and LT. Sidtrack, all from Item Company along with other officers I knew within the Regiment. The Regiment received graduates from the 1949-50 class of West Point, but insufficient numbers to make up for the proposed losses. Due to this shakeup in the company, I was made Platoon Sergeant. I had a Corporal Murray McNeil for Assistant Platoon Sergeant and four pfcs for squad leaders. My Platoon Leader was LT. Sidtract, who was on special duty as the police and prison officer of the stockade. I think I saw him once in the six months before the Korean War started. The pfcs were good and we had a good Platoon and trained hard.

At this time I was in the best physical condition of my life. I had to be the strongest and the best at everything. McNeil and I would go to the movie or snack bar most every night and when we returned we'd get our rifles and do rifle calisthenics to see who would stop first. We also lifted each other from all positions. I'd lie flat on my back with my elbows bent and my hands above my head on the floor. A one hundred and thirty-pound man would step into my hands and I would come up from a lying position to a standing position with my arms extended with him still standing in my hands. At first we only had onlookers, but soon most of the platoon was joining in. When rifle marksmanship began, platoons began rooting for their man. There were three of us who led from the start, myself, Sergeant Fowler, and Clint Nicholes. The more we fired, the tighter the scores became, and when it was all over, I beat the two of them out by one point. That meant a three-day pass from the Battalion Commander and also one from the Company Commander. Competition between Platoons was a great incentive to be the best. My Platoon liked to rub it in when we were tops. They told the other Platoons that all they needed was to get rid of the Sergeants and get Corporals for Platoon NCOs.

CSM Glenn H. Towe, 5th Battalion 68th Armor, 8th Infantry Division, Mannheim, Germany. Last duty assignment before retiring, June 1973.

CSM Glenn H. Towe [Ret'd]

We went into the field for a couple of weeks as aggressors in a Practice Problem when the 2nd Infantry Division "invaded" Hawaii for Operation Mikki. We defended the beach and when the 5th RCT withdrew back across the mountain, my platoon was left as a harassing unit to disrupt operations behind the 2nd Division lines. We tapped into phone lines, got pass words, and even got into one Battalion Commander's tent while he slept. That was a lot of fun and we didn't have a man captured during the entire Practice Problem. The Regiment conducted a test for the Expert Infantry Badge. This was a coveted award for an infantryman because at that time, no one ever expected to get a Combat Infantryman Badge. It commanded the respect of your peers. At the end of the test, only three men from the entire RCT received the Expert Infantry Badge. They were my ex-Platoon Sergeant Bobby G. Sterling, a lieutenant, and a sp4 from another battalion. I had an interesting episode about the EIB which I will cover later. I decided that I needed to improve my education and to ease the boredom of barracks life. I, along with a couple of other men from the Company, went to the Education Officer and signed up for off-post night classes at the Wahiawa High School. The class consisted of about fifteen students all taking collage prep classes. I felt that I could get at least one year of college in the next two years of my current overseas tour. I enjoyed the school and during this period, I also went to the US Army Pacific Chemical, Biological, and Radiation School. This was a two-week course attended by both officers and enlisted personnel. Upon completion of the course, I was appointed Company CBR NCO. I had come a long way in the Company in less than a year. I went from squad leader of a 57 mm recoil-less rifle squad to a rifle Platoon Sergeant and Company CBR NCO.

All this and frequently screwing up, again I felt that I had to soldier twice as hard as anyone else just to keep up. We were spending at least two or three days each week in the field and it was good training. Captain Sutherland was a good Commander dedicated to training and as I look back now, it seems that he knew the Korean War was coming. I know that the training we received saved a lot of lives later. As a Regiment, we were the best trained, best physically conditioned and had the highest morale of any regimentally-sized unit to fight in Korea.

One Saturday afternoon, three of us from school and three young ladies from Wahaiwa, met at the recreation center at Waianae. It was just a few huts, a community shower, and a beautiful beach. There was a small snack stand where you could get ice, cokes and snacks. We carried our sleeping bags, blankets, and a case of beer for the overnight stay. One of the men had a radio that I had never seen before, a Transoceanic model about two feet long and about eight or ten inches square. We lay out in the sun, snacked, drank coke and beer, and talked about school and a little of everything else. The last bus to Wahiawa ran at ten so we walked the girls to the bus stop, said our good-bys, and put them on the bus. They promised to return the next morning.

The three of us slept on the beach that night. The next morning we showered, walked to a greasy spoon for breakfast, and returned to the beach. The girls showed up and we were enjoying a Sunday on the beach, listening to dreamy Hawaiian music. Then our dreamy balloon suddenly went POP. The music from the radio was interrupted by this message: "We interrupt this program to announce that North Korea has crossed the thirty-eighth parallel and is advancing on Seoul, Korea. All members of the 5th RCT report to your units immediately. This is not a drill. We repeat: all men of the 5th RCT report to your units immediately."

THE KOREAN WAR

B y the time we had secured our gear and walked back to the recreation center, there was a duce and a half waiting there for our transportation back to the barracks. We said good-bye and that was the last time I saw any of the girls. At 4:00 PM, the CO had a formation and explained the situation. We were restricted to the Company area until future notice and were instructed to start packing. The restriction was lifted the next morning and we were informed that we'd go to Korea by ship. Since we were short of personnel of all ranks, all records of individuals in Hawaii were screened and all the men who had an infantry MOS and some who had changed their MOS from infantry to other branches were transferred back to the Regiment. All jocks and special assignment personnel also returned to their units. These were Officers, NCOs and enlisted men who had missed all the training we received during the past ten months. In Item Company, Captain Sutherland was transferred to Mike Company as the heavy weapons Company Commander. In my Platoon, LT. Sidtract came back from temporary duty as Regimental Police and Prison Officer; Master Sergeant Chapman came back as Platoon Sergeant; and Staff Sergeant Posey came back as a Squad Leader. These troops had been in desk jobs with little physical conditioning and no infantry training since WWII. The two NCOs were good leaders, but the Lieutenant had been dealing with prisoners too long. He had a tendency to treat the troops the same way as the prisoners were treated in the stockade. I was moved back to Squad Leader of the First Squad. During this adjustment of personnel, there was a blanket promotion of all enlisted men in the regiment. I was promoted to Staff Sergeant. This was of equal rank that I had achieved in the Navy in October 1945. Staff Sergeant Posey still had date of rank on me. We packed and sent our civilian clothing and other personal articles home. We assembled all company equipment that was to go with us and waited for the troop ship to arrive and be loaded. There was an incident during this waiting-period that affected me very deeply. On the May 31 payday, one man from my Platoon, two men from the Weapons Platoon, and a cook went together and bought a car with the Company Commander's permission. Early one morning they were headed back to Schofield from Honolulu with the cook driving when they crashed. All four men were killed. Most likely the driver had fallen asleep. This was the first man that I had lost from my Platoon since I had been in service and it was extremely hard on me, especially since we were headed into combat. I was given the duty of forming a firing squad to render honors as the remains left the Post. I got out my manual and selected the men from the platoon for the detail. SGT Posey came to me and asked if I'd like him to conduct the detail. He had served as Commander of a burial detail back in 1948 when they were bringing a lot of remains of WWII veterans home from foreign cemeteries for burial in the US. I thanked him for his consideration of me. He performed the duty flawlessly and I appreciated it. As they fired their volleys and played taps, tears streamed down my face. These deaths gave me a different perspective on the war in that I now knew what it was like to lose a man from my unit. It also gave me a greater challenge to protect my men when ever possible. That was when I realized that I had a great responsibility to the men under my control that could determine life or death. The responsibility of leadership far outranks the old adage "Rank has its Privileges."

On 16 July we sailed from Hawaii aboard the troop ship the USS Mann for Pusan, Korea. It was a fourteen-day trip filled with classes, exercise periods, test firing weapons and briefings on the progress of the war. The younger troops were afraid the war would be over before they got a chance to earn a Combat Infantryman Badge. The Old Men, as we were called from WWII, were afraid if would still be going on. We didn't wish to be involved in another war. We landed in Pusan in the afternoon of 31 July and bivouacked on a race track.

The following day, we trucked from Pusan through Meson to the front line. We relieved a Company of the 25th Infantry Division on the southwest flank of the Pusan Perimeter. Item Company had the sea on our left flank and King Company of the 5th RCT on our right. The unit we relieved had dug trenches and holes so we continued improving on them. Any time you stopped in the infantry you started digging. This wasn't just a way for the commanders to harass the troops because we were subject to incoming artillery or mortar fire at any time. As often happens with green troops, someone hears a can rattle or sees moonlight on a bush and starts firing. This results in everyone firing and it is difficult to get it stopped once it starts. Our first casualty happened the next morning. The Mess Sergeant had a personal pistol with him and in the process of cleaning it he accidentally shot a young soldier on KP duty.

During the following week we were in constant contact with the enemy. They already knew we were a new unit on the line, so they tried a banzai attack with the bugles, tin pans, and yelling. We were able to stop them without any casualties. This type of attack didn't bother me because we knew where they were and could fight them accordingly. The attack that worried me was the silent one, where they got into grenade-throwing distance before we knew they were there.

Our second night there, I was called back to the Company CP (Command Post) and given instructions to take a man from my Platoon and establish an observation and listening post out about seven hundred yards in front of our lines. We rolled out phone wire as we went to the position I selected. It was a bluff overlooking a small village that was suspected of being a staging area for attacks on our positions. We got into our position just before dark and dug a small prone shelter to partially give us cover from mortar and artillery fire. They patched the 4.2 mortar company line to our phone so that we could register mortar fire on the village.

The Mortar Company fired the first round and I adjusted for the next round. The fire direction center yelled out 'ruptured round.' I looked back and saw this fireball that sounded like a massive train, heading right for our position. We got down in the trenches we had dug and knew immediately they weren't deep enough. Fortunately the round fell about fifty yards from us and none of the WP (white phosphorus or willy peter) fell on us.

A round had split just as it left the mortar tube. This was not uncommon at that early stage of the war. Most of our ammunition was left over from WWII. All of our .30 caliber machine-gun ammo in metallic belts had to be unbelted, the corrosion cleaned off, oiled and rebelted before we could fire it.

I remember one morning, I threw a case of twenty-five grenades and over half of them were duds. We did not get 3.5 inch rocket launchers (they replaced the 2.36 launchers of WWII) and 57mm recoil-less rifles until after we landed in Korea. After the scare, I was able to finish registration on the village. We saw a couple of lights that night and a few soldiers moving around the next day. The four deuces fired a couple of missions for us before we were relieved just before dark that evening. I was glad to get out of there, but we still had to pass through our line after dark and that is always a dangerous situation.

They probed our lines constantly looking for a weak spot. For two evenings I observed two of the enemy move into an observation post on the next ridge. I decided I could get one of them as a prisoner, so I got a volunteer from the squad to go with me and we crawled most of the way to the position and luckily, found both of them asleep. Corporal Rodriguez took care of one while I captured the other one without a sound. We made it back through our line just before daybreak.

The Company was notified and a South Korean Marine Sergeant and a private came up on the hill and took charge of the prisoner. When they left with him, his hands were tied behind his back and he had a commo wire tied between his feet, restricting him to very short steps. They had moved about fifty- or seventy-five yards down the trail when I heard a blast from a burp gun. In a couple of minutes the Sergeant came back up the trail with a big smile on his face. I asked him where my prisoner was and he said, "Sergeant, he run like rabbit."

I completely lost my cool. I flipped off the safety on my M1, stuck it in his chest and said, "You sorry son-of-a-bitch, you killed my prisoner." He saw the anger in my face and started crying, "He run, he run." I told him in plain English, "You are going to go out there and get me a prisoner." He said, "No, no, they kill me." I shoved him harder with my M1 and told him I was going to kill him myself and kick his sorry ass off the side of the mountain if he didn't get started. He realized that I was more dangerous than the enemy at that time and he started on the trail toward the enemy. He made a turn in the trail and I heard one long burst from a machine gun and that closed the book on my prisoner and the South Korean Marine The private, after observing this, ran off the hill. At that time in the military service, cigarettes were just as important as food. Every meal had a pack of four cigarettes and a book of matches. Our first issue of coke, candy, beer and cigarettes came on the afternoon of 9 August. I went to the platoon CP and picked up the supplies for my squad and went to each fox hole and issued the items. A couple of the men traded their beer for my coke and others who didn't drink gave me their beer.

I was watching action along the road in front of our Company position. The Regimental I & R Platoon was running a reconnaissance mission along the road when they were ambushed. They lost a couple of their jeeps and a tank at the small village that I was observing while at the listening post. I don't know how many wounded or KIA that were inflicted on them at that time.

The Platoon Sergeant came over and said I was wanted at the Company CP. When we arrived the Company Commander said he was looking for a volunteer to lead a night attack. He explained that the Regiment was going to attack through the Chinju Pass and go directly to Chinju, which was a North Korean marshaling area for the southwestern front. The 3rd Battalion would lead the attack with Item Company in the point.

I had been chosen to lead Item Company on the night attack. I said okay and waited for the plan of attack. The CO asked me how I was going to conduct the attack. I said I would recon by fire as we moved. I wanted my BAR man and another BAR man from one of the other squads. I told the Platoon Sergeant who I wanted and he said okay. I was asked if I thought they'd volunteer and I said that I knew they'd go with me. The CO said he'd get a tank to support me. That was the plan to lead off one of the most important attacks of the Korean War.

I reported back to my Squad area, briefed the squad on our mission, packed up, and was ready to move out. I still had not tasted one of the beers and I passed up the opportunity. I dropped them in the fox hole, put a piece of cardboard over them and kicked in enough dirt to cover it and moved my Squad over to the assembly area. We spread out, ate, and I checked all the weapons, ammo, and grenades. I also had each rifleman in my Squad carry a couple of ammo magazines for the BARs. We were ready for the fight.

CSM Glenn H. Towe [Ret'd]

My squad crossed the LD (line of departure, the most important time and space element in the Army). This is the starting point of an attack and the final coordinating point before a unit jumps off. We crossed at 2100 hours (9:00 PM) August 9, 1950 and moved out along the road where the Regimental I & R Platoon had been ambushed in the afternoon. We received our first fire from the same village and as the tank moved up to support us, it was knocked out by an antitank mine. We eliminated the sniper or snipers and moved on. One BAR man would fire a short burst of three to five rounds, then we would move fifty or seventy-five yards and the other BAR would fire. We moved like this for the better part of the night. We had fire from our front or flank about three or four times as we moved. Both BARs would open up with about a magazine each, suppressing the enemy fire and we'd move on. Just at dawn, King Company moved through us and took the point.

At daybreak they were hit by an antitank weapon on the road and fire from the high ground on the right side of the road. The CO told me to take my Squad up the right flank of the hill and assist LT. Burk from King Company. I arrived at the top of the hill with two or three members of my Squad that were able to keep up with me. LT. Burk was standing there alone and said, "What the hell are you doing up here?" I replied that the CO said you might need a hand. We looked at each other and laughed because we had taken the vacant hill and his Platoon and my Squad were still making it up the hill. It was a good thing for the two of us that the enemy had decided to withdraw before we reached the top or both of us would have been easily killed.

When LT. Burk and I came down off the hill, Margritte Higgins, a war correspondent, was waiting to get an action report from LT. Burk about how he took the hill. He told her that he had thrown every thing he had at the hill and when he and I arrived at the top, the enemy of at least company-size had withdrawn and carried their dead and wounded with them. The he smiled and said, "Mam, when Towe and I reached the top of that hill, the enemy was long gone, and I don't think there were more than two of the enemy there to start with. It was a wild goose chase and I wish all of our hills would be like that one."

Our Battalion continued to move along the road and railroad track to Chinju. The 555th Artillery and our train sections followed. The enemy had just moved back into the hills as we passed through, then came down and ambushed the Triple Nickel Artillery and trains. The artillery was hit exceptionally hard. They depressed their tubes and fired pointblank as the enemy attacked them along the road. They put up a heroic fight but still lost a lot of men and equipment.

We moved into a small village just before dark on the second night. I placed my Squad in position, got them water and C Rations, and was ready to settle in for the night. Just a few yards from our position was a partially destroyed house. I had noticed a woman with a baby cradled in her arms, sitting in the doorway when we moved into position. She began rocking and moaning so I checked to see if she was injured and found that her baby had been killed when the house was destroyed. She sat there all night gently rocking the baby back and forth and moaning. The moaning was mostly very low, but at times was almost a scream. I felt very helpless knowing there was nothing I could do for her.

Listening to her during the night gave me time to think about my own family, especially since I had a sister about her age who was back home with her first child, a nephew about the age of the dead baby. I knew that as kids we had a hard time during the Depression and I could remember that sister crying at night because she was so hungry. But that was still nothing in comparison to the poor mother sitting there alone all night rocking her dead baby.

Before we moved out the next morning, I rounded up the partial rations we were leaving behind and placed them beside her. She gave me a feeble smile as if she understood and I moved my Squad out with tears in my eyes.

The Regiment converged on Chinju and killed a large number of enemy and destroyed all the supplies and equipment that the North Koreans had assembled for their final push on Pusan. The battle lasted four days, but was the breaking point for the North Koreans on the southwestern section of the Pusan Perimeter. On the night of August 13th, we moved by truck back to our original starting point.

We moved into a low area and a dry wash. I put out security and lay down in the rain. When I awoke, I had an odd sensation in my feet. When I moved them, they felt like they had no weight. I reached down to see what had happened and I found that while I had slept through the rain storm, the dry wash filled with water and I was lying in water up to my waist with my feet floating. It was just getting light, so I checked to see if any of my squad had drowned in the downpour.

The Platoon Sergeant passed the word to move out. He told me to take the Platoon and follow the stream up to the road and wait there for him. He was going to find the mess truck and get us a hot meal. The Platoon Leader was at a meeting with the CO to get our next move. We arrived at the road and I spread the Platoon out while we waited for the hot meal, our first in five days, and we were all looking forward to it with our tongues practically hanging out of our mouths.

About that time a highly waxed, spotless jeep came roaring up with a three-star flag on it. Out jumped a three-star General looking as if he hadn't broken any starch since the war started, spit-shined boots and the works.

"Who's in charge here?" he asked. I reported and said I was. He didn't bother to ask for our unit designation or what we were doing. He looked at me sternly and said, "Sergeant, these men look like a bunch of bums. Get them shaved, washed up, and in clean clothing immediately."

He jumped back into the jeep and was gone before we could bat an eye.

One of the riflemen said aloud, "I wonder where the hell he's been for the last four days." We did get our hot meal, but we moved out again before we had time to shave. A few months later, I read that the three-star General had been killed in a jeep wreck and I was unable to shed one single tear. The action described in the leadoff chapter of this book came at this point in time.

The Third Battalion of the 5th RCT and attached units received a Distinguished Unit Citation, later changed to The Presidential Unit Citation, for this four-day action. The citation follows:

DISTINGUISHED UNIT CITATION

As Authorized by Executive Order 9396 (sec. 1, WD Bul. 22, 1943) superseding Executive Order 9075 (se. III, WD Bul, 1942), citation of the following units in the general orders indicated is confirmed in accordance with AR 200-315 in the name of the President of the United States as public evidence of deserved honor and distinction. The citations read as follows: 1. The 3rd Battalion, 5th Infantry, 25th Infantry Division, and the following attached units: Headquarters Section, Headquarters Platoon, Tank Company, 5th Infantry; 3rd Platoon, Tank Company, 5th Infantry; 3rd Platoon, Medical Company, 5th Infantry; 2nd Platoon, Heavy Mortar Company, 5th Infantry; 2nd Platoon, 72nd Engineer Company (C).

555th Field Artillery Liaison Party, is cited for outstanding performance of duty and extraordinary heroism in action against the enemy in the vicinity of Chinju, Korea, during the period 9 to 13 August.

Under the cover of darkness, this Battalion embarked upon its mission which was to seize high ground in the vicinity of Kogan-ni, then to continue the attack through Pansong-ni, and finally to make contact with the 35th Infantry Regiment and seize and hold the Battalion's assigned sector of the divisional objective along the Nam River. Moving rapidly over mined roads and through enemy-held terrain, the members of this Battalion launched an attack against their initial intermediate objective. Advancing through intense automatic-weapons and artillery fire, the personnel of the Battalion displayed a matchless fighting spirit and, through their aggressiveness and singleness of purpose, they were able to rupture the numerically superior enemy's defense line, inflicting heavy casualties on the hostile troops.

As the Battalion struck out for Pansong-ni, the desperate enemy subjected it to fire from almost every conceivable type of weapon, from small arms to artillery, but with dogged determination, its members pressed forward by forced marches, engaging and defeating the numerous hostile units which attempted to bar their way, regardless of size. Despite the constant harassment of large enemy patrols and individual snipers, the enemy fuel dump, ammunition store, and seven field guns were overrun and captured. After countless ambuscades, the members of this Battalion, even though hampered by a lack of water and vital supplies, seized and held their objective on the Nam River until ordered to withdraw. In the action, the friendly casualties were relatively light despite the furious fighting, but an estimated 450 casualties were inflicted on the enemy. The 3rd Battalion, 5th Infantry, 25th Infantry Division, and the attached units displayed such superlative effectiveness in accomplishing its mission under extremely difficult and hazardous conditions as to set it apart and above other units participating in the campaign. The extraordinary heroism and esprit de corps exhibited by its members reflect great credit on themselves and are in keeping with the most esteemed traditions of the military service.

(General Orders, 239, Headquarters, Eighth United States Army, Korea, 6 May 1952.)

BY ORDER OF THE SECRETARY OF THE ARMY: J. LAWTON COLLINS Chief of Staff, United States Army official:

WM. E. BERGIN Major General, USA

The Adjutant General TRUE EXTRACT COPY

s/H/, S.WAYMEN

2nd Lt., CE

The Company returned to the same positions we occupied before we attacked Chinju and I instructed the Squad Leaders to return to the same positions they occupied before the action. As I checked the other squad positions, I came to the exact hole I had occupied prior to the action just as the Squad Leader jumped into that same hole. I looked at him and said, "By the way, while you're in that hole, hand me my beer." He looked at me as if I had lost all my marbles. "Just rake the dirt off that cardboard," I continued. He finally saw the beer and turned to me and said, "You sure think of everything, don't you." I passed out the beer to the nearest beer drinkers, keeping one for myself and the Platoon Leader.

On August 23, 1950 I was promoted to Sergeant First-Class. Then on the first of September, I was recommended for Master Sergeant. I was wounded before orders were cut for this promotion. Surrender never crossed any of our minds since the time a Platoon of American soldiers had been found slaughtered in a gully with their hands bound behind their backs with common wire. After that news reached us when we first arrived in Korea, we discussed surrender and decided that we would fight until the final man was killed in action. The 5th RCT had one hundred and fifty-one men captured in thirty-five months of combat. Only one of them was from my Platoon who trained in Hawaii. He was a small Hawaiian Japanese by the name of George J Itagaki.

We continued the normal defensive activities, listening/observation posts, patrols, etc. During this period we occupied another high hill where a Company from another Battalion had been kicked off. I had another run-in with the Platoon Leader. He'd check our lines at night and if he caught a man sleeping, he'd jump in the hole and start kicking and stomping him. I talked with him about this action and explained again that he wasn't dealing with a group of prisoners in a stockade. I informed him that a couple of the men had told me that if he jumped into their hole, they would shoot him thinking it was a gook. That was the name given to the North Korean soldiers. He looked at me and asked, "What about you, Sergeant?" I said, "Lieutenant, you know how I feel about you." I looked straight into his eyes for a few seconds and walked away.

On Sunday afternoon, our adjacent Platoon located an infiltrator inside their perimeter. Sergeant Hartley, a Squad Leader, was checking some bushes when the enemy soldier rolled a grenade out between his legs. I saw the explosion as it lifted Hartley off the ground. I hurried over and started to give him first aid before a medic reached him. There was an observation helicopter in the area that landed and I helped Corporal Angelo J Staikos and the medic load Hartley on the chopper skid for evacuation. At one time in Hawaii, Hartley, Staikos, and I had all been in the same Platoon. I was later informed by Staikos that the evacuation was the first helicopter transport of a wounded man in Korea. In the Vietnam War this was called a "dust off". The system we used was the same as the medic choppers used in MASH. That first dust off was the fore runner of the rescue services our armed forces have today that have saved thousands of lives of our veterans and current service men.

Early one morning in September, I was standing in the Platoon CP whistling into the sound power phone to let the company CP know that we had made it through the night okay. Corporal McCassland, my trusted BAR man, was covering the point of the ridge we were defending when a grenade was thrown at his position. It went over his head and he began firing down the path to his front. I was still on the phone and cursing the sleeping operator on the other end when I heard the grenade rolling down to my location. I saw the grenade fall off the rock ledge into my position and as I started to roll out of the hole, the grenade exploded about two feet from my left shoulder. The Platoon Leader and the medic were lying on the ground under a poncho and miraculously, neither of them was hit. I lost all my hearing and most of my eyesight, but could still walk. The medic moved me to the back side of our perimeter and notified the company that he needed a litter immediately. He bandaged my worst wounds, cleaned my face the best he could and we waited for the litter. I was told before I left the hill that I was the only one hit. McCassland got the Gook that threw the grenade plus three or four more for good measure.

The choggy boys (Korean laborers) finally arrived with the litter. I was strapped in and we proceeded down the side of the mountain. My greatest fear at the time was that a mortar round would come in and they would drop me.

The trail was just an old goat path that wound around the mountain. I could see down the side and if they had dropped me, I would have rolled at least three hundred yards or gotten snagged on a rock or bush.

This ended my combat in Korea and started me on the road to recovery and home. I was taken to the Company aid station by the choggy boys. I talked to the CO and First Sergeant and then went on to the Battalion Aid Station where the Battalion Medical Officer checked me over and sent me to the Regimental Medical Station. There the surgeon said that I needed an operation and forwarded me on to a MASH Hospital in Meson. I think that I was given morphine at every stop, so when I arrived at MASH, I was just in and out. It had taken about ten hours from the time I was wounded until I reached MASH.

The Doctor x-rayed me and informed me that he needed to operate immediately. He told me I had a gut wound, but he didn't know how much damage had been done. I was carted into the operating room and as they were cutting my clothing off, a little nurse asked me what size shoes I wore. When I told her size 5 1/2 D, she asked if she could have them. I told her yes and she told the corpsman quickly, don't you dare cut those and proceeded to unlace my boots.

I came out of the operating room and into the recovery room about six the next morning. The little nurse came in to let me know what had happened. The first thing she did was hold up one foot and showed me my combat boot. She told me that they were in such a hurry to get the MASH unit to the combat zone that the smallest boot they had was a nine. She had been wearing her boots with a cushion sole sock in the toe of each. Her shoe size was also a 5 1/2.

She informed me that two fragments from the grenade had penetrated my intestines. The surgeon had to remove a small curve in the intestine and anastomose the two ends back together. They also removed about one hundred small fragments. I had been hit from my forehead to the tops of my boots. Five years later, small fragments were still working their way out of my skin. In 1996, I still had too many metal fragments to take an MRI. I was moved by ambulance to the Pusan Hospital and Evacuation Center. They had inserted a stomach pump and I was also given intravenous liquids and told that I could only lie on my back. At that time they didn't have shunts so each shot and change of the bottle meant a new hole punched in your arm.

At the Pusan Hospital they had to make a decision as to whether I'd recover from my wounds and return to duty soon or be sent to Japan for reevaluation. I was finally flown to Fukuoka Army Hospital, Fukuoka, Japan. This was on a C46 cargo plane that had been converted to a hospital plane. Here again they decided where you should go for recovery. I was flown out the same day to the Osaka Army Hospital, Osaka, Japan. I stayed there for about six days while they waited for me to pass gas which would indicate that my stomach had healed enough to remove the stomach pump.

When we arrived in Osaka, it was the first time I had been on a real bed. Prior to that, it was a canvas army cot or a canvas stretcher. That created severe pains in my lower back and I would plead with the nurses to fold a blanket and put it under my back. Some did and others were afraid it would complicate my wounds. I couldn't have any water at that time so a nurse would give me a gauze bandage soaked in water that had been squeezed out to hold on my chapped lips.

Two nice things happened while I was in Osaka. About two in the morning, a beautiful Japanese nurse came into my room and asked if I would like an alcohol rubdown. I eagerly said yes, but I couldn't turn over so she could reach my back. She smiled and said, "That okay, GI." She started a rub that lasted about forty-five minutes. First, she took a pan of water and a wash cloth and gave me a sponge bath. I didn't know what made her think I needed a sponge bath, but this was the first bath I had since being wounded. Then she started the alcohol rub. She hit every part of my body that she could reach. When she finished I thanked her and she said, "I see you tomorrow night, GI," and she was gone like a flash. I was there for five nights and she returned every night and went through the same ritual. On my last night there, she asked, "How long you stay, GI?" I told her that I would be leaving the next day. She smiled and said, "I be easy on you tonight, GI."

She had a boyfriend in one of the Divisions that had gone from Japan to Korea. He had written her once during the first couple of weeks, but nothing since. I explained the situation in Korea and told her not to worry. I hoped that a letter would arrive soon. She came by to see me the next morning and wished me luck. This was the first time I had seen her except as a shadow in a very dimly lighted room. She stood by the window with the sun streaming in on her hair and face. She was as beautiful as I had imagined she would be.

My stomach had been rumbling all day and night and the next morning I passed a roaring round of gas. The Doctor came to my room and asked me about the gas. I told him about the near explosion. He laughed and said, "Now, that's what I call good news. Let me get this tube out and you can have strained baby food for breakfast." Then he added some good news himself, "Your wound will take too long to heal here, so I am returning you to a hospital in the US for further treatment."

Shortly after a fantastic lunch that consisted of more baby food, I was put back on a stretcher, loaded on a hospital train and was sent to Toyko Army Hospital to await a flight back to the States. On September 12, I flew from Toyko to Hawaii, where I was sent to Tripler General Hospital. The Hospital was located in the same area as the Naval Receiving Station when I was there in 1944. I stayed in Tripler for three days. Here they let me start walking again. I was so weak I had to have help the first few times I got on my feet.

After three days, I was flown out on another converted C54. The stretchers were stacked four high, so once again I was flat on my back and strapped in a litter. About halfway to San Francisco, the captain came on the loud speaker and explained that one engine had gone down, but since we were at the mid point of the flight, he was going to proceed. A large cheer went up from all of us. He said the plane could fly indefinitely on just two engines. The rest of the flight was uneventful to Fair Field Susan US Air Force Base. This was the same base I had departed from a year earlier. We landed about 9:00 AM and all the patients were moved to the Base Hospital. There we were met by three or four movie stars, the Red Cross, and various USO personnel. Ice cream floats, cokes, cakes, and plenty of cigarettes came out of everywhere. We weren't allowed to smoke on the flight, so a camel tasted good like a cigarette should.

They began flying us to our next destinations as soon as they checked our medical records and cut orders. I flew out about 5:00 PM for a long flight across the country to Westover Field, MA. I arrived late in the afternoon and by then I was able to get something more than baby food to eat.

I stayed there overnight and the next morning I was loaded on a one-engine plane that carried only four stretchers and we headed for the US Naval Hospital, Camp Lejeune, NC. This was a Marine Base, but I had no trouble since I had been in the Navy and worked with the Marines in China. We didn't have a phone at home, so I had used the most helpful and courteous volunteers to write and mail letters to my mother at each stop from Pusan to North Carolina.

Around the first of October I was given a thirty-day convalescence leave. I borrowed thirty dollars from the Red Cross, pants, shirt, and shoes from a medic, and rode a bus home to SC. After I had caught up on all the news and learned that my mother had been sent three telegrams from the War Department, first saying I was missing in action, then slightly wounded, and another that stated that I was seriously wounded. At that time all notifications from the Defense Department were delivered by a taxi driver with a telegram.

I had been home about three days and was sitting on the porch with the family when a taxi came bouncing down our rutted road. The driver got out with a sad hangdog look on his face and handed my mother a telegram. When he started to explain, she stopped him and said it's all right, my son is here on the porch with me. The telegram was a notice that I had been killed in action.

While I was on leave, I met Mattie Rimrodt, Marian McGuffin's sister. She gave me Marian's address in Marion, SC. After graduating from high school, she had gone to Marion and started working for a lawyer. I had written her a few letters over the past two and a half years, but nothing serious. Billy Campbell and Furman Cobb were home on convalescence leave also. We were the first veterans of the Korean War to return to Oconee County. Campbell and I were both from Walhalla. At the end of my leave, I reported back to Camp Lejeune and was immediately assigned to the US Army Hospital at Fort Bragg, NC. Then on November 15th, I was transferred to the US Army Hospital at Fort Jackson, SC. There, I was evaluated and given two choices: one, take a hundred percent disability, or go back to duty. I asked the doctor to explain the disability and he told me that the Veterans Administration would re-examine me in about six months and if I had healed up internally, they would most likely cut me to about thirty percent. I asked him what the other choice was and he said if I chose to stay on active duty, I would have a picket-fence-physical profile, all ones. He was not allowed to send me back to duty with a disabling profile.

I decided to remain on active duty, and was sent to the Fourth Battalion, 61st Infantry Regiment, 8th Infantry Division. The Division had just been activated as a training division and was staffed with mostly reserve officers and NCOs who had been recently recalled to active duty. The Battalion Commander was a crusty old Major who had been a First Sergeant at Fort Lewis, Washington when the Japanese attacked Pearl Harbor. He told me that he and a couple of other senior NCOs went to Chinatown and started beating up on some Chinese because the beer made them look oriental. He was reduced in rank and started as a private in WWII. He worked his way back up through the ranks and was given a direct commission in the field artillery.

I was the first Korean War veteran to be assigned to the 61st Infantry Regiment. I was appointed as the Assistant Operations Sergeant and Instructor. While we were getting ready to start training, I was the Receiving and Shipping NCO. I met the trains, buses, and planes to pick up incoming recruits. The company moved them through their introductory phase, physicals, shots, interviews and clothing issue. When this was completed, I shipped them out to where they would receive their basic training.

During this period, Major Matthews asked if I could make a sand box of the training area. I gave him the 5th RCT motto, "I'LL try, Sir." I formed the terrain in sand, then covered it with a light coat of cement. I painted in the roads, ponds, streams, and wooded areas. The Battalion used it for months to orient the troops before they began their field training.

When the Regiment started training, I was assigned as a Platoon Tactics Instructor. On March 11th I was running a Platoon in the attack problem when General Frank McConnell, the Assistant Division Commander, inspected my class. I had put the rocket launcher team in position covering a road junction about two hundred yards away. The General questioned the distance and said that a 2.36 inch launcher would be ineffective at that range. I explained that I had watched a team with the new 3.5 inch launcher knock out a tank at over 300 yards in Korea. He proceeded to question me about Korea and told me I was the first Korean veteran he had talked with.

Well, I had turned the whole Regiment upside down and every one was jumping through their rear ends. The Company Commander of the troops I was instructing called the Committee Chief and reported that I had talked back to the General and the story ballooned greatly from there. They even sent a jeep to the training area for me. The first stop was the committee chief, and the ass-chewing started there; then to the regimental operations officer, the regimental executive officer, and finally to the Regimental Commander. I gave up trying to defend myself and let them rave on. Ultimately, I reported back to Battalion

Headquarters and Major Matthews. He asked me what had happened and I explained the entire conversation I'd had with General McConnell. He said, "I know Frank, so don't worry about it."

In the next day's Division Training Notes, General McConnell praised the Regiment for having a recent combat infantry veteran teaching tactics, one who was using initiative and first-hand combat experience in the field. That evening when I reported back to Battalion, Major Matthews came over to my desk and said, "Towe, how many of those bastards apologized to you today?"

Another learning point: listen to the whole story before jumping to conclusions. Major Matthews assigned LT. Munoz to me as an assistant instructor. I was teaching a class on combat patrol. The patrol was moving along a road and I was covering each obstacle they might encounter. LT. Munoz was at the back of the class reading the field manual and got about two obstacles ahead of me. Then he'd interrupt the class and ask me when I was going to cover a point we hadn't reached in the class. The troops were losing interest after about the third interruption, so I called the LT off to the side and asked him if he would like to teach the class. He answered no. I then told him to go to the back of the class and keep his damned mouth shut.

When the class was over, he informed me that he was going to report me to the Major. I told him that he'd better hurry, because I was going to report him. The First Sergeant came up in a jeep with one seat open and asked me if I'd like a ride in. LT. Munoz came over to the jeep and informed the First Sergeant that he was going to ride in and I could catch a later vehicle. The First Sergeant informed him that he was in charge of the jeep and that he would haul anybody he damned well pleased. LT. Munoz was left standing in the road with a red face. I reported that incident to the Major. He told the SGM to have LT. Munoz report to him as soon as he came in. The Major called me to come in as he read the riot act to the young LT, telling him that he'd sent him along with me hoping that he'd learn something. He told him to take notes during the class and if he had any questions, that I'd be glad to discuss them with him after the class, but he'd better never hear of him interrupting a class again.

I had been dating Marian since I returned from Korea and I finally proposed and she accepted on Christmas Eve 1950. We set a wedding date for August 12, 1951. It wasn't as if we had just met, since we had known each other for over two years. Evidently it was a wise choice for the two of us because we are looking forward to our fifty-second Wedding Anniversary.

We had opened a 61st Infantry Cadre Club, an annex to the Post NCO Club. It was located near the barracks of the clerks in the Post Personnel Office, so we invited them to be members. I was assigned as SGM of the 4th Battalion, 61st Infantry under Major Matthews. The SGM position at that time was SFC E6 and the First Sergeant was First Sergeant E7. On May 27, Major Matthews relieved the Company Commander, First Sergeant, and all the field cadre of the

CSM Glenn H. Towe [Ret'd]

Heavy Mortar Company for inefficiency. He sent me along with Captain Charles N Nielson to clean up the mess, as he said. Captain Nielson was the sharpest officer I ever served under. He'd march the Company to the field in the morning, spend the entire day with them, march them back in and look as if he never broke starch. This was during the summer in Fort Jackson. Captain Nielson appointed trainee James Reynolds as Field First Sergeant and John Lucas as training-aids NCO. I checked the troops and moved trainee Charles Dees into the orderly room as clerk and Omland and two other trainees into the mess hall. We had acting jacks as platoon sergeants and squad leaders. Within a couple of months, the Company Commander and I were the only personnel left in the Company, other than trainees.

First, the troops complained about not getting money that had been mailed from home. The CO told me to get one of my friends from the CID to check it out. They started questioning the mail clerk and directed him to open his foot-locker. All the missing letters were there, minus the money. He also had a wall locker full of cookies and candy that were originally destined for the troops. Next, we had to deal with our cook. I went into the mess hall to check on the noon meal. At that time, we were still cooking on coal stoves. The cook had just put coal into the range and was mixing biscuits with soot still on his hands. I relieved him on the spot. He protested and told me that I couldn't relieve him because he was the only cook. I informed him that either one of the trainees working in the mess could do a better job than he was doing. So go pack your bags and vamoose. That left us with a Mess Sergeant and three trainees in the mess.

The Charge of Quarters called me one Sunday evening to report that a KP had been instructed by the Mess Sergeant to place food from the mess into the trunk of his car. I immediately called the CO and once again he instructed me to call the CID. The investigator went to the Sergeant's home with the list from the KP. He explained why he was there and the SFC went to the refrigerator and removed the stolen food. The load included a block of cheese, bacon, eggs, and many other items. The SFC was also relieved immediately. Later, he was court-martialed and found guilty. He had a wife and seven children, so the Board went light on him. He was fined ten dollars per month for six months. Trainee Omland was subsequently made Mess Sergeant.

The next person in the Battalion to be relieved was SFC Bernard, the First Sergeant of the Tank Company. He was unable to do the paperwork required of a First Sergeant. He was also the kind of Sergeant that knew everything, and if you didn't believe it, all you had to do was ask him. He'd been called before Major Matthews a couple of times while I was SGM. Major Matthews relieved him and he went to work for the Regimental Administrative Warrant Officer.

SFC Sheridan had replaced him as First Sergeant in the Tank company, so one of the first jobs SFC Bernard decided to do was to go to the Tank Company and throw his weight around while pretending to inspect the company administration. SFC Sheridan ran him out of the company with a baseball bat, accompanied by a string of profanity that only a First Sergeant would know. Then he went to see Major Matthews before SFC Bernard got back to the Regiment. The Major listened to the story and headed straight to the Regiment himself. He was dressing down the Warrant Officer when Bernard arrived. SGM Greene told me later that Major Matthews let them know that he had run Bernard out of the Battalion and he never wanted to see him again. At this point, let me end the SFC Bernard story here. A couple of months later, a Master Sergeant got reduced for being AWOL, so the Regiment could promote a SFC to MSG. The Warrant Officer ran the promotion through the Commander before the Adjutant, Captain Giles, or any one else knew the rank was open. MSGT Bernard showed up at the club with his Master Sergeant Chevrons on, threw a twenty on the bar and said, the drinks are on me. He must have been more unpopular that I realized, because not one member of the Regiment would have a drink with him. He wouldn't come to the Company, but would have a private or PFC call me to come to the Regiment about some paper work. He then tried to get on my case by pulling his rank. One time I told him, "Barnard, if you screw around with me, I'll have you sent to Korea." I never thought I would get the opportunity so soon. He let me know that he had friends in high places and he'd never go to Korea. I had a few friends among the clerks from Post Personnel at the club myself. I'd found out early that those young clerks, through friends or other devious methods, could do you in before you knew what hit you. So after the Fort Benning incident, I tried to stay on their good side. You never knew when you'd need their help. I received a call from one of those clerks one afternoon. He wanted to know if I knew of a MSGT that hadn't been in Korea who needed to go. I told him MSGT Bernard needed to find out what the war was all about. He said I thought he might be your choice and hung up. The next day orders came down assigning MSGT Bernard to Korea. Both he and the Warrant Officer put up a fight, but Post said DA approved the assignment and they wouldn't rescind the orders.

The 31st Infantry Division National Guard had been called to active duty and assigned to Fort Jackson for training. Shortly after they arrived, LT. Jepson, SFC McPearson, and I were coming out of the Post PX when two 31st Division Master Sergeants asked us if they could go into the PX. LT. Jepson said it's okay if you're twenty years old. One of them said to the other, bring me a carton of cigarettes and I'll wait for you out here. When we got out of earshot of the two soldiers, I thought LT. Jepson was going to get down and roll. Now those were two MSGTs that were still wet behind the ears. We had a Major General that everyone referred to as Hollywood Harry J Collins. When he came to a football game, his motorcade consisted of four motorcycle MPs and his sedan. Two of the motorcycles were in front and two behind the sedan with sirens screaming. All four laid their cycles down in a cloud of dust. The driver came around and opened the door and the Major General dismounted and headed for the stands. The driver then went around to the other side of the sedan and escorted Mrs. Collins, a beautiful blond Austrian, to her seat alongside the General.

General Paxton and General Collins had an argument over naming the football team. Each threatened to pull their members off the team unless it was named for them. The final name was The Golden Arrow Dixies. We won every game until the play-offs with Carswell Air Force Base. They came into Columbia with a line that could have played pro football. The temperature was about 30 degrees at game time and when they made an end run, it sounded like a herd of horses out on the field. I think every member of their team was at least All Southwest Conference. In June they had an Awards Ceremony and Parade consisting of the 8th and 31st Infantry Divisions. A young widow of a Lieutenant killed in Korea was presented with his Posthumous Bronze Star and Purple Heart. I received the Silver Star and Purple Heart. Marian attended the ceremony. She was seated in the VIP Section and was very impressed. They didn't have a Silver Star, so they borrowed one that had been awarded to LTC Mason for action in the Philippines in WWII. After the ceremony, Marian and I ate in the mess hall.

Captain Nielson transferred and a Second Lieutenant came in as CO. He was a hotshot straight from ROTC. I attempted to assist him, but he felt that he knew all there was to know about Army administration. He had a meeting with the unit fund council and they decided to make an unauthorized purchase from the fund. I told him that the item was an issue item and you couldn't purchase it from the fund. He stated that he was not going to wait for a requisition to go through. I stated that would be an IG gig. He got mad and said, Sergeant, do you think you can do my job? I was mad by then too, so I replied that I could do twice the job with half the training you have received. He told me that there was not enough room in the Company for the two of us and that he was going to see Major Matthews to get him another First Sergeant. I told him to cool down and added, "Lieutenant, don't go to see the Major." He wasn't listening and stormed out the orderly room door. I went out to check training. I came back to the orderly room about two hours later and looked into the CO's office. He had a cardboard box on his desk that he was filling with various items. I asked him what he was doing. He said, "You advised me not to see the Major, but I didn't listen. The Major said the first thing a new Company Commander should learn is to listen to the First Sergeant. He then immediately transferred me over to the committee group. He said to tell you that he'll send you another Second Lieutenant later today."

The new Second Lieutenant must have talked with the one who had just been relieved. He came in and told me flat out, "I don't know anything about company administration, so you and the clerk have to keep me out of trouble."

I had three episodes with the Post Engineers that I remember. The first one occurred when I had Sgt Lucas put in a work order in late August to the Post Engineers to install our heater in the orderly room. One morning in early October, I called the engineers about the stove. I was told to put in a work order. I asked him what happened to the last one. "Oh," he answered, "let me look, yes, we do have the order, but it will be at least two weeks before we can get to the job."

I had Sgt Lucas set up the stove using the same guy wires, screw holes, etc. and the stove worked beautifully. About three weeks later, the Post Engineers came to do the job. They proceeded to chew me out about putting it up. They took it down completely, looked at it, and then put it back up. Then one of the chief assistants came down and got on my case again about doing engineer work.

The second case happened one cold morning when I was checking a barracks and found a plumber sitting in the latrine smoking a cigarette and dropping ashes on the floor. He told me he was taking a break, so I asked him if he'd check a leaking faucet while he was in the barracks. He informed me that he was an outside plumber and that he wasn't required to do any inside work. His tone of voice set me off. I told him in no uncertain words to get his lazy ass out of my latrine, and if I caught him inside one of my barracks again, I'd call the MPs and have him hauled off for stealing. He reported me to the same engineer assistant that came to see me before. We had some harsh words, but I didn't back down. I told him that if one of his men wanted to use the latrine, he was to report to the orderly room first and he would then be escorted anywhere he needed to go.

The best one happened a short time later. The Battalion had set up and marked POV (privately owned vehicle) parking spaces at the end of the street. They were marked as CO, XO, and First SGT for each of the companies and other spaces for visitors. You drove across a shallow ditch and into the space leaving enough room behind you for another car to pull in and still be off the street. I had gone to the PX and when I returned, the assistant engineer was in my parking space. I pulled in tight behind him, set my parking brake, locked my car, and stayed where I could observe him. He went to the Battalion Commander who asked him why he didn't use a visitor's space. His reply was that he was only going to be there a couple of minutes. The SGM called the company and was told that I was not in, but they would see if they could locate me. The entire Battalion played it for all it was worth. About two hours later, the Battalion CO sent word that the engineer was going to call the Post Provost Marshal and have my car towed in. They informed him that I was on the way to the parking lot. He came up really steaming. I said come here a minute. I showed him my sign and asked him if he could read. Hell yes, he replied. I then asked

CSM Glenn H. Towe [Ret'd]

him who the First Sergeant of Mortar Company was. I told him if I ever caught him in one of my company slots again, I would call my friends over at the MP Desk and have his car towed. He left cussing a blue streak, but he never stopped in our area again.

One Saturday afternoon a Sergeant, who had recently returned from Korea wearing a 24th Infantry Division patch, and I were sitting in a beer joint on Main Street in Columbia having a beer. Across the room was a soldier wearing a 1st Cavalry Division patch. He'd already had a couple of beers and was looking for a fight. He came over to the table and looked at the 24th Division patch and started the rumble. The conversation ran like this: Who relieved you at Taegu on 21 July? Answer: 1st Cavalry. Who relieved you at Waegton on 24 July? Answer: 1st Cavalry. Who relieved you at the Nak Tong River on 27 July? Answer: the North Koreans, you dumb son-of-a-bitch. That Cavalry private's mouth dropped open and without saying another word, he returned to his table and continued drinking his beer. I was fortunate to have good clerks who could run the orderly room in my absence. We graduated and shipped the cycle on August 10. We ran another cycle through and got the trainees that we appointed to various positions promoted to SFC before we deactivated Mortar Company on January 24, 1952.

On August 12, 1951, Marian and I were married in her sister Mattie's house on Bear swamp Road, Walhalla, SC. Fifty years later we celebrated out fiftieth wedding anniversary in the same house. We visited her sister and family in Tennessee and another sister and brother and their families in Sandusky, OH on our honeymoon. I had a wreck one night and Major Matthews saved a stripe for me by giving me company punishment and a small fine before the paperwork came from the Provost Marshal's Office charging me with DUI. Major Matthews went with me to see the Magistrate in Columbia, SC but was unable to talk the judge out of the fifty-dollar fine.

When I was Battalion Sergeant Major, I was put in for a clearance. A LT. Colonel from G2 called me in for questions and asked why I didn't enter any credit references on the request. I stated that I had never had any credit before. He advised me to buy on credit and then pay at the end of the month to establish a rating. He said people would say you were the greatest in the world, as long as you didn't owe them money. I received a TOP Secret Clearance that helped me get into a couple of schools and a job later. I have also been in debt ever since.

I was transferred to Headquarters & Headquarters Company, 61st Infantry and assigned to the Committee Group. On January 24th, I reported to the Infantry School, 8th Infantry Division Instructors Course on Infantry Instructions. It was a mixed class of seventy-five officers and NCOs. We moved into the barracks, one for officers and one for NCOs, for four weeks. We had instructions on every subject taught in basic training and in AIT (Advanced Infantry Training). It was a good course taught by the Leadership School Cadre and I learned a lot about how to be an effective instructor by the time I returned to my unit. I graduated number 8 out of the seventy-five students and I was made the leading instructor for machine guns. I loved it because I was using not only the skills that I learned at the instructor course, but also what I had learned from Gunners-Mate School back in 1944 at Brainbridge, MD and while I was Gunners-Mate on the LSM 447. I started with the grease gun and worked through the cal .30 A1 water-cooled, or heavy machine gun and the cal .30 A4 air-cooled machine gun and the fifty caliber machine gun. During this class, I also related that I had watched the North Koreans attack a machine gun section, one heavy and one light gun, for two days and one night. The gunners kept both guns in operation during this period and stacked the enemy up like cordwood in front of their position. I instructed this class for a month before being moved to the 2nd Battalion, 61st Infantry as Battalion Sergeant Major. On Sunday morning, 18 May 1952, at 5:00 AM our daughter Glenda was born in the Fort Jackson Hospital. I've never lived down the fact that I wasn't at the hospital when she was born. I admitted Marian at 3:00 AM and was told by one of the Hospital staff that I might as well go home, since she'll be in labor for four or five hours. Back in those days, you didn't see the patient until after the baby was born. I took their advice and went home and straight to bed. I awoke at six, showered, and went to the neighbors to use their phone. I was told that Glenda had been born about an hour and a half after I left and I'm still occasionally reminded of that time lapse.

The previous SGM had transferred to Germany because he said he couldn't work with the Battalion CO. I found out in short order exactly what he meant.

Lieutenant Colonel Norris was a reservist who had been recalled to duty. He'd been a Professor of English and Literature at the University of Texas before his recall. He usually arrived at the office between eight and eight- thirty. He'd call me into his office for a report on the night's activities. I'd go in, snap to attention and make my report. He'd leave me standing at attention while he gave me a lesson on English usage. The lesson sometimes lasted for thirty minutes. I felt sorry for his students, because he spoke in a monotone and at times almost put me to sleep. Our first run-in came over his choice of ink for his pen. He used Christmas-Tree green ink and I reminded him that papers and documents should be signed with black or blue-black ink. He told me that no SGM or anyone else would tell him what color ink to use.

This ink caused two major flaps. The first was a Subject Letter he wanted sent through channels to the Fourth Army Headquarters about his reserve points. He started the letter with 'Dear Harry' and ended it with 'Sincerely yours.' He told me to have the clerk type it. I looked it over and informed him of the proper format for a Subject Letter. He invited me into his office and explained to me during a thirty-minute session that as a Professor of the English Language, he was capable of writing the letter and I wasn't to question it. I told the clerk to type it as written, but to use the proper format. When it was typed, he signed it with green ink and told me to hand-carry it to Regiment and inform them that he wanted it to go out immediately.

I walked next door to Regiment and gave the letter to Captain Giles, the Adjutant. Evidently Captain Giles had a run-in with him before. He took a red pencil and lined through the Dear Sir and Sincerely yours and drew a circle around the green signature. He gave the letter back and told me to tell LTC Norris that it couldn't go out unless it was in the proper format. LTC Norris headed for Regiment and I went out to check the area because I didn't want to hear him when he returned. The clerk told me later that he returned all red-faced and was told to type the letter properly and that he had a headache and was going home for the afternoon. The next day, he borrowed a pen from the Operations Sergeant and signed the letter.

The next ink incident occurred when his driver went on sick call. At that time, we had a sick-book that both the medical officer and Commander signed when some one went on sick call. He signed my sick-book with the green pen. About two weeks later, we had our IG/CMI Inspection. The Senior Inspector was COL Hill from Third Army in Atlanta. I knew him because this was my third inspection by him. He came in and said, "Towe, how the hell are you?" He then turned to the Sergeant with him and said, "We'll only be a couple of minutes because I know Towe is straight." He glanced at my duty roster and nodded. Then he picked up my sick-book and opened it. I though he was going to have a stroke when he saw the green ink. He looked at me and said, "Towe, who was the dumb son-of-a-bitch that used that green ink?" He was looking at me and I felt that he wanted me to answer, so I said, "Colonel Norris, Sir." Colonel Morris was hovering in the background like a mother hen. Col. Hill threw the book down and left the office without speaking another word. About five minutes later, COL Norris called for me. I went in, snapped to attention, and said, "Yes, Sir. He looked at me angrily and snarled, "Sergeant, I don't appreciate you insinuating that I am a dumb son-of-a-bitch." I replied that I was asked a question that required an answer. He sat there looking at me for about five minutes before dismissing me.

Our nest issues concerned signing in and cover up. I went on leave and was due back for duty the next morning. I called Captain Phillips, the XO, and told him I was back at home and wasn't going out again that night and would he sign me in before he left. COL Norris immediately wanted to know what was going on and said there wouldn't be any cover-ups while he was Battalion CO. So at 11:00 PM, I drove on Post and signed in at 2345 hours. COL Norris had informed me he didn't need a key and that someone would always be in when he got there. I always went in about five-thirty, unlocked the door, plugged in the coffee pot and visited the First SGTs to see what had happened overnight.

I arrived the next morning at a quarter to six and COL Norris was sitting on the step waiting for me to unlock the door. I gave him a cheery "Good morning, Sir," and unlocked the door. He didn't speak, but went immediately to the sign-out sheet. When he saw that I had signed in, he turned to me and asked, "Exactly when did you sign in, Sergeant-Major?" "The time I came in last night, Sir, is on the sheet." Then he told me to come into his office. He explained to me in great detail why no one should cover for anyone. He emphasized that each soldier was responsible to be on time.

And to show how some orders can backfire, the Regimental Commander had instructed all units they would have a sign-out board posted where you could, at a glance, see where the personnel had gone and an estimated time they would return. Both Captain Phillips and I had advised COL Norris of the board and the regimental CO's instructions and we were told that it was none of anybody's business where he went.

The Regiment formed for a Regimental Parade one afternoon in front of the 2nd Battalion Headquarters on the street going up Tank Hill. They formed at 1:00 PM and at about 1:15 PM, COL Norris still hadn't shown up. The Regimental CO came into our Headquarters and asked where COL Norris was and I told him I didn't know. He looked at the sign-out board and asked me if COL. Norris had been instructed to sign out. I said, "Yes, he had been instructed by both the Executive Officer and me." "Well, why isn't he signed out?" the Regimental CO asked. I told him Colonel Norris informed me that it was none of anybody's business where he went.

I was then asked about his duty hours and I told the Colonel that he usually arrived about eight. The next question concerned the time he left for lunch and the time he returned from lunch. I told him that he usually left between eleven-thirty and twelve and returned about two or two-thirty.

"You tell Colonel Norris that I am outside holding up the parade, and I want him to report to me on the double."

About fifteen minutes later, Col Norris came in and asked me if anyone had been looking for him. I informed him that the Regimental Commander was looking for him and I didn't know where he was. He turned pale, grabbed his steel helmet and took off. When he returned, I was called into his office immediately. He said, "Sergeant-Major, you know that you're supposed to cover for the Commander and give an excuse for me not signing out." I looked him straight in the eye and said, "It wasn't that long ago you stood me at attention in this office and let me know that nobody in this outfit covered for anybody else." He said, "Yes, but this is different."

I lost my cool at that point and told him that I didn't see a damned bit of difference in it except that he got his ass chewed out by the Regimental CO. I was fed up with him and knew if I made one slip, I would've had it. When he left the office that afternoon, I called my friend in Post Personnel and said I'd heard there was a levy for Europe. He wanted to know how I knew, since it had only come down that morning. I asked him if there happened to be a vacancy in my rank and MOS, and if so, to put my name at the top of the list. The next morning when I informed the COL at our morning briefing session, he wanted to know how I got on that list. He hadn't approved a transfer for me. I told him as far as I knew, my name was on the list when it came out of the Department of The Army.

I received orders for US Army Europe on 26 September 1952. I took a twenty-day delay en route, cleared Post and went on leave. I arranged for Marian and Glenda to live in Walhalla, SC with her father and stepmother until we could get orders for her to join me in Germany. We moved our meager belongings to Mr. McGuffin's and I spent the rest of my delay en route getting Marian and Glenda settled in for the wait.

I was clearing Finance when I met O.O. Langford, who I thought was lost in a typhoon in 1945.When the barge sank, he stayed on a life raft for a couple of days before he was rescued by a cargo ship going to Long Beach, CA. By that time, the war was over, so he was discharged.

I departed Fort Jackson on October 4, 1952 for twenty-days delay en route before reporting to Camp Kilmer, NJ for surface transportation to Germany. We got Marian situated with her father and stepmother while she waited for orders authorizing her and Glenda to join me in Germany. I sailed from New Pork on the troop ship, USS Darby for Bremerhaven, landing on November 4th. Again I volunteered for head count and had an enjoyable trip over. We went by troop train from Bremerhaven to US Army Europe Replacement Center at Zweibrucken, Germany.

We were the first troopship load of soldiers to be processed through this new camp. There was a 12:00 PM curfew for all of Germany and over the next couple of years it really reduced the NCO Corps there. They explained that if we were late returning from pass, we would be reduced one stripe. There were two or three Master Sergeants reduced to SFC during the three days I remained there.

On 7 November, I went by troop train to Augsburg, Germany, and the 43rd Infantry Division Replacement Company. This was a National Guard Division that had been called to active duty for a period of two years. The 28th National Guard Division had also been recalled and was in Germany. I looked around at all the first three-graders running around and thought they really were loaded with NCOs only to find that most of them were "acting jacks." These were appointed NCOs for duty, but not a promotion for pay purposes. I was reassigned to Company K, 169th Infantry Regiment, in Furth, Germany. This was a suburb of Nuremberg which was a large city. I went by train to Nuremberg where I was picked up by a driver from the Company and driven to Johnson Barracks. This was the home of the 3rd Battalion of the 169th Infantry. It was a very small Post, with just enough room for the Battalion. We had a PX, barber shop, GYM, NCO, and EM Club. It was just a couple of blocks from the William O. Darby Post. This was a large complex with military housing, large PX and everything a soldier and his family needed. I had been in K Company about three days, when all the new NCOs had to report to Monthieth Barracks, Headquarters of the 169th Infantry, for an orientation by the Regimental CO. He didn't welcome us, but instead threatened us with reduction. He looked around at all the stripes and said, don't come in here thinking that you're going to change things. We have a top-notch unit here and I intend to keep it that way. If you get out of line, I'll have your stripes. Sadly, the last part of that statement was very true. He busted about forty NCOs in a two-month period. I will say one thing for Colonel Craig, he wasn't partial to anyone. He reduced his own Sergeant Major for coming through the gate twenty minutes late.

At Johnson Barracks, we had unit police for gate guards. The gate was a large metal gate that swung across the entrance. On the wall above the hinged end of the gate was a large clock. When the clock hit 23:59 and thirty seconds the guard started closing the gate. It was slammed shut at exactly 2400 Hours. Anyone who didn't get in was written a ticket automatically, and if he was a NCO, he also lost a stripe. I have seen men running for the gate and ricocheting off of it like a shell fragment because they were five seconds late. When I arrived in King Company, I reported to Lt. Sigmund Newman, the CO, and again I almost let my big mouth over-load my little ass.

During our conversation, Lt. Newman informed me that K Company had qualified eighty-two percent of the company for the Expert Infantry Badge. Without a thought as to how it might have sounded to him, I said, "Bull shit." He sat back in his chair with a startled look on his face and finally said, "What do you mean?" I quickly took stock of what I'd said and then explained my remark. "Sir, two years ago, I was in a Regular Army Infantry Regiment, the 5th RCT, the best-trained Infantry Regiment to fight in Korea. We were given the test by Army Regulations and we had three men who qualified for the Expert Infantry Badge. One was my ex-Platoon Sergeant, SSG Bobby Sterling, A West Point 2nd LT. and an E4, both from other battalions. I explained that I had never heard of a unit qualifying over fifty percent of the unit as expert marksman.

He explained to me about being a National Guard unit and everyone was looking forward to going home. There were three Regular Army NCOs present when I arrived in K Company. SFC Thorton was the First Sergeant, SFC Dettoria was Mess Sergeant and SFC Wojchowski was Communications Sergeant. When I completed my processing, I joined the Company at Hohenfels Training Center, where it was undergoing winter-training exercises. I met the First Sergeant and he said I was going to the 3rd Platoon as Platoon Sergeant. I was replacing SFC Johnson who would be going home soon.

SFC Thornton introduced me to SFC Johnson. I told Johnson that I'd like him to continue running the Platoon while I observed for a couple of days. He said it's your platoon, you run it. That pissed me off and I told him that I could damn well do it. I checked Johnson out and found he was really only a Corporal acting as a SFC. He was as worthless as tits on a boar hog. I went to the CO to get those SFC stripes removed, but no dice. Apparently, he had relatives in high places and everyone was afraid to touch him. I put him in the rear of the Platoon and when we marched, he followed three paces behind the platoon.

I remember one Saturday morning we were having an inspection by the Regimental CO. Johnson was standing inspection three paces behind the platoon. The Colonel asked, "What is that man doing standing behind the Platoon?" I replied, "Sir, he is too sorry an individual to be a part of the platoon, so I keep him three paces behind them." The Company CO almost fell over, but nothing else was ever said about it.

I never found out if it was Regimental Policy or not, but when a person reached sixty days of his date to return to the US, he turned in all his equipment, including his weapon and field gear. He then sat in the barracks and did nothing. They didn't bother to get up until the snack bar opened for breakfast. The first morning we were back from Hohenfels, I went through the rooms getting the Platoon up for reveille. All the short-timers said, "Mache Nix, I'm ETS," and stayed in bed. About fifteen minutes later when I found them in bed, I turned the bunks over. I was informed later to let them sleep in, so I moved them all in one large room and closed the door. The room was never inspected and looked and smelled like a pig sty. All this was going on when we were less than an hour's drive from the East German Border. At times I would think, if it weren't for getting my ass killed, I would like to see the Russians come after those 'Mach Nix" bastards. Mach Nix was German slang for "I don't care" and ETS was Army for "End Term of Service."

Another problem we had at that time was with the truck drivers. When we went to the field or were put on alert, we received our transportation from a truck company. This would usually require a duce and a half with trailer. Most of the time we received good drivers, but occasionally we would get a new driver who couldn't drive the truck, much less back it with a trailer attached. We were required to Combat Park all vehicles. This meant they had to be backed off the road or down a tank trail or firebreak cut through the forest. If you were unfortunate enough to have a driver who couldn't drive, then the Platoon Leader or Platoon Sergeant were the ones who got chewed out. After receiving two duds in a row, I called the Motor Sergeant and got lined up for a driver's test. Since I was in the MPs in Vienna, I'd always had a driver's license for any vehicle I might have to use, so I was licensed to drive up to a five-ton truck. Then I went back to the Platoon and informed my Platoon NCOs that they were to get licenses. A couple of them refused, saying that they were not truck drivers. I tried diplomacy to no avail. I finally went to the Company Commander and explained that we never knew when one of the drivers would get sick or another emergency arose that would require someone else to drive. He agreed with me and put out an order that all Platoon Sergeants and Squad Leaders would get licenses. The same two NCOs who had refused to get licenses before, went to get tested and intentionally failed the test two times. Their excuse was that the test was so difficult they just couldn't pass it. I went to the CO again, but this time I took them with me. Each of them owned a POV (privately owned vehicle) and was licensed to drive it in Europe. I explained to the CO that the written parts of both tests were about the same, so if they couldn't pass the test, their licenses should be pulled until they could be retested, and at the same time be tested for a military vehicle license. He agreed and gave them an order to either have military vehicle licenses in a week or turn in their POV license until they could be retested. The next day they both got their licenses. They were pissed off at me for a few days, but I didn't care. As far as I know, none of the NCOs ever had to drive, but a couple of times we did have to back the trucks into position. I continued that policy as long as I was Platoon Sergeant and also as First Sergeant.

Lt. Dan E. Shilling was the XO. He came to me one day and asked if I had ever made a sand table. I said that I'd made one in Fort Jackson covering the training area. He asked me if I'd assist him in making a display for the Company to enter in the Division "Golden Rifles Display."

It was the leadoff of the Division Company annual testing. Our display was judged best in the Division and the CO and XO were elated. I think this might have helped save a stripe for me. I went to the club or the movies regularly, but went into Furth only once before Marian came over. I went with a couple of other Sergeants to eat and have a couple of beers. At 11:00 PM, I started looking for a taxi for the five-mile ride back to Post and there wasn't a taxi on the street. I looked until 11:30, then went back into the bier halle and asked if they had any available rooms. Luckily, they had one left, so I took it.

Before I went up to the room, I called the Company CO and explained what I'd done. He said I should get back immediately and I told him that it was too late. If I came back now, I would be caught at the gate, so either way, I'd lose a stripe. I knew that the message-center truck ran at about 5:30 AM, so I got out on the street the next morning and caught the truck and got in the back with the mail bags. They drove through the gate and the guard asked the driver if he had any passengers and he said no. I got out when the truck stopped around the corner at Battalion Headquarters. I went to the Company area, changed into fatigues, and stood reveille. Nobody ever asked where I was at bed check or anything else.

SFC Thornton entered the Army in 1933 and was assigned to the Horse Cavalry. He stayed with them to the end of WWII. Then he went to a military school as an ROTC instructor, teaching riding and caring for the school's horses.

He was lost when it came to administration. All he wanted was to go back to the Military Academy and be a stable boy.

At that time, DA decided that every company in the Army should have an Administrative Warrant Officer and they were appointing senior NCOs as Warrants. Back at Fort Jackson, Major Matthews had talked to me about a direct commission when I first joined the 61st Infantry. I explained to him that due to my limited education, I would take my chances as an enlisted man. I also explained that my CO in Korea had informed me that the Battalion had three battlefield promotions and asked me if I would like him to submit my name to the Battalion CO for one of the spots. He told me if I took the commission, I would be transferred to another Company in the Regiment. Again he wanted me to take a Warrant when they opened up once more, but I declined a second time.

On February 11th, I was appointed Unit Administrator with duties of handling all the administrative duties of the Platoon Leaders, so that they could spend more time training the troops. This job was a snap after being First Sergeant and Sergeant Major.

In early spring when all the snow had melted in the southern areas of Germany, the 43rd Infantry Division Commander decided that we should have a police-call along the Autobahn. This was to be between Nuremberg and Munich and from Munich to Augsburg to Stuttgart. Our section was from the Danube at Inglestadt and back to Nuremberg. Other regiments covered the other sections. At that time, there was very little traffic on the autobahn. I remember a couple of field problems when we set up blockades on the autobahn and checked all vehicles for aggressor forces.

The most miserable night I ever spent in the field was in the same area. The Regiment had a maneuver area and river-crossing site on the Danube near Inglestadt. We were to cross the river in rafts and attack and hold the high ground across the river. We bivouacked in the vicinity of the crossing site and the mosquitoes were large black ones that came upon us in swarms like gnats. They would land on you and as you tried to brush them off, they just sat there and kept sucking your blood. The only way to get rid of them was to squash them where they sat. All of us looked like we had been in a brawl with blood all over. We dropped all of our equipment except for our weapons and a poncho on our ammunition belt. Our LD (line of departure) was the river edge at 10:00 PM. We had secured our rafts about 1000 meters from the edge of the river and carried them to the river through grass and reeds about six to eight feet tall. It was a hot night, so by the time we struggled with the rafts, rowed them across the river, then attacked about three hundred meters up a hill, there wasn't one of us who had a dry stitch on him. We placed the Platoon in a defensive position and laid down all our weapons and finished up about 2:00 AM. They said we had accomplished our mission and called off the problem. A heavy fog rolled in and it was impossible to see more than ten feet. You located other men by voice. We were in a hay field that had been recently mowed and we tried to sleep on the stubble. Nights along the Danube can be very cold, especially when you have sweated a lot and are wet all over. You roll up in a poncho and it is like entering an ice box. I would lie down for a few minutes, go to sleep, and wake up cold, then get up and pace around in circles before lying down again. We ate our cold C rations for breakfast and moved alongside a road to wait for trucks to pick us up. About 9:00 AM the sun burned off the fog and just as it began shining through, a German girl came down the farm road on a bicycle. The men started whistling and made all sorts of catcalls, and she just pedaled faster. Her dress blew up around her waist and all she wanted to do was get away from there. She pedaled faster and faster and let her dress fly. I'm sure that must've been the most frightening morning of her life. She probably rode there every morning and for all those whistling and screaming GIs to appear out of the fog must have been terrifying. I have spent some cold nights since then, but I put that one down as the most miserable. During the night just to keep warm I frequently thought of the time about five years before when I had been swimming in the Danube River at the nude beech in Vienna.

On February 24, 1953, Marian received orders for her and Glenda to join me. Now all they had to do was get passports and wait for a port call. She sold our car and kept the money for us to purchase a car when she arrived in Germany. On April 7th I was assigned quarters at 16 Schleichstrasse, Eibach, Germany. It was one-half of a duplex German house with a basement, an upstairs, and attic. The three of us were lost in it since the only apartments we ever had consisted of two rooms. One was a living room and bedroom combination and the other room was a kitchen-dining room combination. I was issued about a one-hundred-piece set of Rosenthal China, a lead-crystal service and a drawer full of German silverware. This was what they called confiscated housing. The other side of the apartment had two entire families living in the same type of unit. We enjoyed our stay in Eibach and made a lot of German friends. Our daughter Glenda learned to speak German before she learned English. We'd go to a restaurant and she'd show off by going around and speaking to all the people we knew.

The fireman of our building, Joseph Koric, was hired by the US Army. He was a Yugoslavian who had been brought into Germany as slave labor when he was fifteen years old. At the end of the war, he was left on the street to fend for himself. He thought that all his family had been killed during the war and because the Soviets were occupying Yugoslavia, he was afraid to go looking for them. I visited him in 1973 and he had gone back home and located all of his family. He had married a German and they had a daughter, so he remained in Germany. Joe introduced Marian and me to the local population. I became a member of the local Rod and Gun Club and we were both honorary members of the Fellowship Club.

Those clubs rotated hosting a party each month. Marian and I went to all of them. Joe was a good dancer, so he and Marian danced most of the night while I talked with the Germans. I was on duty one Saturday night and Marian went to the party with Joe. A large hog had been killed for the occasion and there was fresh ground raw pork sausage as a specialty. The Germans went wild over it, piling it on bread and eating it as a sandwich. That made Marian sick just seeing it so they left early.

We owned the only car in the group so it was Marian's job to be taxi driver and get them all home. When Marian arrived we purchased a 1942 Mercedes Touring Car. It had belonged to the German Army and you could see the outline of where the Swastika was painted over. Most of the time we ended up at home with ten to twenty guests from the party for breakfast. I did the cooking, nothing fancy, just a good American breakfast of toast, jelly, bacon, eggs, and plenty of coffee. It was Marian's job afterwards to drive them all home.

After about a year and a half, we became eligible for Post housing in the William O. Darby Kasern. We fought to stay where we were and we finally won. We were allowed to live in the same house for our entire tour.

When all the National Guard went home, we started a rough training program. I kept a calendar for the last six months of 1953. We were in the field overnight or away from Johnson Barracks on field exercises for one hundred and thirty-four nights.

When we were in garrison, we had our duty roster duties. Because of the shortage of officers and Company Charge of Quarters, this included Regimental Staff Duty NCO, Battalion Sergeant of the Guard, Battalion Staff Duty NCO, Battalion Courtesy Patrol, and Company Duty Officer. You might come in for three days after twenty days in the field and have roster duties for all three nights.

Here's an example of how tired you could get: we came in about eleven AM one Saturday morning after being in the field all week. I checked to see that all field equipment had been washed, inspected all weapons, made out the Platoon pass list and other tasks required before I even thought of a shower. I finished up about 4:00 PM. I decided to shower and go to the club for a steak and a beer before heading to bed for some much needed sleep. I showered, got into my Class A uniform and made one final check of the Platoon area. By then, it was 6:00 PM. I decided to wait until about 6:30 or 7:00 P.M. before I went to the club. I laid back across my cot for a couple of minutes. When I awoke I looked at my watch and it was 6:30 PM. I got up, felt nice and relaxed, and went to the latrine. I walked around the end of the barracks, past our mess hall and to the club. I walked up to the door of the club and it was locked. That seemed strange for the club to be locked on a Saturday night. I walked back to the mess hall to find out what had happened. I went in and the cook asked me,

"Sergeant Towe, how would you like your eggs this morning?" I stopped in amazement and it finally dawned on me that I had slept around the clock. I replied, "Thanks, over easy, as usual."

The Platoon Sergeant's job is one of the most demanding in the army. The Squad Leader has eight men to care for, while the Platoon Sergeant has thirty-eight. You have the four squad leaders to assist you, but you live with the Platoon and know each man. The First Sergeant has the four Platoon Sergeants and Section Sergeants as a buffer between him and the troops. It's the same for the XO and Company Commander.

Every time I got a pass or leave, Marian and I traveled and tried to see as much of Europe as we could. During this tour, we made one trip that especially stands out for me. We drove from Nuremberg to Heidelberg, Metz, France, and on to Bastogne, Belgium. They had just completed the Battle of the Bulge Memorial that was dedicated to the Allied Forces. Everything there was "Nuts" after General McAuliffe's reply to the German's demand for surrender. From there, we went on to the Rhine River and Remagen, where the US Forces captured the Remagen Bridge. At that time, a part of the bridge was still in place.

Our Mess sergeant was SFC Joe Dettoria. His wife, Virginia, and daughter, Victoria (Vicky), came to Germany before Marian and Glenda. He invited the senior NCOs to come to his house on Saturday nights because of the curfew. We were covered because if an alert was called, we could be reached by phone and we were off the streets. As the dependents started to arrive, Virginia was like a mother to them. The men played pinochle and the women baked and talked. Everyone remained there until 6:00 AM when we were able to get on the street again.

We had a First Cook that worked for SFC Dettoria, whose wife came over shortly after Marian. The first Saturday after they arrived, everyone gathered at the Dettoria's and he told us about his wife and the taxi driver. He met the train when she arrived and they were in a taxi heading for their apartment. He and the driver were in a conversation when she asked, are you German and he answered yes. She said, I can understand every word he's saying. So the Cook answered, you should, you damn fool, he's speaking English. She didn't deny it so it probably was the truth.

The US Army was integrating at this time. Our Battalion was to exchange soldiers with an infantry unit of the 2nd Armored Cavalry Regiment that was stationed at Murrell Barracks on the other side of Nuremberg from us. We were to select a percentage of our troops to be transferred to the 2nd AC and they were to do the same. The troops were supposed to be good soldiers with no history of unit punishment, VD, or AWOL.

When we received our black troops, I got two men that I remember, SFC Dixon and Private Tolliver. SFC Dixon was from Alabama and one of the best soldiers I have ever known. I met him in the hallway and he asked me which of the squad rooms I'd like him to stay in. I said, you are my Assistant Platoon Sergeant and you'll stay in the two-man room with me. I was never sorry that I had him in the room, although it caused me a lot of extra work.

He was sharp as a tack. He was about 5-9 or 10 and 160 or 170 pounds and looked like a wedge from the heels up to the shoulders. His shoes were spit-shined like mirrors.

He could slide his foot under a girls dress and tell you the color of her panties. I gave up trying to be the better-looking soldier and just tried to hold my own with him. We talked a lot about the integration and the effect that it had on soldiers of both races. The young soldiers accepted the integration better than the civilian population. We had very few problems in the barracks, but each man continued not to socialize off post. SFC Dixon said that this was the first time most of the black soldiers had ever been treated as equals and they had trouble handling it.

The Officers and senior NCOs went out of their way to see that desegregation of the army worked and you can still see the results of that effort in the military services today. SFC Dixon told me that all the troops we received from the 2nd AC were good men except for Private Tolliver. He was one that they sent to us just to get rid of him. He resented authority and accused everyone of trying to take advantage of him because of his color. Dixon also told me not to argue with Tolliver and to let him take care of any situation that might arise.

Toliver's Squad Leader reported that Toliver refused to clean a commode. I went to the latrine and told Toliver that I didn't want any trouble with him and to clean that commode as he was told. He said, "Ain't no damned white man going to tell me to put my hand in that damned commode." He squared off as if I was going to fight him.

I suddenly realized that I had been in this kind of situation before. One Saturday morning back in Hawaii, I told a man in my squad to clean a commode. He refused and I got a rag and scouring powder and scrubbed one side of the commode. Then I told him to get his hand in there and clean the damn commode. He whirled around as if to hit me. I caught his arm and before I knew what happened I had him bent over the commode when temper and temptation got the best of me. I put enough pressure on his arm to force his head into the commode and then I flushed it.

He went to Captain Sutherland and reported that I tried to drown him in the commode. The CO asked me what happened and I told him that the Private swung at me and I caught his arm rather than hit him and he fell head first into the commode. The CO told him to get back to the Platoon and clean the commode the way I showed him.

Later that afternoon when I went to the orderly room to pick up my pass, First SGT McGuire called me into his office and said he and the CO had a good laugh after we left the CO's office. Just as Toliver squared off, SFC Dixon tapped me on the shoulder and said, Top wants to see you in the orderly room now. The inflection on the 'now' let me know I should get out of there fast. I said okay and headed in that direction. Just as I arrived at the orderly room, Tolliver came in with a bloused eye and said that SFC Dixon had hit him. About that time SFC Dixon came in and told the First Sergeant that Tolliver swung at him and his foot slipped and he hit his head on the commode handle. That cooled Tolliver off since he couldn't cry racial prejudice. About two weeks after that incident, the CID came to my Platoon to ask me to point out Private Tolliver's wall locker. They searched his clothing and found two marijuana cigarettes in his Ike jacket pocket. They arrested him on the spot and that was the last time I ever saw Tolliver.

At that time, beer was the recreational pastime of choice and drugs were not common in the military. The only time I had come close to drugs prior to this incident was once in China when the three of us decided that since we were in China, we should try opium. There were opium dens all over the cities of China at that time. We went down the steps into a den and looked around. The place was dirty and the stench of the opium pipes almost knocked your head off. They had one- and two-deck cots with dirty blankets on them and they were occupied by old men, the derelicts of years of opium use. All of them were just skin and bones and most looked as if they were on the verge of death, or death warmed over. I looked at my buddies and said, "Let's get the hell out of here." We made a beeline for the nearest bar down the street and proceeded to get roaring drunk. That was the closest I ever came to using drugs of any type.

During the spring, most of the National Guard soldiers departed along with Lt. Newman. Thornton received orders to return to the states for retirement. I was still Unit Administrator and we had four Master Sergeants in the Company and Captain Bell was the new Company Commander. On September 10th, Captain Bell called a meeting of the Platoon Sergeants including me.

Sergeant Thornton was leaving and Captain Bell had to decide who'd be the next First Sergeant. He asked each of the Platoon Sergeants if they'd like the job. MSGT New said that he didn't have the education for the job and it'd be difficult for him to do the administration work required in the Platoon. Sergeant Spears was next. At that time, he was enrolled in a basic education class so that he could re-enlist. MSGT Groves said that he couldn't do the job and MSGT Miller also declined the offer.

MSGT New told the CO, "Let Towe do it. He's been doing all the administration work anyway." The CO asked me if I'd take the job. I replied, "Only on one condition, Sir. There are four Master Sergeants here who outrank me, but if I am going to be the First Sergeant, then I don't want any of them trying to pull rank on me."

The CO said, "Okay, then its settled."

I was First Sergeant again. The thing about rank was for Miller's benefit.

He had been promoted from private to Master Sergeant in one year in Korea. I don't know if he was deserving of the rank, or if he just got it for being there. He had a habit of trying to pull rank on anyone with less rank than he had. For example: his Ike jacket was dirty, so he borrowed a SSG jacket to wear on pass. He came into a beer stube where SSG Evans was having a beer and started an argument. He told Evans that he was giving him a direct order to shut up, saying I'm a Master Sergeant. Evans said, where are your chevrons? Miller looked at his sleeve, turned and left. He caught a cab back to the barracks, changed into his dirty jacket with MSGT chevrons, and then caught another cab back to the same bar and again pulled his rank on Evans. He was a poor Platoon Sergeant and a sorry soldier. I had a couple of minor run-ins with him when I was unit administrator.

One Saturday morning, I checked his pass list and he had exceeded his quota. I sent the list back to him by the clerk with instructions to correct it. He came flying into my office, leaned over my desk and told me that he was a MSGT and I didn't fuck with his pass list. He had on a shirt and tie, so I came up from behind my desk, caught him by the short end of the tie and gave it a jerk. This shut off his air supply. Still holding onto the tie, I led him into Captain Bell's office. I told him that Miller was pulling his rank again. He told me, "Loosen Miller's tie, he's turning blue." I let go of the tie and Miller loosened it to where he could breathe.

Captain Bell asked, "Towe, what's the problem?" I told him what Miller said when he came into my office. His remarks were then directed to Miller. "Miller," he said, "I offered you the First Sergeant's job and you said you couldn't do it. I'm also warning you that you are doing a piss-poor job as Platoon Sergeant and if you ever think of pulling your rank on anyone else, I'll see that you lose at least one stripe. Now get your ass out of my office."

The Army had promoted so quickly in Korea that there was an excess of Master Sergeants everywhere but Korea, oddly enough. They continued to promote them there but rotated them to the states and on to Europe. A good example of this was the number of soldiers in the mess field that were promoted to Master Sergeant. The Company Mess Sergeant was a SFC, so there were very few positions for a Master Sergeant. There was only one MSGT position in an infantry regiment. At one time, we had twenty-six Master Sergeants in the Regimental Food Service Section alone. They all felt that it'd be degrading for them to go into a company as Mess sergeant so we had a food inspector for just about every Company in the Regiment. This was a three-year tour of duty and my only hope was to keep the five stripes I had.

About 9:00 PM in the evening of January 13, 1954, I received a call from the Regimental Staff Duty Officer that I was to report to the US Army Intelligence School, Oberammergau, Germany, the very next day to attend Combat Intelligence School. I was to report to the Nuremberg Train Station at 5:00 AM and a Sergeant would meet me there with my orders and train ticket. I had no idea where the hell Oberammergau was or why I was going to school there. All I knew was that someone had screwed up and I had to cover for them. I got out a map of Germany and finally found the village. It was up on the mountain above Garmish, one of the Military Recreation Centers.

I packed and Marian got me to the station the next morning at 5:00 AM. A Sergeant had my ticket and orders for a 5:30 AM departure. I arrived in Oberammergau at about 8:00 PM. I was taken to the mess hall for hot soup and sandwiches, then up to my room. The class consisted of sixty students, both officers and NCOs. The class lasted for four weeks and I had a really good class on map reading.

I thought I knew maps pretty well until I made a fifty-eight on the first test, and that score was well above average. After the test, the instructor said he gave the test to get our attention before he started teaching map reading and it wouldn't count in our final class standing. We also covered combat intelligence, top secret document control, and operations of the S2 or G2 Intelligence Sections in garrison and in the field.

I was able to catch a ride with someone back to Nuremberg one weekend. We drove up Friday night and returned on Sunday evening. This gave me a chance to see Marian and Glenda for a couple of days. This was another school where if you kept your grades up, you could leave on pass Friday night rather than go to study hall on Saturday. I graduated number five in the class.

One Saturday morning it started snowing about 5:00 AM and it continued to snow all day. The flakes looked as big as silver dollars and the snow kept up all night. They shoveled out a walkway to the mess hall, but it was like going through a tunnel. We were told that it had snowed sixty-two inches. There was a student parking lot that I could see from my window. It looked completely level with just a couple of tall antennas protruding through the snow. The village of Oberammergau was completely snowed under. About Wednesday or Thursday evening, a couple of us went down there for dinner at a Gasthaus. They'd plowed the street and dug tunnels from the street to the door of the business establishments. All sidewalks were totally impassable.

I returned to K Company from school and was transferred to Regimental Headquarters. This was located in Montieth Barracks in Nuremberg and I was assigned there as the Intelligence Sergeant in the S2 Section. And with all this, I also had a Top-Secret Clearance. I worked with Lieutenant Colonel Gardener and MSGT Kemp, who were the complete S2 Section. MSGT Kemp showed me the necessary duties and the importance of the Top-Secret vault. This was where all Intelligence-Sensitive documents were stored. Each page, supplement, annex, sketch, or map relating to that document was carefully logged in. When you signed out a document, you logged out every part and piece, and when the document was returned, it was logged back in the same way. He also introduced me to the map room. The maps were not classified, but when stored together in the map room representing a sector, they became classified as confidential material. COL Gardener and MSGT Kemp were a great help in receiving and signing out documents and when any operational changes were made in our area of operations, each change had to be logged in or out. Another duty of the S2 Sergeant was to type all requests for clearances.

MSGT Kemp finally rotated back to the states and that left the Colonel and me to run the office. During this period, we wrote lesson plans and conducted long-range patrolling and map reading. We'd get a helicopter to take the students out at night and drop them off in pairs. They had to find their location and reach check points to pass the exercise. When we went on field exercises, COL Gardener and I shared the watch and maintained the intelligence log. We got little sleep, but we managed to survive and I enjoyed the work very much.

COL Gardener returned to the states and a Major Pearce was assigned as the S2 Officer. He was the only black officer that I had trouble working with during my entire military career. When the Regiment went to the field, the S2 section requested maps from Corps to cover the area we would be training in. Some of the FTX or CPX (Field Training exercises) and (Command Post Exercises) covered many miles and up to twenty-five or thirty map sheets. They had to be assembled in sets. Some problems required up to a hundred sets and then you had to sign them out. Without any help from Major Pearce, I was working myself to death. The Major suggested that I use his driver in the map room and I explained that he didn't have a clearance. Major Pearce told me not to worry and that he would get me some help.

One morning a black MSGT by the name of Lewis reported to the section for duty. I was happy to see him and especially when he said he could type. Then he dropped a grenade on my bliss. He didn't have a clearance and couldn't get one. All the help I got from him was to watch him read a comic book for a couple of hours each morning, then to lunch until about three or four. Since our office was classified, we were required to do our own house keeping.

One afternoon as I headed for the map room, I asked MSGT Lewis if he'd empty the trash cans and sweep the floor before leaving for the day. I knew I'd be in the map room until at least midnight. The next morning when Major Pearce arrived at the office, he called me into his office and asked me to close the door. I had no idea what was going on, but thought maybe we were going to conduct a secret exercise. Then he said that MSGT Lewis had reported that I had given him an order to empty the trash cans and sweep the floor. Major Pearce informed me that I wasn't to give MSGT Lewis any orders since I was only a SFC. I flipped my lid and asked him what the hell MSGT Lewis was expected to do. "You said you were getting me some help and the only thing he is cleared for is to read a comic book and sweep the floor." I also told him to send the help back where he came from. He dismissed me and a couple of days later, MSGT Lewis was gone. On May 24, 1954, the 43rd Infantry Division was sent back to New England and the 9th Infantry Division was activated. The only thing that changed was that suddenly we became the 39th Infantry Regiment, 9th Infantry Division. Our grape leaf shoulder patch was changed for the 9th Division patch and our Regimental Crest was also changed and we became AAA O Soldiers.

Things did not improve during the summer because we were in the field most of the time. Major Pearce would come into the S2 tent in the morning, check the map and the intelligence log, criticize some aspect of my work of the previous day, then leave the area. His driver told me that they'd go out where nobody was likely to find them. Major Pearce would then sleep the rest of the morning. Most of the time, he didn't check back with me until the evening. He came in for maybe fifteen minutes and was off to bed before I could blink my eyes. I was lucky that some of the operations crew would keep watch on my radio and let me get a couple of cat naps during the night.

We went to the field for two weeks the first of November and the routine was unchanged between the Major and me. Major General Booth, the Division Commander, had inspected the 60th Infantry Regimental S2 Section one morning and found that the S2 Sergeant had slept instead of keeping the S2 log up to date. The Sergeant was busted one stripe on the spot and instructed to report to the General's Office when he came out of the field to sign the papers. This information went through the Division with the speed of any good rumor along with instructions to be on our toes.

I was on watch one morning about one AM when I received a report from a long range patrol that an enemy Platoon was at a road junction about thirty kilometers from our left flank. I plotted the coordinates on the map as a possible sighting and logged the time, location, and source of the message in the log. Then at 4:00 AM, I received a call from Jayhawk, (Corps HDQS) that a reinforced platoon of enemy paratroopers had jumped into the same road junction as the previous report. This confirmed the first sighting and I plotted the Platoon's location on the map and made an entry into the log. About 8:00 AM, we received word that General Booth was on the way to our location. Major Pearce came rushing in and wanted to know what was going on so I explained the night's activities to him. He looked at the location of the enemy Platoon and said, "That's a mistake." He moved the Platoon down to our left front and said, "Now, that makes a better-looking picture."

When the General arrived, the Major hovered around him like a fly near a fresh cow pile. General Booth looked at our map and asked who was on duty this morning? I answered that I was. He asked me if I received any messages about a platoon on our left flank. I answered yes, Sir. He said why is that Platoon not over here, Sergeant, as he pointed to the crossroads. I replied that the Major had moved it and he asked why. I replied that he said it would make a better-looking picture.

The Major was getting paler as the conversation went on between the General and me. Then the General asked for the log. I handed it to him and he said, you have it logged correctly, Sergeant. He turned to Major Pearce and said step outside with me. Major Pearce was gone about fifteen minutes and returned looking green and like he was ready to upchuck at any minute. He called me over to the side and wanted to know why I didn't cover for him. I explained that he knew about the Sergeant in the 60th Infantry and I didn't feel like getting busted over him trying to make a better-looking picture. You never touch the map, so why did you do it today? He indicated that he would get even with me for causing him to get his ass chewed by the Division CG.

When we returned from the field, I went to see LTC Moriaritti, the Regimental Executive Officer. He had been the Committee Chief that I worked for at Fort Jackson when I was NCOIC of the Machine-Gun Committee. I explained the situation between Major Pearce and myself and expressed a desire to return to a rifle company as a Platoon Sergeant or Squad Leader. He said the ATM Platoon (Anti-Tank and Mine Platoon) was having trouble and he asked me if I'd be willing to go there and see if I could work with MSGT Cross and get that Platoon up to standards. I said, yes, Sir and was immediately moved from the S2 Section to the ATM Platoon.

The ATM Platoon was known as the "Ash, Trash and Manual Labor" Platoon. No one knew what the duties of the Platoon were. When we went to the field, we were the work detail for Headquarters and Headquarters Company. I was assigned duty as the Assistant Platoon Sergeant. I talked with MSGT Cross about setting up a training schedule like the long range patrol training we set up in the S2 Section. We went to the S3 Section (training and operations) and got them to schedule our training. We'd give a Squad Leader a map, coordinates of a bridge, and tell him to set explosives and prepare to blow the bridge. We used mock ammo charges for training purposes. We had a good training schedule and were able to train most of the time while in garrison.

This was a summer in Germany that it rained just about every day. In the field we set up the three ring circus that made up Regimental Headquarters. We dug latrines and since we had the only three-quarter-ton trucks with wenches, we also became a wrecker service. All three of our squads went from one stuck jeep to another, winching them out of mud holes.

The Regimental Commander was a tall man at least six-six and had the longest neck of anyone I ever knew. Each Commander of an army unit had a call sign. It was a code word used in radio communications. These call words came from Corps Headquarters and someone there must have known Colonel Roberts, because his call sign was "Turkey-Neck Six". He demanded that we have a two-holer for his latrine. Every time we moved, the first thing we did was dig a latrine and set the two-holer up for his use. I never knew why he wanted one with two holes. No one of junior rank was allowed to use his latrine. Maybe he felt that if another Regimental Commander or the Division CG should drop in, they could sit side by side and discuss tactics.

At that time, we poured diesel oil in the latrines each morning to keep the flies down. MSGT Cross had an 'eight ball' in the platoon who took care of COL Roberts' latrine each morning. It was scrubbed down with soap and water and diesel oil was poured in the hole in the ground. One morning, this private got a can of gas and poured it in the hole. He said it was a mistake, but any way, he just happened to flip a cigarette into the hole and that created a fire that destroyed the Colonel's latrine. The entire Platoon caught hell for that minor mistake.

There was a training area in Nuremberg that engineer units could use. You were allowed to set off one-quarter pound of explosives in this area. MSGT Cross reserved this area for the ATM Platoon to practice setting off live explosive charges. We had finished our regular training one day when he decided to set off a cratering charge. This was a forty-pound charge to blow craters in roads. I warned him that he'd get his ass in trouble. He said everyone on the range is gone so no one will ever know that we set off the charge.

He had members of the Platoon dig a hole for the charge and then connect a fuse and primer cord to the charge and set it off. I think just about everyone in Nuremberg heard the explosion. The German Police, Game Wardens, American Military Police, and many American Officers descended upon us before we could load our gear and get out of the area. Those people came as if they had been in bleachers watching a demonstration. MSGT Cross explained that he thought it was a practice charge with a very small amount of explosive. He wasn't court-martialed, but we were restricted from that training area.

In January 1955, I was sent to The US Army Engineer School at Murnau, Germany for the Mine Warfare and Demolitions Course. I enjoyed this school because a lot of it was hands-on training. We learned the formulas for all types of explosives, including their use in fruit orchards. We also covered the laying of mine fields and booby traps and recording them. I graduated as Superior Student and number two in a class of eighty enlisted men. A college-educated Corporal beat me out by half a point. This school came close to changing my career. When I graduated they changed my MOS from Infantry to Engineer. On August 18, 1955, I received orders for the 4th Armored Division at Fort Hood, Texas. I had sold our Mercedes and bought a 1951 Pontiac Catalina Custom Coupe from another Sergeant, so I started processing out and getting ready for our move back to the States.

Marian did a lot of driving with her friends on shopping trips, sightseeing, and any time anyone wished to go somewhere. I remember that on one outing, Marian and three friends let the top back on the Mercedes for a trip into Nuremberg for lunch and shopping. There was one intersection where three major streets or highways intersected and two streetcar lines crossed. They were all laughing and enjoying the outing until Marian made a turn onto the streetcar tracks instead of the street. This caused the streetcars on both lines to stop. This in turn blocked the three major streets and resulted in a traffic jam that tied up half the traffic in downtown Nuremberg. A squad of German policemen came, looked at the mess and muttered "dumb Amerikanisch." It took about fifteen minutes to get the mess cleared up. The police didn't give them a ticket. They just told Marian to stay in Furth. During this tour I became a camera bug. I bought a German Robot automatic camera. Joe Dettoria and I spent a lot of time taking pictures and traveling over the country-side visiting bierhalles on Saturday afternoons. I set up a dark room in the attic and really spent a lot of evenings there baby-sitting Glenda while Marian and a next-door friend of ours went to the movies.

When I received orders, I went to the Post Engineers and had them make me a wooden box for shipping my slides and viewer home by US Mail. I had over two hundred slides of places we had visited since Marian and Glenda arrived in Germany. I wanted them to arrive in SC by the time we did so that I could show them to our families. On August 30, 1955 they discontinued all ATM Platoons in the Infantry Regiments and I was transferred to Headquarters Company, 3rd Battalion, 39th Infantry Regiment for duty with the Pioneer and Ammunition Platoon, back at Johnson Barracks. On October 3, we terminated quarters at 16 Schleich Strasse, Eibach, Germany and reported to Bremerhaven Port of Evacuation for surface transportation back to New York. Saying good-by to all the good German friends we'd made over the past two years was very hard for all of us because we never expected to see any of them again. They threw a big going-away party for us and we had a Sunday afternoon drop in for them. Both affairs drew a large crowd and many tears were shed by all. We sailed from Bremerhaven on the USS Darby on October 8, 1955, and arrived in New York on the 17th. Marian was seasick most of the trip and Glenda was all over the ship. When we docked we picked up our car and headed for SC. It was a two-day drive down and everyone was anxiously awaiting our arrival. We went to Marian's sister Matt's house first. On the second day we were home and I received a card to pick up my package from the post office. I picked up my box and noted that one side of it was broken open. When I arrived back at Matt's and opened the box I found that all my slides and my slide projector were missing. I had wrapped them in my top coat and a couple of suits that I wanted to wear while at home on leave. The only things missing were the slides and projector. Most of the film I had shot while we were on vacations in different countries of Europe was gone. Since that time, I have never trusted the postal service. I know they have a lot of good dedicated men and women working for them, but I also know they had one sorry son-of-a-bitch in their midst. I filed a claim and they paid me for the projector and the price of ten rolls of film.

Everyone was crazy over Glenda who was three-years-old and a big show-off. Marian had worked for a lawyer while she was waiting for a port call to go to Germany, so she decided to remain with Matt and work again. I'd report to Fort Hood, look over the housing situation and come back to SC for them at Christmas.

I reported to the 504th Replacement Company, 4th Armored Division on November 22, 1955. The next morning I reported to the Personnel Section for assignment. The Personnel Sergeant said he was glad to see me because the Engineer Battalion was in dire need of a Platoon Sergeant for the Bridge Platoon. The Battalion was on maneuvers in Louisiana at that time and would be gone for another month.

I said, look, the nearest I've ever been to a bridge was to cross it on maneuvers. I'm an infantryman. Do you have any infantry here? Then I explained how I received an Engineer MOS and told him that not knowing anything about bridge building, I could give the wrong order and get someone seriously injured or killed. He said let's talk with the Personnel Officer. We went in and he explained the MOS situation, also stating that I was the first NCO that had ever wanted to change to the infantry. The Personnel Officer said, go ahead and change his MOS and send him to the 512th Armored Infantry Battalion. To show you how hard it was to get the Army to admit a mistake and correct it, the AIBs in the 4th Armored Division were supposed to be the 51st, 52nd and 53rd Battalions. When the orders were cut activating the Division, someone made a typographical error by typing a numeral 2 onto the 51st, making it the 512th AIB.

I reported to Company D of the 512th. The Company CO was 1st LT. Don E. Taylor. The Company was preparing to receive their first troops for advanced infantry training. The Company NCOs would teach all the subjects including firing at ranges for the eight-week cycle of training. They had good senior NCOs. 1SGT Blue was a good top kick and looked after the permanent party and the troops.

MSGT Pete Vowell was the Field First Sergeant and the most complete Infantry NCO I've ever known. He enlisted in the army in 1940 at the same time they started the draft prior to WWII. He joined the 15th Infantry Regiment, 3rd Infantry Division in Fort Lewis, WA. He knew Audie Murphy but they weren't in the same company. He went into North Africa, Sicily, and the Anzio Beach Head in Italy. He had been shot through the neck and talked with a lisp. He had the Silver Star and a couple of Purple Hearts from WWII. He was in Japan on occupation duty when the Korean War started and was sent to Korea as a Platoon Sergeant with Task Force Smith in July 1950.

While in battle in Korea, he told me someone gave the order, "every man for himself." He didn't know if it was a rumor or not, but he called his Platoon together and explained that if they wished to survive, they had to stay together and take care of each other. When they reached the Pusan Perimeter, his Platoon was intact and only a couple of the men had been slightly wounded. He was a leader that I'd go into combat with any day. The last time I saw Pete was ten years ago. He was seventy-four years old and had served two tours in Vietnam as a Battalion Command Sergeant Major. To keep in shape mentally and physically, he stood at rigid attention for an hour each day.

We spent the month of December writing lesson plans during the day and cleaning the barracks at night and on the weekends. The last unit to occupy the barracks left them in a mess, so we were getting them in shape for the incoming troops. LT. Taylor lost the respect of his NCOs by leaving us scrubbing latrines and barrack walls and floors in the evening. He'd go home for dinner saying he would be back around eight to inspect the barracks. Around nine, MSGT Vowell would call his quarters to see when he was coming out. His wife informed Vowell that the LT was tired and sleeping and she didn't wish to disturb him. She told us all to go home.

I caught a ride from Fort Hood to Westminster, SC with MSGT John Sullivan and his family. They were on their way to NC for Christmas. We had a nice Christmas ourselves. Glenda had Santa Claus at Matt's house and then we had Christmas Dinner with my family.

My mother always told Marian that she was glad that she had married me because she was always afraid that I would marry one of those "ferners" (her word) and she knew that she'd have to love her like a daughter. My mother was a good teacher. She taught us all the basics of good living, including not lying, stealing, or cheating anyone. She hated gossip. I remember once when I was home on leave from WWII, I had gone into a beer joint in Westminster, SC for a beer. When I arrived home my sister said that one of the neighbors had come to see Mama, and told her she should talk to me when I got home. She had seen me going into a beer joint. My mother told her that I had been fighting a war for two years and I deserved a beer if I wanted one. It wasn't anyone's business, especially someone who had kept two grown sons out of the army to take care of her. My sister said the neighbor left with her ass on her shoulder and never visited my mother again. I returned to Fort Hood with Marian and Glenda after Christmas and we started house-hunting. Killeen, Texas was a small farm/ranch to market town. It had boomed during WWII and died again when Camp Hood was closed after the war ended. Then they put two armored divisions there and everyone was scrambling for quarters. Some men were commuting from Waco to the north and Austin to the south. That was about seventy miles in one direction. Some families were living in tank crates that landlords had thrown up just to fleece the GIs.

We looked at one house for rent that consisted of three rooms and a kitchen. The walls between the rooms were made of cardboard boxes. I remember one was nailed up with the words "Pure Lard" showing. He was asking $75.00 per month for that monstrosity. We saw a nice place at 718 Hall Street, but decided we couldn't afford it. We drove around and finally stopped for a sandwich and figured out our budget. We decided that if we cut every expense to the bone, we could go as high as $90.00 per month.

We drove back to the house and talked to the owner. He told us we looked like a decent couple and they liked children, so he'd rent to us. We were both holding our breath because we knew that he was going to say at least a hundred and we could never swing that. He said 75 dollars and we almost shouted with joy. We moved in on December 29 and celebrated New Year's Eve by going to Sears and buying our first TV. We paid for it with the money we saved by not having to pay $90.00 for rent. We started 1956 in a new home with a new TV. We lived in that home the whole time we were in Killeen and he lowered the rent by $10.00 the last month we were there because we took such good care of his house.

LT. Taylor had a bad habit of giving orders without considering the results. The trainees were issued an M1 rifle and bayonet. We drew all the other weapons we were training with from the Post Weapons Pool and locked them in the arms room at night. Lt. Taylor decided that an officer would open the arms room each morning and check the weapons out. He made a duty roster assigning an officer for each day of the week. On Monday morning, I went to the arms room at 6:30 to draw machine guns for the class and the officer wasn't present. MSGT Vowell marched the Company to the range leaving a weapons detail for me. The requirement for firing was that the first round had to go down range at 8:00 AM sharp. At 7:30, Lt. Taylor came in and chewed me out for standing around in the Company area and not on the range.

He asked me, "What the hell are you doing here, Towe? Don't you realize you are the primary instructor?"

I replied, "I'm waiting to get the weapons, Sir."

He said, "Who the hell is on duty today? His head will roll if we are late getting the first round off."

I said, "You are, Sir." He turned beet-red and went rushing to the arms room.

Sergeant Vowell had everything set up on the range, so we threw a couple of guns into position and fired off a couple of blasts at 8:00 AM on the nose. When we came in from the range that day, the weapons-issue officer roster was gone and in its place was a directive saying that the NCO in charge of the class would sign for the weapons. Another one of his orders backfired on him. We were on the 60mm mortar range and I was teaching a concurrent class on the methods of laying the mortar. The class was about two hundred yards behind the firing line. I needed about two minutes to finish my subject when LT. Taylor went by in a jeep. I finished my class and gave them a break. MSGT Vowell came trotting up and told me the CO was pissed off and wanted to see me on the double. I trotted down to the firing line and reported.

Lt. Taylor started a royal-ass chewing. He let me know that breaks started at ten minutes to the hour, not a minute before or a minute after. Then he began shaking his finger in my face, snarling, "If you ever fail to give a break on time again, even if you are in the middle of a sentence, I want you to stop and finish the sentence after the break. And if you don't, I'll have you busted for disobeying a direct order." Then he turned and walked off.

For each cycle, we went to the field for two weeks of field-training and bivouac. The march out called for each Platoon to encounter an enemy obstacle, eliminate the obstacle and then take a break while the other platoons leapfrogged through. As it happened, my Platoon was to lead off. D Company, being the first unit to go to the field since the 4th Armored Division started training recruits, everybody and his uncle was out to see us off.

This included the Three-Star Corps Commanding General, the 4th Armored Division Major General, The Combat Command C Colonel, the 512th AIB CO, the LT. COL, including all of their staff. The area was crowded with about as much brass as there were troops. Our LD (line of departure) was the top of the first hill on Turkey Run Trail, a tank trail. We were to cross the LD at 0800 hours. I told FSGT Blue and MSGT Vowell that we'd just hit the ambush at ten minutes to nine.

That was break time and Lt. Taylor had never said anything about canceling his order to me about breaks, so I was going to give my Platoon a break exactly at ten minutes to the hour. They said, "Towe, you don't have the balls to do that." I went to LT. Taylor and synchronized my watch with his. I crossed the LD right on the money and my Platoon looked sharp, keeping the proper distance as they had been trained. I had instructed them when they heard my whistle to drop, roll over, and light up. On the second whistle, they were to come up firing and charge over the hill. We were ambushed as scheduled and I got the three rifle squads on line and started the assault on the hill. My watch said 08:50 and I blew my whistle. Every man fell as if he had been shot, rolled over, and the smokers lit up.

Blue and Vowell laughed later when they told me what happened on the hill, The Corps Commander asked the Division CO what the hell was going on and it was passed down the chain of command to the Combat Command C and the Battalion CO. He asked LT Taylor and he in turn asked MSGT Vowell. Vowell said, "Sir, it looks like they are taking a break." Lt. Taylor said, "Go and find out exactly what the hell is going on."

Vowell trotted down to where he could yell at me and I told him we were taking a break. He trotted back up to LT. Taylor and reported. LT. Taylor told him to tell me to continue the attack. MSGT Vowell relayed the message. When I blew the whistle, the Platoon came up as if they had been puppets on a string, firing, yelling, and practically flying over the hill.

There was only one person that ever asked me why I gave a break at that time. As we waited for the remainder of the company to pass through, the Assistant Division Operations Officer, a LTC, came up to where I was sitting on a rock. I reported and we sat together.

He said, "Towe, I have inspected your classes for the past six weeks and I know you're a combat veteran and a damn good instructor. Would you explain why you gave a break during the attack?"

I told him about the incident on the mortar range.

He said, "I figured something like that because I knew that maneuver was well planned. Your Platoon hit the ground and came back up with such precision not often seen, especially in trainees."

As long as I stayed in D Company, LT. Taylor never revoked that order. Since no one had been in the infantry training area for about ten years, we really had to watch for rattle snakes. The first night that the troops moved to their tents, they found about five rattlers. After that, all tents were struck each morning and tied up in trees. I never thought of snakes at night as I moved through the area with my platoon without a care, but during the day, I had to see where I put down each foot. We were very lucky because we didn't have one single snake bite during our entire field training.

You know that you can learn something new every day if you just listen. An example of this follows. One Saturday morning, we were cleaning BARs (Browning Automatic Rifles) after our range training. I made the comment to SSG Robinson that we'd be there all afternoon getting the carbon off the pistons of these gas-operated weapons. He said, "Don't worry about it. I'll take care of that." I had been working with weapons on rifle ranges, in combat, and as an instructor for twelve years and had never learned how to get carbon off a gas-operated weapon.

He turned around and called two trainees over. He gave one of them a handful of change and told him to go to the dayroom and bring back some cokes. He then told the other trainee to get him two clean butt cans. At that time we had #10 tin cans all over the area because so many men smoked. When the trainees returned, he poured three or four cokes into the two butt cans, put all the pistons from the BARs into the cans, and then said to me, let's go get a cup of coffee. We went to the mess hall for our coffee and he explained that carbon was cooked-on fat and coke would dissolve fat. When we finished our coffee, he got a rag and took one of the pistons out of the coke and wiped the carbon off with the rag. I stood there looking like a fool, thinking of all the hours I'd spent getting carbon off weapons.

As time went on, I'd become one of the senior SFC E6s in the Army. With all the Master Sergeants that were promoted in Korea, about the only promotions available were blood stripes (stripes from someone who got reduced for misconduct), and these were few and far between. They usually went to someone in higher headquarters who brown-nosed his way to a promotion. I had been promoted to SFC in August 1950. There was a Master Sergeant reduced in the Battalion for being AWOL, so the blood stripe was open.

The promotion was cut and dried for the Personnel Sergeant. He and the Personnel Officer were pretty tight. They had discussed it with the Battalion CO and he went along with them. All they had to do was wait for Division to notify them to promote someone. The Battalion CO transferred and an interim CO, Major Hughey, came to the battalion to fill in before the assigned CO arrived.

The group from personnel approached Major Hughey about the promotion. He wanted to know why they weren't promoting a 1SGT for B Company and they explained that the Personnel Sergeant was doing such a good job. The Major didn't buy it and said if you promote him, you'll lose him because his job only calls for a SFC. He said I don't know anyone in the Battalion, so let's start with date of rank and promote a 1SGT for B Company. There was only one SFC in the Battalion who out-ranked me. He was the training-aids NCO who'd always worked around the Operations Section.

The Major called him in and said he'd like to promote him to 1SGT and send him to B Company. He added, if you can't hack it, we'll reduce you without prejudice and send you back to training aids. The SFC declined the offer of promotion and later explained there were too many strings attached to it.

I was the next NCO to be called in and was asked the same questions.

I jumped at the offer and said, "Yes, Sir, I'll be glad to go to Company B as First Sergeant."

He looked at my record and said, "Towe, you shouldn't have any trouble in B Company since you've been First Sergeant and Sergeant Major a couple of times before."

He dismissed me and I went out floating on air. I reported to Company B, on July 13th and was promoted to 1SGT E7 with a date of rank of July 17.

The next day, they asked Marian and me to report to Major Hughey and they pinned 1SGT stripes on my arm. LT. Taylor told 1SGT Blue that he didn't understand how they promoted me without talking to him.

1SGT Blue answered, "Lieutenant, there are a lot of things in this Army that you don't understand."

I reported across the street to B Company as the newest 1SGT in the army after six years in grade and almost thirteen years service. I didn't know at that time I was in for another long dry spell.

I reported to LT. Hernandez, the CO of Company B and received a warm welcome. I'd arrived just in time to help him prepare the company for an IG/CMI reinspection. The Company had failed their annual inspection. This second inspection was about twelve days away so we started burning the midnight oil. I made new duty rosters from the date of the last inspection, ran corrections in the morning report, checked the unit fund and barracks, mess, and supply. We covered all areas except the condition of the troops, haircuts, and uniforms.

I talked with the manager of the cleaners and arranged for credit so that each man could have a fresh suit of khakis for the inspection. I checked the trainees for a barber, but no one had experience in cutting hair. I called a company formation to see who had money, or could borrow it from a friend for a haircut. I sent all those with money to the barber shop. I was left with about sixty men. I went to the supply room and got out the Company barber kit and arranged for one of the Sergeants to send the men needing haircuts to me in groups of five.

I started cutting hair about two in the afternoon and finished about 7:00 PM. I learned as I went. It wasn't hard for a GI haircut at that time. It only required going straight up the sides and back of the head. What hair that was left on top, you put a cap over it and the soldier looked respectable.

The next morning, my right hand was swollen and sore as hell from using the manual clippers all afternoon. Two days later we passed the reinspection with flying colors. The IG commented to the Company Commander on the fine appearance of the troops.

The Division CG decided that since we were giving passes to the trainees, they should be able to let their parents and friends know if they're going to be on duty or not. Due to sick call, appointments, AWOL, and emergency leave or pass, it's almost an impossibility to keep your duty roster current for four or five days, much less ten days. He directed that duty rosters would be posted on the bulletin board for the period covering the coming weekend and the following week through Sunday. To keep the roster correct, it was necessary to revise it each day. I had two duty rosters, one for the inspections and one I kept in my pocket that I used daily.

We had a 2nd LT who never entered an office without sitting on your desk, regardless of how many chairs were around the room. I'd asked him a couple of times not to sit on my desk, but it just went in one ear and out the other. One Thursday I had all my duty rosters, appointment book, and other papers needed to make up the ten-day duty roster and get it posted on the bulletin board by 6:00 PM.

This Lieutenant came in and almost got in a prone position on my desk, scattering papers everywhere. I was burning, but never said a word. I came up from my chair with a good grip on the desk and turned it and the Lieutenant over onto the floor. I walked out and went to the mess hall for a cup of coffee to cool down. A few minutes later the Company Clerk came in and asked me what happened. I said, why. He told me the Lieutenant had called Post engineers requesting another piece of glass for the top of my desk and was sweeping up glass from all over the room.

I went out and observed a class that was in process before going back to the orderly room. My desk was back on all four legs, the floor was clean, and all my papers neatly stacked in the center of the desk. I had to get them all back in order before I could continue work on the duty roster. This incident was never discussed between the Lieutenant and me. I later heard that he told a group of Officers in the Officers club to keep at least two paces from a First Sergeant's desk.

The Company Commander informed me that he allowed the young soldiers' wives to congregate in the dayroom while their husbands were training. I disapproved of this, but to no avail. It was too late in the training cycle to change the rules. I probably enhanced the morale of the husbands, but was a pain in the ass for everyone else. Somewhere between ten and twenty wives arrived in the dayroom many mornings before we had a chance to get it cleaned up from the previous night. Three or four of them would share one room at the Post Guest House, but there was no place for them to hang out during the day except in our Company area. I got the cadre together and laid the law down. If I ever heard a rumor that one of them made a pass at one of the young girls, I'd have him before the old man and gone from the Post before the sun set. We got through the cycle with no problems, but were lucky.

We had a man go AWOL about the third week of the cycle by the name of Claypool. I wrote all the usual letters as required and was waiting for the end of thirty days so that I could drop him from the rolls as a deserter. Before I could drop him or he returned, I had to report him each day as an AWOL.

At 4:00 PM on the thirtieth day of his AWOL, a veritable mob descended upon Company B. They were led by a civilian lawyer, a First Lieutenant from the Judge Advocate General's office, a chaplain, and Private Claypool, in person. The Company Commander was out in the area somewhere, so I sent the clerk for him. The lawyer told me they wanted to get the matter of the AWOL cleared up, so that Claypool could get a three-day pass and spend the weekend with his new bride before she went back home. He was telling me that Private Claypool had wanted to get married before being shipped out and hadn't intended to stay away for the full thirty days so as not to be listed as a deserter.

The CO and clerk came in and I told the clerk to call the MPs to come and pick up an AWOL. They started talking all at once, wanting to know why I was calling the MPs. I explained it was standard operating procedure.

The lawyer proceeded to piss LT Hernandez off by asking him in a sarcastic tone: "Exactly who is running this Company?"

LT Hernandez's answer was in the same tone, "The First Sergeant."

He turned to the clerk and said, "Call the MPs as you were told."

The lawyer turned back to me and asked in a polite tone, couldn't we discuss calling off the MPs? I told him since I had already notified them, Private Claypool would have to be placed under their authority. The MPs arrived in force and asked me, Top, where is the AWOL? I pointed to Private Claypool and they duly placed him under arrest.

The lawyer asked if he could have a few words in private with his client. He was informed he would have to get clearance from the Provost Marshals Officer before he could talk with the prisoner. They all left at the same time. LT Hernandez asked me about any possible repercussions from the action we had taken. I assured him we had acted according to regulations. To the best of my knowledge, Private Claypool received six months in the stockade.

I had a very pleasant experience while I was in B Company that allowed me to help the Army and a trainee at the same time. A couple of Sergeants approached me about one of our trainees, Private Rosenthal from Princeton, NJ. They wanted to know what we could do with him because in their estimation, he'd never amount to be a satisfactory infantryman. They said he couldn't fieldstrip a weapon and couldn't even tie his boots.

I talked to some of the other trainees in the Platoon about Rosenthal. They said he tried hard, but just couldn't do anything right. They carried him through all the inspections and on-hands training. One of them asked Rosenthal who dressed him each morning before he went to school. He replied, my valet. A reserve Sergeant who had taken the first eight weeks of basic with Rosenthal at Fort Dix, NJ stated that the first day they were at Fort Dix, Rosenthal was using a safety razor and chopping at his face trying to shave. He showed Rosenthal how to use the razor properly.

I also talked with the other trainees in Rosenthal's Platoon. They all said that he tried harder than any other man in the Platoon. I also learned he had a photographic memory. Each night he went to the bulletin board and checked the references for the next day's training. Then he got a field manual and read all the subjects. When asked a question in class, he always answered the same way: Sergeant or Lieutenant, Fm 23-5, chapter 6, paragraph 4, page 96 states that... and then he would recite the material verbatim.

I sent for Rosenthal to bring his M1 Rifle and report to my office. I put a blanket on my desk and asked Rosenthal to fieldstrip his M1 for me. I didn't say a word, but watched him struggle until he got it apart, but he was unable to re-assemble it. This seemed strange to me, since I could do it in a few seconds blindfolded. Then I asked him to tell me how to assemble it. He went through the entire procedure step by step, as I assembled the weapon.

After this, we sat and talked for about an hour. He was probably the smartest and best educated man I ever met and had the least common sense. He explained that he had a man servant or valet since he was born. They took care of his every need from birth until he was drafted into the army. He was chauffeured in a limo to and from classes from kindergarten through college. Here is where the army failed him. He could speak, read, and write seven foreign languages fluently and had a Master's degree in English. He was a Professor of English and Literature at Princeton University.

I asked him if he was trying to get out of the Army. He said if he'd wanted, he could've avoided the draft, but felt obligated to serve his country. He intended to do the best he could for two years. I told him I felt the Army could make better use of him than as a rifle man. I asked him if he'd like another assignment. He answered he would go anywhere and do anything the Army wanted him to do. I told him that after work call tomorrow morning to report back to me and I will see what I can do about getting him another assignment.

The next morning we walked up to the Personnel Office and I explained the situation to the Personnel Sergeant. He asked us to come in and talk with the Personnel Officer.

After I explained Rosenthal's background and education, the Personnel Officer asked him if he'd like to get out of the infantry. Rosenthal replied that he'd go anywhere the Army desired to send him. He was told that the Army had been looking for men like him for months, and how would he like to serve the rest of your two years in Paris, France. Rosenthal smiled and said that would be great.

He was going to be sent to SHAFE, Supreme Headquarters Allied Command as an interpreter. They asked me if I could get him cleared from Post and ready to leave that afternoon. I said yes, what time? They said 4:00 PM. They wanted to fly him out of Temple, Texas that evening. We returned to the Company and I assigned him to a Sergeant to take him around and have him packed and in the orderly room by 3:00 PM. I had Rosenthal sitting in front of the Personnel Sergeant's desk at 3:30 PM. Rosenthal thanked me and I wished him luck. I thanked the Personnel Sergeant and Personnel Officer and left the office feeling great. I had helped both a soldier and the US Army all in one day.

I decided that I'd enjoy being a helicopter pilot, so I volunteered for flight school, but never got off the ground. When I went for my physical, the doctor informed me that my hearing problems from the grenade in the Korean War would be bad enough for him to ground me if I was already on flight status. The hearing loss continues to be a problem today. About ten years ago, the VA gave me hearing aids for both ears and in 2002, I was rated 30% disabled for hearing impairment.

MSGT Pete Vowell went to Fort Worth, TX, to see COL Boyle. He was the Regimental Commander of the 172nd Infantry Regiment, 43rd Infantry Division in Munich, Germany, when Vowell was in that unit. COL Boyle was the PMS&T (Professor of Military Science and Tactics) of the Fort Worth High Schools. Pete wanted to work for the Colonel again and was accepted.

Upon his return to Fort Hood, he came to see me to tell me COL Boyle wanted to speak with me. He had another job open and was looking for a good NCO to fill the spot. I discussed this with LT. Hernandez and he told me to go ahead and try for it. So off I went to Fort Worth to see COL Boyle. He wrote me a letter of acceptance and asked me to hand carry it through channels to Fourth

Army in San Antonio, TX.

Everyone up the line explained that due to shortages in my grade, they had to recommend that it be disapproved. The Division Personnel Officer, who I had gotten to know quite well, told me the same thing, but that slot was a Fourth Army slot and they would be the approving authority on whether I go or stay. I drove to Third Army Headquarters with my request for reassignment to the Fort Worth High School System. They told me to go home and start packing, orders would follow. During this period, our son Kevin was born in the US Army Hospital, Fort Hood, TX, making him a true Texan. Again I got in hot water with Marian because I wasn't in the hospital when one of our children was born. Her water broke at approximately 3:00 AM, so I got Glenda up, grabbed Marian's bags and headed for the hospital. This time I didn't go back home and go to bed. I was told it would be a couple of hours before the baby arrived, so I drove to B Company with Glenda. I carried Glenda to the mess hall where the Mess Sergeant fixed her a bowl of cereal while I went outside to hold reveille. During reveille, the clerk came out and told me that the hospital had called to let me know that I was the proud father of a baby boy. I turned the formation over to the Field First Sergeant and Glenda and I went back to the hospital to face Marian about my being AWOL when Kevin was born.

I decided that a coupe was not good transportation for a family of four so I went shopping for another car. I found a 1956 Chevrolet station wagon that I could afford so I drove it to the house to show Marian. The doctor had advised her not to drive, but she decided that once around the block wouldn't hurt her. That drive almost delayed our moving. It was almost all she could do to get from one room to another for four or five days.

The Fourth Armored Division had cut orders on me the day after I returned from San Antonio, so I was busy clearing Post. I loaded the station wagon with our belongings and headed for Fort Worth early in the morning. I reported to COL Boyle and was assigned to North Side High School. I was to work with a MSGT Booker from Hearst, Texas, who was retiring at the end of the school year. I rented a two-bedroom duplex just across Highway 80 from the school. It was very convenient, but so small you couldn't cuss a cat without getting hair in your mouth. When you sat four people at the table, you couldn't open the stove door.

We were treated as faculty and paid sixty dollars a month for our services. I was assigned a home room made up of all ROTC students. This required roll call, collection of all funds, keeping grades, and posting report cards. We attended all faculty meetings and school extracurricular activities. We trained rifle and drill teams and participated in and conducted meets. I enjoyed working with the young people. It was like conducting basic training, but to a group of boys about two or three years younger. We taught all the subjects you would teach in basic training except for the bivouac period spent in the field.

CSM Glenn H. Towe [Ret'd]

The dress code has changed over the years. The ROTC students were allowed to wear uniforms every day. The boys wore slacks and button-type shirts, while the girls wore dresses or skirts and blouses. You'd think jeans would be the fashion, but not in Fort Worth High Schools. The girls weren't allowed to wear denim skirts except on Western Day. That day everyone wore jeans, western-style shirts, cowboy boots, and a hat. There were six schools in the system, so we had our rifle team meets on a weekly basis rotating between schools. The drill team had two or three meets a year with all High School ROTC units in the area invited. We were required to have the cadets usher at all football games. They were in uniform, but we had to wear civilian clothing.

I had a good gray topcoat from Germany, so all I needed was a hat for rainy weather. I bought a gray wide-brim Stetson to go with my topcoat and slacks. One Friday night after supervising a game in the rain, I stopped in a small supermarket on the way home for milk. I went in as usual, but the cashier and night manager must have thought I was a gangster. She pointed at me as I entered and he shadowed me the entire time I was in the store. He even came up behind me when I went to check out. He must've had a pistol in his jacket because he never removed his right hand from his pocket. I was more nervous than he was. Someone could have come through the door causing him to start shooting. When you feel someone has a gun on your back, you move very carefully.

Since we had spent the previous Christmas at home, we decided to save my leave time and stay in Fort Worth over the holidays. Being the new kids on the block, Vowell and I were selected to go to Fort Hood for the senior ROTC summer camp. That was an eight-week vacation. We worked with the reception committee the first two days, then the tactics committee for four days, and the rest of the time was ours.

During those eight weeks, I quit smoking for the first time after smoking continuously for fifteen years straight. I didn't smoke for two solid years before I started again. I quit at least once a month for a couple of hours or up to two months at a time occasionally. This continued for the next eighteen years before I finally stopped in 1976. I hoped that was for good. Quitting smoking was the hardest thing that I ever tried to accomplish.

There were about fifteen senior NCO instructors assigned to the system and about half of them were undoubtedly the biggest group of bitchers I've ever served with. No group of privates could compete with them. They cried about every thing; the school system didn't pay them enough; they shouldn't have a class room; the school required them to attend meetings; the students wouldn't behave; and anything else you could imagine.

During this period, I sat through one of the shortest debriefings after a major inspection ever held in the US Army. COL Boyle had a deep gravel voice and one that when he spoke, you listened. The Fourth Army Inspector General

Team spent about four days inspecting our six schools and departed on Friday afternoon. After they departed we had our debriefing. We were in the conference room at the downtown office. COL Boyle entered, attention was called immediately and we all snapped to. COL Boyle said be seated, gentlemen, but he never sat down himself.

He looked around the room carefully and then said, "Men, the good Lord gave you two eyes and two ears and only one mouth and that should mean something to you."

He did a left face and walked out. Everyone sat there in stunned silence with their mouths open. No one called attention at the departure of the CO. After he left, all the big gripers began saying, I didn't say anything. I wondered who he was talking about. The inspection report came down and we made the necessary corrections and returned it. The inspection was never discussed by COL Boyle.

We had a bowling team and belonged to the Carswell Air Force League. I didn't care that much for bowling, but wanted to support the team, so I agreed to be the supernumerary. That was a big mistake. The four years that I was a member of the team, I bowled more games each year than any member of the team. I carried an average of 165 give or take for the entire four years.

There was one member of one of the Air Force teams who constantly ran his mouth off. He was always in a hurry and rushed everyone to speed up the play. One Sunday morning his impatience caught up with him. While driving on one of the main streets of Fort Worth, he stopped behind another car at a red light. The light changed and the car in front of him hesitated for a few seconds prior to moving on. He slammed down on his horn with a big blast to get the other driver to go. That was a bad move. The other driver casually got out of his car and walked around in front of this Air Force Sergeant's car. He pulled out his pistol and put three bullets through the hood and into the engine.

He then got back into his car and drove off. The Sergeant was so shocked he couldn't even identify the other car to the police. The report appeared in the newspaper and all the bowlers really got on his case at the next league meet.

At the end of my first year at North Side, MSGT Booker retired and MSGT Lancaster replaced him. Lancaster wanted to coach the rifle team because it was a sit-down job, so I continued to coach the drill team. We never won the city meet and when it came to statewide competition, you could forget it. There was a Catholic School from the southern part of Texas that fielded a full Infantry-size Platoon and they came to drill. They did the standard dismounted Army drill for a couple of minutes and then competition-type drill for about fifteen minutes. They never did the same movement twice. All the riffles and passing of the rifles were done with absolute perfection with never a hesitation or a single bobble. They placed first each of the four years that I was there. They were the best drill team that I've ever watched and that includes colleges and universities.

We received two riffed (Reduction in Force) officers who needed a couple of years service to retire. They were SSGT Wood and SGT Gilligan. They were both products of the Senior ROTC system. I would have ended up in this category if I'd taken a battle field commission or gone to OCS (officer candidate school). Therefore, I feel that I made the correct choice when I decided not to be commissioned.

MSGT Colclasure and Sgt Gilligan introduced me to golf, a sport that I've enjoyed for forty-five years and still play occasionally. Colclasure was a good golfer with about a five handicap and Gilligan shot in the low eighties. They were good teachers, but they put me through the mill the first few rounds we played. I remember one time when I hit into a deep dry wash and my ball rolled into a large corrugated steel pipe. I asked Colclasure about laying it out and he insisted that I had to hit all shots as they lie. After about ten or fifteen strokes and both of them laughing so hard they were about to drop, they informed me that I could have a drop. Then they explained some of the rules of golf and Gilligan gave me a rule book. Over the years, I played some decent rounds and at one time I carried an eight handicap.

I remember that one Sergeant from the ROTC unit at TCU always called Colclasure begging to play with us. He blamed everything about his game except himself. The last time he played with us, he'd called and said that he had found his problem and corrected it and was ready to play. His golf and his temper had not improved and the new set of woods had not improved any of his problems. The course had large metal pipes with the hole-marker welded on top. He hit a big round-house slice and threw his driver in disgust. It wrapped itself around that pipe and he grabbed his bag and walked up the hill toward the club house without ever looking back. He never played with us again.

The high light of my golf game was when I played eighteen holes on a regulation course with only seventeen putts. I one-putted seventeen holes and chipped in on the other hole. At that time I could hit about a 25 or thirty yard chip shot in my back yard, so I chipped up to two hundred balls every evening and it paid off. Also, when I arrived at the course for a round, I went to the putting or chipping green and practiced until my tee time. Shortly after I retired, I played thirty-two rounds in one month while playing in four states.

There were some good perks that came with our duties, if you wished to take advantage of them. I had always enjoyed sports, so when the local universities asked for cadets to assist in ushering, I was always at the top of the list. We'd furnish ten or twelve cadets and get a couple of passes for the entire tournament. We assisted TCU at the Fort Worth Invitation Golf Tournament. That was the first time I had been to a pro tournament and I fell in love with it and the golfers.

My all time favorite was Sammy Snead and I also got to watch Arnie Palmer and Jack Nicholas as they started on the tour. I remember being on the fourth or fifth hole when Arnie came to the green. He four-putted and I thought, what's he doing out here? That was probably his last four- putter in his entire career.

Later, I had the opportunity of seeing the Masters for about six years. That was when you could go out to the Masters Course in uniform and see a day of golf for $2.50. My first year in Augusta, the Army provided guest houses for visitors and a large detail of troops to assist in the operation of the tournament. I volunteered one year as a driver in the parade. The request called for NCOs in white dress shirts and Khaki trousers. I drove one of the beauty queens and received a season pass for a two-hour ride with another beauty queen.

I'd take a five-day leave starting on Monday prior to the start of the Masters and was on the course from early Sunday morning until the last ball was hit the following Sunday afternoon. Some of the golfers threw some lavish parties and no one was invited, but the people just showed up.

Doug Sanders was a flashy dresser. Every golf suit he had was color coordinated from cap to shoes, and his parties were like his dress, the best anybody could ever dream of attending. I did this routine for five years. I still go to Hilton Head occasionally for a day and enjoy seeing the younger golfers play. I feel the legions of golfers are from the forties through the sixties.

One year, I had invitations from SMU for ushers for the Cotton Bowl, the home games for TCU, and The Fort Worth Rodeo. I enjoyed all of these perks. The Fort Worth Chamber of Commerce also hosted a Teachers Day each year. We were divided into groups and visited different businesses for a day. I visited the Fort Worth Stock Yards and the Famous Cattleman's Steak House. They served a steak that I called an NCO steak, as big as a shelter half and as thick as a second lieutenant's head. I also visited the Fort Worth Candy Factory where they served lunch and gave each of us a box of chocolates.

When I went to summer camp, Marian, Glenda, and Kevin went to Walhalla, SC for the summer and visited with our folks. In the summer of 1959, they went home for a niece's graduation from high school. After camp, I caught a bus and headed for SC and visited my folks and Marian's people.

Jane, the niece who had graduated, and Joretta, a classmate, were dragging around and complaining that they had no money for a graduation trip. Marian invited them to go to Texas with us. They jumped at the chance to get away from Walhalla for a month. We drove to Fort Worth and Marian gave them the keys to our car. They hit every drive-in around Fort Worth and had a ball. To illustrate the change in times, when their month was up, we put them on a bus for SC and never thought anything unusual about it. Now I would hesitate to make the same trip myself. Both Jane and Joretta are grandmothers and still talk about their graduation trip.

Marian and I always tried to give Glenda and Kevin everything possible with the money available. The Army pay then was the same as it is now, considerably below the civilian level. The only difference now is that most of the lower ranks are living on food stamps. Marian insisted that they have good clothes, so we financed a new Singer Sewing Machine so she could make some of their clothing. She made all kinds of clothes including dresses for Glenda, suits and shorts for both of them, skirts and blouses for herself, and shirts and shorts for me.

We took vacations when I had a pass or leave. One of our trips is still discussed when the four of us get together. We took a four- or five-day trip to San Antonio, TX, and the kids insisted that we stay at a motel with a swimming pool. We attempted to explain that our money was limited, but they didn't give up on the pool. We went to the commissary and picked up milk and dry cereal for breakfast, bread, lettuce, tomatoes, and lunch meat for lunch, and we'd eat the evening meal out. We figured that the money saved on the two meals would enable us to have a pool.

I had a large ice chest, so we packed up and headed for San Antonio. We spent the day between driving and sightseeing at a cave and the water show in San Marcus. When we stopped for lunch at a roadside park, neither of the kids wanted a sandwich. They wanted to go somewhere for hamburgers instead. When we told them it's either hamburgers or a pool, they ate. Marian always insisted that we go to all the educational places, so we toured the Alamo, the river walk, and a couple of museums and churches. We returned to the motel for our sandwiches each day.

Glenda and Kevin say they remember the trip and the sandwiches, but never realized that money was so scarce. They remember the new clothes and having things at home like all the other kids. They now jokingly tell people that their mother dragged them screaming and hollering to every castle, museum, garden, church, and cathedral in every village, town, city, or country they were ever in. Now they are happy that she did.

During the summer of my second year, Pete Vowell was reassigned to an Infantry Unit and was transferred and I was moved over to Paschal High School. The duty was the same except that now I had a normal homeroom. There were twenty-seven girls and one ROTC cadet in my homeroom. Here, we were required to assist the male teachers to patrol the hallways and dining area. Pete had warned me that some of the physical education students would put me to the test.

My first day there they counted cadence as I walked into the building. There were three ring leaders who would lock arms and walk up and down the hallways elbowing the other students out of their way. The first time I met them in the hall, I moved over and they came after me, giving me the shoulder and laughing. I warned them not to try it again. The next day I met them once more and decided that I wasn't going to run from them for an entire school year.

I continued walking in the center of the hall as they came on. Their intention was to walk over me. I braced and gave the center kid a hard right to the solar plexus that doubled him over. The other two just stood there holding him up as he gasped for air. I ordered them to take him to the bathroom and bring him around and if I ever saw them in lockstep again, I would do the same thing. Word got around quickly and I never had any more trouble after that.

One thing I remember distinctly from the homeroom was the girl who sat in the front row right opposite my desk. I knew that it had to be intentional because I was able to tell the color of her panties each day for two solid years.

During my third summer at Fort Worth, the Dallas High School ROTC system had arrangements with Fort Walters, Mineral Springs, Texas for a high school summer camp. The only thing the Army furnished was the tent area, mess hall, and training sites. The camp lasted for a month and all of our cadets who desired to go and could afford the cost were invited. The only support we gave them consisted of two NCO instructors.

I instructed map reading and tactics for about six days total. There was a SSG from Dallas who wanted to be Mister Mortar himself. He let everyone know that he was the final authority on the 81mm mortar. I think he'd been teaching the mortar classes for about five years. The mortar range was set up for firing the 81mm tear-drop with a charge one. Everyone left him alone while he showed the cadets his skill in firing the mortar.

One morning about 11:00 AM, all hell broke lose at Camp Walters. Military Police, ambulances, and everything else headed for the camp commissary. A couple of us went over to see what the commotion was all about. An 81mm tear-drop round had fallen through the roof and skidded along the concrete floor of the commissary, just barely missing a couple of women shoppers. One of the women fainted and the other thought she had been hit by the mortar round. Everyone wanted to know if the round was a dud and would explode if moved. One of the NCOs from Dallas went in and got the round, explaining that it was an inert round and would not explode. That afternoon the mortar expert vanished and didn't return for the remainder of camp.

Subsequently, the Defense Department came out with two super grades, Master or First Sergeant E8 and Sergeant Major E9. These were two additional grades to shoot for and I wanted a shot at them. The ROTC Department at the Fort Worth High Schools only called for an E7 so I decided that it was time for me to change assignments.

For the next three or more years, the Master Sergeant's stripes were up in the air. During this period I was a First Sergeant, Master Sergeant, Sergeant First Class, and Platoon Sergeant, all as an E-7. It changed back and fourth according to the job you were performing. I saved a poem that said it all about the E-7 mess.

CSM Glenn H. Towe [Ret'd]

A SIX STRIPER'S PRAYER
By MSGT Jack C Wall, Sr.
Recruiting Station, San Francisco

O Lord I pray, deliver me
From busting back to SFC.
I've had these stripes for 16 years,
I've paid for them in sweat and tears;
How can they now, at this late date,
Give my six stripes to a young E-8?
I've grown so used to them, somehow,
I'd be lost without them now.
But now they give me five to wear;
My pride is hurt, I'm in despair,
So, dear Lord, won't you hear my plea?
Don't break me back to SFC.

The Army, in this modern day,
Has streamlined my six stripes away,
There can't be given any thought
To who gets hurt; change must be wrought;
In atomic war, there is no place
For sentiment or social grace.
No longer can they take the time
To think of men long past their prime;
There really isn't time to be
Concerned with a few old goats like me,
So, Lord, I pray on bended knee;
Don't break me back to SFC.
Long years ago it would've been a pipe.
To have bucked those kids for that sixth stripe
But I've had the course, it's plain to see.
I ask you Lord, to hear my plea;
I can't start over; it's too late
To try to buck for that E-8
They say old soldiers never die,
But DA wishes that we would try.)
That'd solve the problem of what to do
With us old goats who are nearly through.
I don't much care what they do with me;

But please, O Lord, not back to SFC!

In January, I was called into the PMS&T's office and was asked if I wanted to be placed on a retention list for another year in the school system. Marian and I had already decided on a move, so there was no hesitation with my answer. I definitely wanted to be transferred at the end of the current school year. I received a telegram at about 7:00 PM on Saturday night, June 27, 1960, informing me that I was being transferred to the 1st Battle Group, 15th Infantry, 3rd Infantry Division, in Bamberg, Germany.

That was a great relief, especially for Marian. Because my last tour was in Germany, I felt sure I was due another tour in Korea. We had made our plans with that assumption. Marian and the kids liked Texas, so they would remain in Fort Worth, while I was in Korea. We both had enjoyed our time in Germany. When we located Bamberg on a map, it was only forty miles from our previous assignment there.

Marian and I became good friends with MSGT Pete and Net Vowell. They had a son, Mike, who was about eleven years old. They lived in a house trailer at that time and encouraged us to buy one. We got the bug and started shopping in earnest for a home of our own. We found one that suited Marian, but I thought it was too large, measuring eight by forty-eight feet. We almost never found a place to park it. Most units at that time were about thirty-six to forty feet. We located a lot out on Lake Worth, where the owner allowed us to park with the front extended out into the street.

When we received orders for Germany, that changed our plans about Marian, Glenda, and Kevin remaining in Texas. Marian got in touch with her younger sister who lived in the Keowee Community of Seneca, SC. We could park our house trailer in her yard and Marian and the kids could live there. Glenda and her cousin Rachel could go to school together until they received a port call to join me in Germany.

I checked with the Army and they'd reimburse me fifteen cents per mile for the movement of our trailer. I checked the companies who pulled house trailers and their rate was thirty-five cents per mile. That was when I decided to pull it myself behind my station wagon. Everyone told me I was a fool to try it with an automatic transmission. Being a little on the hardheaded side, I didn't listen to them. I proceeded to read the want ads for used towing equipment. I found a hitch, overload springs, and electric brakes and turn signals. It wasn't any trouble finding a garage that would weld the hitch to the frame, so I was ready to go. I also had a Studebaker coupe. Marian and the kids used the station wagon and I drove the Studebaker to work.

We decided Marian would drive the Studebaker with one kid and I would pull the house trailer with the station wagon. I wrote each state requesting permits to pull the house trailer through that particular state. I heard from each state except Georgia. I complied completely with all the instructions I'd received. We said good-by to everyone in the trailer park. As we left, everyone that wasn't working lined the street to wave good-by and see if I was going to be able to move the trailer, or say I told you so.

It took a few miles to get the feel of the load and realize how long it was. With a forty-eight foot trailer and twenty-two foot station wagon, my unit was seventy feet long. I found it best to start off in the number one or lowest gear on the automatic shift and then change gears the same as with a stick shift, except you didn't have a clutch. We went through Texas and Arkansas and almost to the Mississippi River before we stopped.

We parked and stayed in a motel for the night. We ate breakfast at the motel and headed for Mississippi. I stopped at the Mississippi Highway Patrol checkpoint for my permit as instructed. I had to wait until after 9:00 AM to wire Jackson for the permit. Marian decided to drive on to Greenville, Mississippi, and call Net Vowell and talk with her for a few minutes while she waited for me. Glenda stayed with me and Kevin went with Marian. When I finally received the permit, I drove on through Greenville without seeing the Studebaker or Marian. I continued to drive until about 2:00 PM without any sign of Marian and Kevin.

At that time, US 82 across Mississippi was a two-lane highway, so there was no way I could've missed her. Glenda was hungry, so we stopped at a gas station for a coke and crackers. When we came out there was a state trooper at the trailer. He asked me if I was Glenn Towe and I answered yes. He told me Marian was at a Highway Patrol Station about sixty miles up the road. He called and had them wait there for me. We still laugh over our chase across Mississippi. She thought that I had passed her while she was talking to Net Vowell or taking care of Kevin. So she stepped on the gas to catch up, not realizing that she was pulling farther away from me. When I reached her, it was time to quit for the night. We stopped at a motel in Alabama just before we reached the Georgia state line.

The next morning, I was stopped at a checkpoint by a Georgia State Trooper. He asked for my permit and I explained that I'd never received it from Georgia. He checked my other permits and my leave papers. He commented on my being a First SGT and said he'd been in the Korean War, too. He told me I could do one of two things, leave the road at the next town, go to the Western Union Station, send a wire to Atlanta, and then wait a couple of hours for a permit, or I could just drive on. He also told me if I did drive on, not to mention that I'd been stopped before. He also warned me to watch myself when I went through Gainesville because the bastards there like to write up service men. I thanked him as we shook hands. He wished me luck in my next assignment and we were on our way again.

I went through downtown Atlanta and even now, when driving in Atlanta, I still remember pulling that seventy-foot rig through there. I sat on the edge of my seat as we passed through Gainesville and gave a big sigh of relief when I crossed the bridge entering South Carolina. We traveled US 123 from Atlanta to Seneca, SC. We stopped in Richland, SC, and visited briefly with my Dad who was grading lumber at a lumber yard there. He was surprised and very happy to see me.

We drove to a church near Mary Lou's and Kirby's house and parked the trailer there for the night. I pulled the trailer into her yard the next day. Kirby and I leveled and blocked the trailer and I dug a trench and connected the commode to their septic tank and laid drain pipe for the washing machine. One thing I learned from that trip was the long trailers are easier to back up than the short ones. That was an experience that I'll never forget, just knowing that I had the ability to move that rig halfway across the country. That was before any interstate highways or bypasses were built in the United States. The highways in most cases went through the downtown business districts or the main streets of the smaller towns.

We visited my father and mother and they too, were very glad to see us and the kids. I often think of the character and standards they passed on to me, especially my mother. To her, being poor didn't matter because she had us six children to love and take care of. She wanted us to have everything better than she did and that would only happen through hard work. She taught us to be honest in all our dealings and to take the consequences of our actions bravely without trying to blame others for bad decisions. She also taught us to share with others who had less than we had and never belittle anyone. These teachings had an effect on all of us kids. I was the only one who ever landed in jail and that was for driving under the influence. None of us ever used drugs and I was the only one who ever drank more than a few beers at one time. Each of us was only married once and each of us, except my youngest brother, continues to live with our first spouse. None of us was overly religious, but all believed in God, Country, and love of family. Considering today's standards, I feel that she did exceptionally well with her third-grade education.

My parents had always wanted a place of their own, so when I went into the Navy I sent money home each month for them to buy a place. They were not eligible for an allotment, so this came out of my fifty-dollar a month pay. I continued to send money home until after Marian and I were married.

On September 8, 1960 I left South Carolina driving the station wagon and reported to the Overseas Replacement Station at Fort Dix, NJ on September 10, 1960. My stay at Fort Dix was uneventful. I went to the NCO Club for dinner a couple of times, but never left the Post. This was quite a change from my first stop in NJ while waiting for transportation to Europe. I eventually reported to McGuire Air Force Base on September 15 for air transportation to Frankfort, Germany.

We made an overnight flight, stopping once in the Azores to refuel, then on to Frankfort. The pilot announced that we'd be flying directly over Paris, but the weather was cloudy. Soon the clouds cleared, however, making a hole just over Paris and I had a perfect view of the city from my window seat. We landed in Frankfort at approximately 8:00 AM on Saturday morning. I was processed through the Frankfort Processing Center and was given a rail ticket for Bamberg, Germany. I was with the NCOIC (NCO in Charge) when he called Headquarters, First Battle Group, 15th Infantry, 3rd Infantry Division, telling them that I would arrive in Bamberg at 7:00 PM and to have some-body meet me at the Bahnhof (Rail Depot) and also to notify the mess hall to save chow for me.

At that time I felt that everything was going well, not knowing that I was headed into a nightmare weekend. The German trains run like clockwork, so we arrived in Bamberg on the minute. I went to the passenger waiting room for my escort and transportation to my new assignment. There was no one waiting there for me, so I checked outside and there were no military vehicles to be seen anywhere. I sat and patiently waited for about a half-hour before walking around again. There was still no sign of any military personnel.

I suddenly remembered to call 83 for an English-speaking telephone operator. I told her I needed to contact Headquarters, 15th Infantry, and she patched me through immediately. A Specialist 4 answered the phone. I identified myself and told him I've been waiting at the Bahnhof for transportation. He informed me that he knew nothing about my arrival, but would find someone to pick me up. About thirty minutes later, a Medical jeep arrived and the driver drove me to Headquarters.

The Specialist 4 found me an empty bunk on the third floor of the Headquarters building and told me to report to the Personnel Office in the basement at 8:00 AM Monday morning. He showed me the mess hall and we found nobody there had been notified to save chow for me. I did manage to get two slices of bread, a slice of cheese, and a quart of milk.

The room was occupied by six Sp 4s, Pfcs, and Privates. They all came in at different hours and were very loud and totally drunk. By Monday morning, I was in the mood to take no crap from anyone. I reported to the Personnel NCO, a SFC. After I gave him my orders, he told me to go out and have a seat in the hallway and he'd call me when they finally decided where to send me. I informed him that I wanted an assignment to a Company, not the bunch of crap I've had to put up with since arriving here.

At that time, the Personnel Officer came over and told me to do exactly what the Sergeant had instructed. I said, "Lieutenant, I was assigned to this unit as a Platoon Sergeant and if you don't want me, just say the word. I still have my damned bags packed and I know some infantry unit in Germany would like to have me. Therefore, both of you can go straight to hell as far as I'm concerned." Just at that moment, a voice from behind me said, "Lieutenant, you and Sergeant Wolf both shut your mouths and don't utter another word."

I looked around and saw the Battle Group Sergeant Major standing there.

He said, "Sergeant Towe, I'm Sergeant Major Greene, the Battle Group SGM, and I'm very happy to have you here. Let's go up to my office and have a cup of coffee."

We sat in his office and he explained what had happened. There was a Specialist 6 from the Medical Detachment on duty as the Staff Duty NCO for Saturday. He was an alcoholic and Sergeant Major Greene told him that if he screwed up my arrival, he'd have him busted to private. They had the Executive Officer's driver scheduled to pick me up at the depot, take me to a private room, and after I'd cleaned up from my trip, he was to deliver me to the NCO club for dinner with the Sergeant Major and his wife.

He apologized to me for my unseemly welcome to the Battle Group and told me to report back to his office the next morning for orientation. He called the First SGT of Company A to send a vehicle to get me and my duffel bag. (The above is a good example of what happens when someone drops the ball. The Sp6 was reduced one stripe for being drunk on duty).

The First SGT came in with me to meet Captain Dowie, the CO. CPT Dowie was with a British Light Infantry unit during WWII and received his commission through OCS. He was a good officer after you adjusted to him. I was assigned to the Third Platoon and didn't have a Platoon Leader. The next morning I reported back to the Battle Group Headquarters as instructed. There were about six or seven of us new members in the Sergeant Major's Office. He told us we were to spend the day in the 15th Infantry Museum and introduced us to a SSG who was the Museum Curator.

He then took us to the top floor of another building where the museum was located. We went into a small theater where he spent the first hour giving us a brief history of the 3rd Infantry Division and the 15th Infantry Regiment. I remembered some of the history from being in the 3rd Infantry Division briefly in 1948. I also learned a lot of the 15th Infantry History from MSGT Pete Vowell. After his orientation we watched the movie "To Hell and Back" with Audie Murphy. I had seen the movie before, but this time it meant more to me because I was going to be a member of the 15th Infantry.

The Army changed the configuration of the Infantry Division, giving it a Pentomic concept. Everything was in fives. There were five rifle companies in a Battle Group and they did away with Battalions and Battalion Headquarters. I felt that this hurt the Officer Corps greatly because there wasn't any command position from Captain, Company Commander to Colonel, and Battle Group Commander. Major and Lieutenant Colonel positions were staff and executive officer slots. This deprived them of command experience.

After the movie, we joined the Battle Sergeant Major in the mess hall for lunch. The Battle Group CO stopped in for a brief welcome to the unit. After lunch, we were escorted through the Museum and all the exhibits were explained to us and all questions answered adequately. We were dismissed about

CSM Glenn H. Towe [Ret'd]

3:00 PM and I returned to A Company. I went to the supply room and first drew my field equipment and then the arms room to be assigned an M1 Rifle. All the old Army Units at that time had high morale and a lot of esprit de corps and competitiveness. I remember a running competition between us and the 2nd Armored Cavalry Regiment that was across the street from us.

Organization day was a big thing for both units and you had to watch your ass closely or be made a fool. There was always a parade in the morning and organized athletics, ball games, etc. in the afternoon. The Officer and NCO Clubs had formal military balls and there were always special activities at the Enlisted Men's Club.

We had a Rock in front of Battle Group Headquarters with the Battle of the Marne in World War I etched into it. It was painted blue and a show piece for the Battle Group. One year they failed to post a guard on it and someone from the 2nd AC came over and painted it a Cavalry yellow. The Infantry vowed to get even with the Cavalry and at the 2nd AC Organization Day Parade, the Infantry sneaked in a crew, distracted the AC Commander's jeep driver and painted his jeep wheels Infantry Blue. There was the Cavalry Commander passing review with Infantry Blue wheels on his jeep.

Another time occurred just before the AC Commander gave the order to pass in review. A loincloth-clad wild Indian riding bareback at breakneck speed pulled his horse up in front of the CO and threw a spear into the ground with a sign attached that read, "WE DID IT BEFORE AND WE CAN DO IT AGAIN." The Indian then rode off in a cloud of dust. Things like this gave units competitive spirit and increased morale tremendously.

I only had one run-in with CPT Dowie. On our first field-training exercise after I joined the Company, we were conducting a Platoon in an attack problem. At that time the battle group had a maneuver called the "Lawn Mower." The squad consisted of two fire teams. When they went into the attack, one fire team moved ten to twenty yards while the other team provided covering fire, then the other team moved ahead. This movement was repeated until the objective was overrun.

The objective in this case was about four hundred yards to the top of a small hill and CPT Dowie selected my Platoon to go first. We moved out and quickly overran the objective. I reformed the Platoon and moved back to the starting point. The other two Platoons were in the rear conducting concurrent training.

When we arrived at the starting point, CPT Dowie said, "Towe, run it again." We moved up the hill as we did before and moved back to the starting point.

He said, "Run it again." We went up the hill once more while neither of the other Platoons had run the hill and my men were dragging ass.

This time when he said, "Run it again," I blew my top. "Captain, what the hell do you want? All you've said was 'Run it again,' with no critique or any comment. My men have busted their asses and their tongues are hanging out and all you can say is 'Run it again.' Tell me what the hell you want us to do." His reply was, "Towe, all I want to find out is whether you have the balls to be one of my Platoon Sergeants. When you stood up to me for your men, I knew then you were made of the right stuff. Now, take your Platoon to the rear and conduct concurrent training for the rest of the day."

A couple of months later we were in a Gasthaus having a beer and he told me I was a good Platoon Sergeant because I had not complained for myself, but for my men. In November, we were making a night march during a problem in a local training area when I stepped into a rut and twisted my ankle. The crack from the ankle sounded like a rifle shot and I fell down like a ton of bricks. I was walking alongside MSG Wheeler, the Weapons Platoon Sergeant. He immediately called for a medic. One night about fifteen months later, MSG Wheeler and I were walking up a snow and ice covered road in Hohenfels, when he slipped and went down on one knee. We went to the mess tent for a cup of coffee, but he said his knee was still hurting and he'd decided to see the medics. He had cracked a knee cap and was in traction for over six months. The last time I saw him, he was still walking with a cane.

As for my ankle, the medic arrived promptly and gave me a pain killer. He put on a splint and said he was sending me to the dispensary with a broken ankle. I was placed on the medical jeep and driven to the Post Dispensary for medical attention. At the Dispensary, the doctor had my ankle X-rayed and found that I had a fracture. He told me to go to my company area for the night and return the next morning on sick call. They dropped me off at my barracks and I crawled up two flights of stairs up to my room.

The next morning, I got one of the men from my Platoon to see a medic and get me a crutch. I made it to the mess hall with difficulty because of the pain. I then got the CO's driver to drive me back to the Dispensary. They X-rayed my ankle again and informed me that I only had a sprain, but they'd put me in a walking cast. I asked why, with only a sprain. I was informed that in many cases, a sprain could give me a lot more trouble than a break. The cast was to stay on for six weeks. During the following week, I was back in the field with my platoon, cast and all. They had to replace the cast twice because I was in the field during wet weather.

The first week that I had the cast on I received notice that my car had arrived in Bremerhaven and was ready to be picked up. I took a train up and drove my car back. I had some trouble using my left foot for both the gas and brake. I returned on a Saturday, so I drove on to Furth and looked up Joe Koric, a good friend of mine and Marian's from our last tour in Germany.

Over a good schnitzel and a couple of German beers, we covered the past five years in short time. He had a sister-in-law who lived in Bamberg, so he was eager to see Marian and Glenda again. I spent the night with him and Frances and returned to Bamberg the next afternoon.

In December, we received a new First Sergeant, Jim Legg, a veteran of the 82nd Airborne who made a glider landing in France on D Day. We became good friends and golfing buddies and to this day still exchange Christmas cards. His wife was planning to come over after the first of the year. To discourage enlisted personnel from bringing their families over before government housing was available you were instructed to rent a house before they'd issue your dependents a port call. This required you to pay rent on a house or an apartment for a couple of months before your family arrived in the country. I didn't want to wait a year before Marian, Glenda, and Kevin joined me, so in December of 1960 I rented a house on the German economy and applied for Marian to join me.

Marian received notification in November that she would receive a port call for January. In December, she received notification to report to Fort Hamilton, NY for surface transportation to Germany for her, Glenda, and Kevin. They sailed from New York on January 13, 1960 aboard the USNS General Patch. Marian was seasick for about half the trip. Glenda was also sick the first day. Kevin was the trouble maker. It took two GIs to keep track of him. He was there one minute and gone the next. They were constantly looking for him all over the ship.

I took ten days leave to get Marian and the kids settled in. One of the first things we did was go to Furth to see Joe and Frances Koric. On this trip, Marian again got acquainted with the European PX System. The kids were back in school and found that the military school system was far ahead of the schools in South Carolina they attended prior to leaving for Germany. We lived in the first apartment until May and we were getting anxious to move. When the snow melted, we found that we were living over a trash dump. SSG Kramer from our Company, moved to temporary quarters so I rented the apartment on Spegiallgraben Strassa that he'd been living in and remained there until October when we moved into temporary quarters. We had the entire attic of an apartment building. It had at one time been bachelor officers' quarters, with a kitchen, bath, living room, and about ten bedrooms. We stayed there for three months before being assigned permanent quarters.

Marian and I have always taken advantage of our assignments to travel and learn about the area we lived in. The following is an example of so many GIs and their families failing to take advantage of their situations. The CO and all key NCOs drove to Hohenfels Army Training Center to coordinate a support mission we were to perform in late November. On the return trip we stopped in a German restaurant for lunch. The Supply Sergeant, who had been in Bamberg for almost three years, asked me where the latrine was. I told him to go back through the hallway and he'd see it. A short time later, he returned and said I found one that said Herren on the door, but didn't find one for men. I thought he was joking at first, but then I explained that Herren was the German word for men and Damen for ladies. He went back again.

As we ate lunch, I talked with him about his tour and family. He and his wife had eaten dinner in Bamberg only once during the past three years. They had taken a week's vacation in Garmish, a beautiful small town and one of the US Military Recreation Centers located in the German Alps. They'd stayed there for two nights and returned to Bamberg without seeing a show, taken a tour, or leaving the hotel bar. I found out the two of them sent their kids to the movies and they sat in the NCO Club for three years and bitched because there was nothing to do. That was a constant gripe from a lot of the enlisted men. They just sat there like robots complaining there is nothing to do here.

I had forgotten about the Germans and Christmas Eve. SFC Binion, a Platoon Sergeant and I went to Furth to spend Christmas Eve with Joe. All the Germans go home for Christmas and all stores, restaurants, and bars close by 1:00 PM. SFC Binion and I got to Furth in time to have a beer with Joe before he and Frances headed out in the country to spend Christmas with her family. We came back to Bamberg and the club was closed. The only place in Bamberg to get something to eat was the Bahnhof. You could get bread, wurst, and a beer there. After that, I went to the barracks for a good night's sleep and missed the arrival of Santa Claus. On the Monday morning after New Years, Captain Dowie, in a sadistic move toward NCOs with hangovers, informed us that we would go on a hike. In the British Light Infantry, they moved at just under double time and for people with short legs like me, it was an "airborne run". This was the first and only time while I was with him that he moved that fast. We moved out at 8:00 AM sharp and had a ten- minute break at the end of each hour. We arrived back at the barracks at 11:50 after covering sixteen miles. I made the run, but never want to do it again. During the next few months, I became the final Platoon for all "eight balls." First, I informed them if they were sharp and kept their noses clean, every man had a chance at the overnight passes for the Platoon. I treated them in a fair way and they soldiered for me or they were gone. We had been the best Platoon for over two months when the Company received a new 2nd Lieutenant straight from ROTC. I was called to the orderly room and the CO introduced me to my new Platoon Leader, 2nd LT. Sinclair. He informed the LT that he was getting the best Platoon in the Company and expected him to keep it that way.

We went up to the Platoon and I pulled out my little black book and said, "I'd like to give you a run-down on each of the Squad Leaders and the men."

He said, "That won't be necessary, Sergeant, since you're not in the Chain of Command. I'll be dealing with the Squad Leaders directly and if I need anything from you, I'll let you know."

I said, "Thank you, Sir. I'll be around if you need me."

I went down to talk to the First Sergeant. On Friday afternoon, Top called me to the orderly room and asked me if I had authorized Friday night passes. I informed him that was the Platoon Leader's decision. My policy was a GI party each Friday night with no passes, and everyone gets ready for the inspection. Three of my four Squad Leaders were sent to me the same way as the men, so I expected them to pull the wool over the Lieutenant's eyes.

I went out in the hallway the first Friday evening the Lieutenant was there and found part of the Platoon in Class A uniforms. I asked what was up and a Squad Leader said they had talked with the Platoon Leader and he said they could have passes and then cleanup in the morning. I went home early and got a good night's sleep. I went in the next morning for reveille and found that the entire Platoon was "drag-assing around." I kept my cool and did as I was told by the Lieutenant. He came in about seven and was just as happy as if he had good sense. He really thought everything looked good. When I was in charge, the only man that walked on a floor in the Platoon with his shoes on was the CO when he came through during inspection. The floors were polished like a mirror, along with all shoes, and every piece of clothing and equipment was in its proper place.

This morning, it looked like a wind storm had hit the barracks. I was standing in my room when the CO came through. He didn't say a word to me, but I could tell that he was highly smoked.

When the Inspection was over, the 1SGT called over the speaker for me to report to the CO on the double.

I reported to the "old man" and his words were, "Towe, what the hell happened up there? You've had the best Platoon for months and this morning you went from top to under the damn basement."

I told him that the new Platoon Leader had informed me that I wasn't in the "chain of command" and if he needed anything from me, he'd let me know.

The 1SGT had come in with me, so the CO turned to him and said, "Get that damned dumb 2nd LT. down here on the double."

He didn't say a word while we waited for the Lieutenant, just sat behind his desk and boiled. The Lieutenant came in looking as if he expected to get an award for his performance as Platoon Leader that morning.

The CO came out of his chair and said, "Lieutenant, where the hell did you get the idea that the Platoon Sergeant wasn't in the chain of command. He is the chain of command. You had better get that through your thick skull now and remember it if you wish to be an Infantry Leader."

The Lieutenant said, "I, ah," about three times in succession and the CO said, "I want you to listen and listen closely to what I'm going to say. I sent you to Sergeant Towe because I knew he could teach you how to be a great Platoon Leader. Now I'm going to give you a choice, and if SGT Towe agrees to keep you in the Platoon, you can stay in the Company. You will follow Towe around, take notes, and observe how he leads. You will not interfere with any actions he takes, and at the end of the training period, or the day, you can ask your questions. You will not be the Platoon Leader, but merely an observer. You can accept these conditions or pack your bags, it's up to you."

Then he turned to me and asked if that was satisfactory to me.

I replied, "I'll be glad to work with the Lieutenant, and he did say he wished to stay in the Company. He realized that if he was relieved from duty after less than a week in his first assignment, he might as well just hang it up."

We were dismissed and the Lieutenant said, "Let's go upstairs and talk."

I said, "No, let's go to the mess hall for a nice cup of coffee."

We sat in the mess and talked until lunch time and covered many things. He apologized and said that he should've talked with me before. I told him that it wouldn't have done any good for me to have talked with him sooner, because he had a chip on his shoulder and the sooner he got it knocked off the better. He followed my every step except to the latrine for the next four weeks. He stood reveille and retreat with me. He wanted to know about every man and why we were the 8-ball Platoon.

One day I said to him, "Let's go see the old man." He immediately wanted to know what he'd done wrong. I said nothing, it's just time we had a talk with him. Top showed us in and the CO wanted to know what I wanted. I told him that I felt that LT Sinclair was ready to take over the Platoon. Lt. Sinclair nearly went into shock. He was prepared for an ass-chewing and ended up as Platoon Leader. We worked together as a team for a couple of months and I enjoyed having him in the Platoon. The Platoon Leader was transferred from one of the other Platoons and the CO moved LT Sinclair to that Platoon, leaving me again without a Platoon Leader.

One day we were in the field and the CO called me over and told me the Battle Group Commander, COL Wills wanted to talk to me. I went to a clearing in the woods where COL Wills was sitting on a log. I reported and he asked me to have a seat. My brain must've almost boiled over trying to figure out where I had screwed up this badly. A Full Bull Colonel doesn't travel twenty miles out in the boondocks to sit on a log and chat with a Platoon Sergeant.

I sat and waited as he started talking. "Towe, I am well aware of the fine job you're doing with all of those maladjusted young soldiers we've been sending you and I want to thank you."

Then he dropped the bombshell about why he was out there. "I want to ask you for a favor," he said. "You can say yes or no after I explain the situation to you."

I said I understood.

"We have a Lieutenant in the battle group by the name of Jason Hoffman," he continued. "LT Hoffman has been assigned to two platoons in two different Companies and the Platoon Sergeants have refused to work with him. Furthermore, the Company Commanders don't wish to assign him to a different Pla-

CSM Glenn H. Towe [Ret'd]

toon in the Company. LT Hoffman doesn't know the meaning of the word 'tact'. He's headstrong, and doesn't listen to his Platoon NCOs. I think with the right supervision, he could become a good officer and as you well know, we need good officers in the army today. I feel that with your capabilities as a noncommissioned officer, you can lead and guide him into becoming a good officer. Should you decline the challenge, and I know it is a great one, then I'll move to have him separated from the service. Take a couple of days to think it over if you wish."

After that build-up by the Battle Commander, I said, "I don't need any time, Sir. I'll take him."

The Colonel stood up, we shook hands, and he said, "Thanks, Towe, I hope he doesn't disappoint both of us." When I received LT Hoffman as Platoon Leader, my Platoon of castoffs had been training very hard for weeks for the Rifle Platoon Tests. The Tests were conducted by a group of officers and NCOs from another unit, to see which Platoon in the battle group was the best. We were to be tested in the assembly area, approach march, Platoon in the attack and defense, a night withdrawal, night march and organization of a defense at night. This was to be conducted over a twenty-four to thirty-hour period. We were the only Platoon without a Lieutenant as Platoon Leader.

No one except our Top Sergeant and the Commander gave us as much chance as a snowball in hell, but we continued to train. They had a battle group program that awarded outstanding soldiers a four-day R & R in Berchtesgaden. I told the CO and my Platoon if they made a good showing, I'd take them on R & R as a Platoon. When LT Hoffman arrived, I met him, the CO, and the 1SGT, in the orderly room. He said that he was glad to be there and take the Platoon through the test. I told him and the CO that he didn't know the men and the training that we had conducted for the test. It wouldn't be fair to the men to change leaders two days before the test. The CO agreed with me and LT Hoffman cooled his heels until the test was over.

We ran a grueling test for about twenty-eight hours without more than a catnap between phases of the operation.

The only points we lost were from a Squad Leader who was sent to me with problems. In the attack phase of the test he couldn't physically keep up with his squad. This had no effect on the proficiency of the fire teams, but cost the Platoon points.

The other points lost were caused by me. SFC Hedges was the weapons Squad Leader and a damned good NCO who knew his machine guns as well or better than I did. I selected him to go back as the advance party to receive the defense order. He was to meet me and the Platoon after our night march and assist me in setting up the defense. Since SFC Hedges knew the guns and how to lay a final protection line, I placed the remainder of the Platoon and didn't check the machine guns. The guns were laid properly, but I failed to check them. This cost us our other points and the title of number one Platoon. We lost by one-half point and some people said we should've won.

Still to come in second out of twenty Platoons and without a Platoon Leader, I was proud of all my 8-ball soldiers. Quite a few of the battle group felt that it would be a mistake to send a Platoon of characters such as I had to a place like Berchtesgaden. The other Platoon NCOs declined to go because they were either married or had German girlfriends in Bamberg.

When the CO went to the Adjutant to make arrangements for us to go, the only date they'd give us was the twenty-sixth of the month. They knew that all the privates would be broke and unable to go. I told the CO to set it up and we'd get the money. I called the Platoon together and explained the situation and asked them how many wanted to go. The count was nineteen. The next thing I asked them was how many had money for the trip. Three of them answered in the affirmative. I told them not to give up yet.

I went to the American Express, the Military Bank in Europe, and talked with the manager. I explained our situation and waited for an answer while he thought it over. He said, "Sergeant Towe, this is the most unusual request for a loan that I've had in the past ten years here. You must be proud of those men to go out on a limb like this for them. I'm going to go out on that same limb with you because I know this is for a good cause and I'm sure you'll stand by your word and repay the bank." He loaned me $320.00 on the strength of my signature and, as he said, an honest face.

I had discussed this with Marian and her only comment was, "That is more money than you make in a month. I hope you know what you're doing." We went to Berchtesgaden and were given rooms in a US Army hotel and meal tickets for four days. There were only two incidents of interest that occurred during the four days. One of the '8 balls' went to the Officer's Club and was telling every one he was a Lieutenant who was the Platoon Leader of the best Platoon in the 15th Infantry. They called the MPs and he was taken to the MP Station. They sent two members of the MP patrol to talk with me. I rode down to the station with them and after talking to the Desk Sergeant, they released the '8 ball' to me on the condition I keep him out of the Officers Club.

The other incident was just about as stupid. Two of them were in a Gasthaus and got in an argument over who was the best soldier during the test. They started fighting each other. The bartender called the MPs and was in the process of tossing them out when the MPs arrived. He threw them both into the arms of the two MPs. Again the MPs came up and gave me a lift to the station and then drove all three of us back to the hotel where we were staying. The Desk Sergeant assured me there wouldn't be any DRs (Delinquent Report) issued and he only had one thing to say to me, "You must be crazy as hell to bring a group like that here and turn them loose."

I surprised every one in Bamberg when I arrived back without a DR or any

AWOLs. On payday all sixteen of the men came to see me immediately after they were paid and paid me in full. They thanked me and most of them wanted to give me interest on the loan. I went to see the manager of the American Express that afternoon with their money. He tore up the paperwork and wouldn't let me pay the interest.

LT Hoffman stayed with me for about four months and then went on to a staff job. He couldn't read a map and was too proud to ask questions or admit it when he was wrong. I remember one field problem that we were on when our Platoon was in the attack. He insisted on running the Platoon without any help from me or anyone else. After the Platoon attacked the hill, the CO called LT Hoffman on the radio and told him the attack looked good. LT Hoffman was all aglow until the CO added there was only one thing wrong, you attacked the wrong side of the hill. I told Marian that LT Hoffman could enter a florist and buy a bouquet of roses and when he got out to the street, he'd have a bag of horse manure.

I had one major run-in with him. We were to support a European Rifle Match and he assigned me to the target pits. I explained to him about the hearing loss I had from the grenade in Korea and advised him to get someone else to run the pits. He accused me of malingering and ordered me to go to the pits. First, I went on sick call to get my ears checked and a set of heavy ear plugs. I then operated the pits as instructed. From doing jobs like that, today I have 30% hearing in the left ear and less than 60% in the right.

I was visiting SGM Jim Legg in Georgia a few months after I retired and we called LTC Hoffman. He was living in Atlanta and had retired as a LTC. The only thing he wanted to talk about was my trying to pull a fast one on him about my ears. I never told him about my hearing loss or that I was the one who kept his ass from being kicked out of the army.

The Platoon went to Hohenfels for a month. This training area was large enough for us to conduct live-fire field-training exercises with our track vehicles. We loaded out track vehicles on rail flatcars and shipped them by train to Hohenfels. We were then convoyed there by truck. We had been in Hohenfels for about three weeks when the POWERS TO BE announced that the Battle Group would march home. That would be a ninety-three mile hike with full field-gear and crew-served weapons. They had it plotted out for three days. That's over thirty miles a day, which means that we'll have to hike for twelve hours each day at the march rate of two and a half miles per hour. I figured that we'd have to go about fourteen or fifteen hours per day.

We started training by making hikes of three to six miles per day besides our other training. We planned on leaving Honhenfels on Wednesday morning and arriving about two or three miles from Bamberg on Friday evening. We'd then march to the Post Saturday morning. This march will give you an idea of the leadership, discipline, training, physical condition, morale, and esprit de corps of a good unit. We asked for volunteers to pull KP duty for the trip instead of hiking and got no takers. Everyone wanted to make the hike, including the professional goof-offs. The off-duty cooks agreed to pull KP until someone fell out on the hike, or decided to volunteer for KP.

We had a Battle Group formation in a parking lot on Wednesday morning. The Battle Group Commander gave us a short pep talk, turned to the Battle Group Sergeant Major and said, "Sergeant Major, march the troops to Bamberg. The officers and I will bring up the rear of our respective units." He saluted the Sergeant Major and moved to the rear of the formation. The Sergeant Major and staff NCOs stepped off and we were on our way to Bamberg. We moved for fifty minutes and rested for ten until lunch. We then stopped for an hour.

During this period, I along with all other NCOs in the Company checked everyone for blisters and sore feet. We also wanted to see if anyone desired to pull KP. At the end of the day, everyone was again checked for sore feet. The mess hall provided a helmet of hot water to anyone desiring to soak or wash his feet. The medics opened blisters and taped up sore limbs and advised a couple of people to join the mess crew. There were still no takers. Each of the three days we did the same routine and some of the men's feet were getting bad, but no one volunteered to drop out. I was the only one in the company who had a box of corn starch in his pack. The only thing I had ever found to keep me moving was to frequently dust with corn starch. I think I provided the starch to half of our company and some to other companies, also.

On the second day, the Mess Sergeant picked up a dozen boxes when he went to draw rations, so we had plenty of starch for the remainder of the hike. Able-bodied men helped the walking-wounded, the men with really bad feet, by carrying their packs and sometimes their weapons.

When we marched through the front gate at the barracks, the Division Band was playing and I think every dependent of all the personnel on the Post, plus a large number of German civilians were on hand to welcome us home. In Company A every man who started the hike in Hohenfels marched through the gate in Bamberg and nobody had ridden not even one mile. I know a couple of other Companies matched our record. Only a few men were evacuated by the medics and at least 95% of the Battle Group completed the hike. When 1SGT Legg dismissed the Company, he told them bedroom slippers would be the uniform of the day for the following week.

We had some changes in Company A. 1SGT Jim Legg went to Battle Group Headquarters as Sergeant Major and 1SGT Casey came to the Company and replaced Jim Legg. LT Hoffman went to Company XO and I was again left without a Platoon Leader. We changed from a regular infantry unit to a Mechanized Infantry Battle Group. That meant we changed our method of getting to the objective. We'd ride instead of walking.

This also meant that the Platoon had the responsibility for maintaining four-track vehicles. I got a driver's license for track vehicles and on occasion I drove the track when I wanted it in a position where the regular assigned driver wouldn't go. When I did this, the Squad Leader would always say abandon ship; he's crazy to put that track in there. I never rolled it over, but came close a couple of times.

The Armored Personnel Carrier M113 was a rolling-maintenance problem. It would throw tracks in a frozen field and we were always having trouble with the alternator going out. The alternator went out on one of my tracks, so I put in a work order for the part and the track was placed on deadline. We were required to check on deadlined vehicles two or three times a week. I always got the same answer; your alternator has not come in. Colonel Wills put out the order that no vehicle would be cannibalized and the parts used on another vehicle.

On my way home from Nuremberg one evening, I stopped at the NCO Club in Erlangen for a sandwich and ran into a Motor Sergeant that I had known in the 39th Infantry in Nuremberg in 1954-55. We were talking about track vehicles and parts and I commented that I had a track down for five weeks waiting for an alternator. He told me to wait a few minutes and he'd get me one. He left and returned in about five minutes with the alternator. I thanked him and headed home feeling good. I would finally get my track off dead- line.

The next morning I went to the motor pool and was stopped by the Maintenance officer, a Lieutenant that I'd had words with before about my deadlined vehicle. He wanted to know what I was doing and I said I had an alternator and was going to get my track off deadline. He told me I had to give him my alternator and it would be put on another vehicle that had been deadlined longer than mine.

"Like hell, I will," I said. "You had nothing to do with my getting this alternator. Our mechanic and I will put it on my vehicle."

When we arrived at my track, I was informed that the Battle Group Maintenance Officer had a mechanic remove about five parts off my track. That was when I went looking for that Lieutenant. I reported to him and told him I needed to talk to him about my track.

He said, "I don't have time to listen to you and your complaints."

I answered him quickly, "Lieutenant, you cannibalized my vehicle and you had better damned well listen to me and listen good. I expect you to have all the parts that have been removed from my track back by tomorrow morning or I am going straight to COL Wills and report that you cannibalized my vehicle and probably a lot of others."

He started to turn red and I knew that I had him by the balls, so I squeezed.

"That is your problem and I'm telling you I'll be here with this alternator at 8:00 AM tomorrow and when I put this alternator on, I expect to drive that track. I'm going to call the SGM this afternoon and have him make me an appointment with the CO for tomorrow morning because I don't think you can come up with the parts."

He said, "Don't go to see the SGM. I'll see what I can do."

I went down at 8:00 AM the next morning and the driver and I put the alternator on and he drove the track over to the wash rack to clean it up.

The Army Supply system was set up to work like clock work. You put in a work order and received what you needed, but unfortunately, it didn't work that way.

An example of this was expendables. They had a list of cleaning supplies that you requested, but it was impossible to work within the system. The Company was allowed four mop heads per month for the mess hall, four Platoons and all the headquarters sections; 12 pencils, 1 twelve inch ruler, and 3 brooms and other items needed for normal operations. To beat this system, I would go to the Class VI store and buy two fifths of PM Whiskey and drive to Nuremberg where I had a German friend who would trade the whiskey for two five-gallon cans of OD (olive drab) paint, something we couldn't get for our vehicles. I returned to Bamberg with the paint. I would give one can to the Motor Sergeant and carry the other can across the street to a Sergeant in the 2nd Armored Cavalry Regiment. He had an arrangement with a German in Hanau where he got expendables the same way I got paint. I gave him the paint and he supplied me with the expendables I needed for the Company.

My mouth just about terminated my career one morning while we were on a FTX (field training exercise). We had bivouacked one night and the next morning I moved my Platoon out for an attack. I left the bivouac area on my route of march down a firebreak in the forest. The Germans always had firebreaks and we used them frequently. The Assistant S2 Officer came roaring up in a jeep, and as the saying went, the most dangerous thing in the army was a 2ND LT and a map and this one was in a vehicle. I reported and he asked me exactly where I was and I showed him my location on his map. He said that can't be right. I explained to him that I'd left the bivouac area, went down a firebreak, crossed the stream, turned left and was here at this firebreak and the stream. He answered in a sarcastic manner, "Sergeant, evidently you don't know where the hell you are." I answered, "Lieutenant, I'm not the son-of-a-bitch that's lost."

I prided myself on my map reading. The last thing a leader wishes to do is get lost and march his unit around in circles all day. My Squad Leaders called me 1/100,000 Towe because most of the time, I used a 1/100,000 scale map instead of a 1/25,000, especially after we went mechanized. I never thought about that run-in until one day the officers and senior NCO were to go recon a defensive position on the East German border. The First Sergeant informed me that my clearance had been revoked by Division. I was shocked and couldn't imagine what I had done to warrant that action. An Officer or NCO without a clearance is a handicap to any unit because he's in constant contact with classified materials. I told Top I was going to see SGM Legg and he said, "Good luck."

I was told that the Lieutenant that was Assistant S2 had rotated back to the states and separated from the army. As the Lieutenant was leaving, he'd laid a stack of request for clearances on the CO's desk and asked him to sign them. He said he'd drop them off at the Division G2 Section when he cleared there on his way home. They were all on the same type form, so the Colonel signed them without knowing that there were about seven clearance revocations mixed among the papers. By the time word got back to Battle Group Headquarters, the Lieutenant had been separated from the Army. The Lieutenant had revoked the clearances of everybody he'd had a run-in with, including me and another NCO. There were five Lieutenants involved, three of them West Pointers.

They had a rule in the Officers' Club that anyone coming in during "happy hour" and sitting down with his hat on would buy a round. The Lieutenant refused to go along with this and they picked him up and threw him out the door. It took a few days for me to get a secret clearance, but my top secret status was gone forever. I never really needed it again anyway.

In December, the Battle Group CO called LT Hofffman in and asked him if he'd like to be the CO of Company A. According to Jim Legg, Lt Hoffman told the Colonel that he would under one condition and that would be to transfer 1SGT Casey, who had asked for a transfer to the 2nd AC Regiment and I would be his 1SGT. 1SGT Casey transferred and I became First Sergeant once again.

You had to sit on top of LT Hoffman all the time or you'd have a mutiny. He tried as hard as any officer I ever served with, but he was headstrong and never thought any problem completely through before acting. We were getting ready for our annual AGI/CMI inspection and he came to me to see what I wanted him to do.

I said, "Go to the Officers' Club, get yourself a good dinner and I'll see you at six in the morning."

I never thought he'd go, but he did. The Colonel and his lady were there having dinner and he asked LT Hoffman what he was doing there, and didn't he have an inspection in the morning? His reply was that I'd told him if he'd go to the Club that would be the most help he could be to the Company. We passed in flying colors and I stayed out of hot water on that recommendation. LT Hoffman stayed as CO until June and was replaced by 1st LT Bradshaw.

LT Bradshaw was a full-blooded Indian from a reservation in Oklahoma and a ROTC Graduate from Notre Dame. I asked him one day how a wild Indian got into Notre Dame. He said that his high-school graduating class consisted of him and one other student. There were two scholarships, one to Notre Dame and the other to a college in Oklahoma. Since he had the best grade average, he got first choice and selected Notre Dame. He joined the ROTC thinking it would be an easy subject and he graduated as a 2nd LT. He said all he knew about an orderly room was enlisted men went there to receive Company punishment and officers to get an ass-chewing and he didn't want either one, so I would have to give him some guidance. LT Bradshaw was a good officer and a completely different personality from LT Hoffman. Anytime he wasn't sure about something he'd ask questions and that impressed the NCOs. He never got excited or raised his voice even when you knew he was boiling after someone had screwed up. The men always came first and he did everything possible to make their lives a little easier.

LT Bradshaw wanted to know everything about all the troops, so he decided he'd like to see some of the bars that the troops frequented while on pass. He asked SFC Binion and me to show him around. The first three or four bars were very quiet so we just looked in and moved on. We decided to have a beer in the next one so we went in, sat at a table and ordered a beer. There were two young women sitting at a second table over from where we were seated. One was Khonen Strasse Annie, who every GI in Bamberg knew. As soon as we sat down, she started making loud obscene remarks about us. They went something like this, "You NCOs are the reason the privates have so much trouble. You brownnose and ass-kiss the officers. All of you are sorry sons-of-bitches."

This went on for four or five minutes and I got fed up with it. I got up and went over to their table and asked in a polite manner if she'd please shut up. She said, "You sorry brownnosing bastard, you don't tell me what to do." I told her that I had rather be a brownnosing bastard than a Battle-Group whore and started back to our table. She came at me from behind with one of those tall, thin, glass German beer steins. SFC Binion yelled, "Watch out!" but it was too late. She hit me just over the right ear and the glass broke. She continued down with the broken glass, cutting a gash from over my left ear and down and around under my chin. Before anyone could stop her she was out the door.

LT Bradshaw said let's get out of here before the MPs arrive. He drove me to the dispensary to get me patched up. The medic on duty was Sp 5 Nakedhead from the same tribe and reservation that LT Bradshaw came from in Oklahoma. Nakedhead cleaned out my wound and put about fifteen stitches in the side of my head and neck and a bandage that covered the whole side of my head. Then LT Bradshaw and SFC Binion drove me home to Marian.

She had a fit and thought I must be half-dead from the size of the bandage. LT Bradshaw calmed her down before leaving. Three days later I returned to the dispensary to get the bandage changed and I had to see a German Contract Surgeon. He got all upset when I told him who had stitched me up. He called Sp 5 Nakedhead in and wanted to know why he wasn't called to sew me up. Sp Nakedhead said, "When SFC Towe came in, you were drunk and passed out in the back room and I wasn't about to let you work on a friend of mine." After that, I got the Company medic to change the bandage and finally take out the stitches. This time my mouth almost got my head cut off and it looked like I'd never learn to keep quiet.

The winter of 1962-63 was the coldest winter for Europe in a hundred years. It started snowing about the first of October and we didn't see the ground again until April. In the housing area, huge humps of snow could be seen where cars were frozen up and buried. Most of them couldn't be cranked again until spring. The Rhine and Danube Rivers froze over and looked like canyons where the ice came up like large boulders. This stopped all barge traffic on the Rhine and we depended on this transportation for coal for the boilers that heated the barracks. The Army used 18-wheel semis to haul coal from France. The company set up a room with a cot for the driver to take a four-hour nap while we unloaded the coal through a coal chute into the basement. We were ordered to have a detail on standby twenty-four hours a day to unload the trucks and a cook in case the driver wished to eat. We had four hours to get him back on the road.

In February, 1963, we went to the field in support of a tank battalion field-exercise in the Bad Kissinger-Schweinfurt area. When we left Bamberg on Monday morning, the temperature was 2 degrees Fahrenheit and the high for the week was 10 degrees. We ran tank-infantry tactics, attack, defense, road marches, and screening exercises. The Tank Battalion returned to their Post at night and came out again the next morning. The Tank Battalion Commander asked if we'd like to go into the Post and sleep on the gym floor. LT Bradshaw called our battle group operations and they said no, stay in the field. Our greatest fear was frostbite which was a cardinal sin in the infantry. Usually, when you had two or three cases of frostbite on one field trip, someone usually got relieved of command.

On one night in the middle of the week, we got a weather report that the temperature would drop to 33 degrees below zero. That is really frigid, especially when you haven't been issued Arctic clothing and your vehicles don't have heaters. LT Bradshaw came to me and asked, "What are we going to do? If the troops crawl into those tracks, or sit down by a tree, they'll freeze to death."

He called operations again about using the gym in Bad Kissinger and again got a negative answer. Stay in the field, they said.

We had a small general purpose tent, with a diesel heater and a kitchen fly which is a canvas tent top without sides. I recommended that we walk the troops all night, so LT Bradshaw said, if you think it'll work, go with it. I got the Mess Sergeant and let him know that I wanted hot coffee, soup, and sandwiches all night. Next, I called for the Platoon Sergeants and squad leaders and explained the situation to them. They were to form their units in single file and the file would move through the warming tent in a slow shuffle making an S formation in the tent as they moved through. Then in single file, they'd pass the kitchen fly and pick up coffee, soup, and sandwiches if they wanted them, and continue in the circle until they came to the warming tent again. The squad leader would account for his men to the Platoon Sergeant each time he came through the tent. Should a man be missing, the Officers, Platoon Sergeants, and I would search for him.

During the night, about three or four men cut out of the line, but we found them before they received any cold injuries. There was a hell of a lot of bitching, but we got through the night without a single case of frostbite.

We had eleven slight frostbite cases during the week, most of them facial from exposure to the wind by track drivers or wheel vehicles with the windshields folded down, a standing order while we were in the field. LT Bradshaw and I were never asked about the frostbite cases after we returned to Bamberg.

We had a new Lieutenant in the Company with additional duties as Mess Officer. Apparently, he wanted to exert his authority and get shot out of the saddle by LT Bradshaw. One afternoon, the Mess Sergeant caught up with me about 4:00 PM and wanted to know what to do about the evening meal. We'd been moving all day and would like to have chow ready for the troops when they arrived in the bivouac area for the night. The menu called for mashed potatoes and liver. The potatoes were no problem, but the liver was frozen solid. It would take from two to three hours to get the liver thawed enough to slice it. I asked the Mess Sergeant about the egg supply and he said we had plenty of eggs and bread. I told him to slice the potatoes for hash browns, toast the bread on top of the stove and fry eggs to choice. He said he'd be ready to serve by 5:00 PM.

When the Company arrived, I told LT Bradshaw what the Mess Sergeant and I had planned. The eggs were frozen and looked like boiled eggs when they were broken and put on the stove to fry. You waited for the eggs to thaw and flatten out before you turned them over. The new Mess Officer came up and wanted to know who changed the menu and I explained what I did and why. I further added that my radio had gone out, so I was unable to clear the changes with him or the CO. He told me it wasn't my responsibility to change the menu and not do it again.

I was standing with LT Bradshaw when the Mess Officer came up to LT Bradshaw and informed him there wasn't any meat item on the menu and he wanted his meat ration for the meal. The Indian cool LT Bradshaw had shown in other encounters went through the ceiling.

He turned to me and said, "Towe, do you have a meat unit in you pocket?" I reached in and pulled out a can of beef stew and handed it to LT Bradshaw along with my P38 can opener.

LT Bradshaw opened the can and handed it to the Lieutenant and said, "Here is your damned meat ration, now eat it."

The Lieutenant turned red and said, "Yes, sir, I'll go warm it up."

LT Bradshaw said, "Since we're in the field, eat it as it is."

He handed him a plastic spoon. The Lieutenant stood there not saying a word. He was trying with all his might to get the frozen stew out with the plastic spoon.

As the 1SGT, I always had a 5/4 ton truck at my disposal for use in the field to carry chow, mail, ammunition, and other supplies to the Platoons. During the winter, I always carried a bottle of good cognac in the truck and gave a shot to any of the officers or NCOs that I came across. I also did the same for an occasional private if he was near by. When you are cold and miserable any thing warm helps. I'm not talking about a four or five shot slug, but a good nip.

I went to get the Mess Officer, who was also the XO, and the Supply Sergeant once when their jeep broke down. There was about three feet of snow on the ground and it was as cold as a witch's tit in the Klondike. When I arrived both of them were cold and shivering, so I got out my bottle of Hennessy Three Star and offered them a drink. The Supply Sergeant took a nip and passed it to the XO. He refused and informed me that he was putting me on report. I also gave the driver a shot and then called the motor pool for a wrecker to pick up the jeep.

I drove the XO and Supply Sergeant to the Company CP. When we arrived, I went to let LT Bradshaw know that I had taken care of the vehicle and picked up the XO. The XO came over and said that he wished to put me on report for having a bottle of liquor in my truck. LT Bradshaw asked him if I had offered him a drink and he said yes.

Then the CO told him, "Top has had that bottle in there as long as I have known him and I have yet to see him take a drink, but I'm sure he's given away gallons of good cognac to the officers and men. When he offered you that drink, that was his way of accepting you into the Company and you should be proud that we have a Top Sergeant that cares enough about the troops to try and build up their spirit in weather like this. Now will you forget this incident and have a drink with Top and me?"

He accepted the drink and after that he looked forward to seeing me around.

LT Bradshaw had a wonderful sense of humor. We received a new 2nd LT who was a large young man who waddled when he walked. One time he came into the CO's office while I was in there and the CO asked him how he was doing with the men in his Platoon. He said he was getting along good and the men had given him a nick name, Baby Huey. LT Bradshaw asked him if he know who Baby Huey was and he answered no.

"It's a big dumb duck," LT Bradshaw said, smiling. The Lieutenant turned red and left the office.

Then LT Bradshaw said, "I shouldn't have said that, but it was too good to pass up."

On June 19, 1963, I received orders from Company A, 4th Battalion, 2nd Training Regiment, US Army Training Center, Fort Gordon, GA. I was to be in a First Sergeant slot again. In Germany you couldn't go before a promotion board if the Department of the Army had scheduled a First Sergeant to fill the position. For the past eighteen months I'd been in a First Sergeant slot that someone in the States was supposed to fill. For some reason no First Sergeant ever showed up, so I did the job. Once in that period, I was notified that the slot in company A was not filled and to report to Division for a promotion board on the tenth of the month. On the fifth, I received word not to come. The Department of the Army had scheduled another First Sergeant in. When I left the unit, he still hadn't showed up. I was sitting there with eight years in grade and had been in and out of the orderly room and battalion headquarters for fourteen years as First Sergeant or Sergeant Major.

Marian and I had a wonderful tour of duty while in Bamberg. When I could get leave or a pass, we traveled with the kids when school was out. At other times when I went to the field, Marian and Marta Legg, Jim's wife, went on trips together. When we went to the field for an extended period of time, I'd get a PFC or Sp4's wife to stay with the kids and get them off to school. This would give the young wife something to do with no grocery or utility bills while her husband was in the field. Marian and I'd give her a few extra dollars for baby sitting.

Marian and Marta went to Garmish several times and Marian learned to ski on one of their trips.

Joe Koric and I'd go down into Austria for two or three days when we had a chance. We always stayed at this hotel up on the side of the Alps. They had a swimming pool and the water came down a flume from melting snow on the mountain. If you needed an eye opener in the morning, all you had to do was just slide into that pool. It was so cold, I always felt that I had forgotten to break the ice before diving in.

Marian and I took Glenda and Kevin to Chiemsee, a US Armed Forces Recreation Center, for their first ski trip. We put Kevin's skis on first and then Marian and I were both occupied with Glenda's skis. When we turned around, Kevin was gone. We were on a levee, so Marian went one way and I went the other, but no Kevin. We came back to Glenda and I found ski tracks leading down a steep bank and into some trees. I went down the bank and found Kevin buried about three feet into a snowbank.

After an afternoon on the beginner's slope and a stop in the snack bar, we got a sitter for the kids and Marian and I went to the ballroom for dinner. We knew the Leggs were friends of the recreation center manager, but we didn't know they were going to let the manager know we were staying there. This was during Fasching Season. Fasching to Germany is the same as the Mardi Gras is to New Orleans. We had been to a lot of Fasching parties before, so the crowd did not surprise us, but the reception did. We were met at the door to the ballroom, presented with mask and crowns and given the honor of being the King and Queen of Fasching. Then everyone in the ballroom wanted to dance with us. That was a good weekend trip and everyone enjoyed it.

We decided that we needed a new car before we returned to the States, so we purchased a 1964 Pontiac Bonneville convertible before leaving Germany to be picked up in New York. We had the use of our station wagon until I drove it to Bremerhaven a few days before we went to Frankfort for the trip back home.

On July 19, Marian, Glenda, Kevin, and I reported to Rhine Main Air Force Base for air transportation back to New York. We stayed there for three days before our flight was due out. We boarded a four-engine propeller air-force transport plane for the trip back to the U.S.A. I think that was the noisiest flight I've ever taken. We flew the northern route and were able to see the great northern lights. We stopped for fuel in Shannon, Ireland, but were prohibited from leaving the terminal. This was about a two-hour stop.

We then loaded up again and flew to Gander, Newfoundland. We were unloaded about four in the morning, once again. They had to wait about two hours before they could find some one to fuel the plane. The waiting room was like a huge warehouse with not even a coffee stand open. After about four hours we loaded again, this time for the final leg into McGuire Air Force Base in New Jersey. We picked up our luggage and went to a motel. We cleaned up and went to New York to pick up our new car. The GMAC office was near Times Square, so Marian and the kids got to see the Times Building. The New York agent drove us over to New Jersey where we picked up the car. Then we drove back to the motel for the night and departed for SC the next morning.

We stopped overnight in VA and arrived at Mary Lou's house about 7:00 PM. Marian had written Mary Lou that she had two surprises for her, so when we stopped there, Mary Lou ran to the car wanting to know where they were. Marian had platinum hair and the convertible, and Mary Lou thought we had a set of twins. The laugh was on both Mary Lou and Marian. We spent about a week visiting and catching up on three years of family news.

Marian and I drove to Augusta, GA. I went on Post and located my new unit and then we started looking for mobile home courts and checking on schools. We found a space at Mars Hill Trailer Court outside of Gate 5, Fort Gordon, GA on Highway # 1, Hephzibah, GA. The kids would go to Hephzibah School. We had the trailer pulled down a couple of days before I was to report in. I'd decided the pull from Fort Worth to Seneca, SC was enough to do me for a life time. We packed our belongings and used the remainder of my leave to get set up. I was always ready for duty the day I reported in. It always surprised me when NCOs reported in and then wanted a few days off to get their family situated.

On August 23, 1963 I reported to Headquarters, 4th Battalion, 2nd Training Regiment for duty. I reported to the Sergeant Major and he asked me if I needed a few days to get settled. When I said no, he said they weren't sure where they wanted me, so he told me to come back in three days. I went home and cooled my heels for three days, wondering what the hell was going on. I finally reported back to Battalion Headquarters after the three-day delay and the Sergeant Major told me the Battalion Commander wanted to speak to me. We went into his office and I reported to him. He hemmed and hawed a while as to what to do with me, then said, "We have a good ole boy as First Sergeant of Company A that's doing a good job and we're trying to get him promoted to E8. We're having trouble getting waivers for time in service and time in grade. What I would like you to do is go down there and work for him until we can get him promoted." I asked him about the waivers and he told he had six years service and five months in grade.

I said, "May I ask the Colonel a question?"

He replied, "yes."

I said, "If you were assigned to a Battalion and had been asked to be the Executive Officer under a Lieutenant Colonel who you outranked by three days, would you take the assignment?"

He turned red and said, "No, that'd be a different situation."

I said, "To hell it would. My date of rank is just as important to me as yours is to you. I have eight years in grade which is two years longer than SFC Peterson has been in the army and you're asking me to go to work for him?"

He replied, "That's all, Sergeant. Go outside and wait."

A couple of minutes later, the Sergeant Major came out and told me to go back home for another three days. When I returned after that second delay, I was informed I was assigned to Company D as Field First Sergeant.

Captain Danner was the Commander and Penwell was 1SGT. I did a lot of soul-searching during the next three months about retiring because I'd have my twenty years completed in November. I knew that with my retirement pay of only $162.50 a month, I'd have to go out and get a well-paying job just to make ends meet. I still felt there was an opportunity for me to be promoted and to be patient for another two years and see what happens. That was one of the smartest decisions career-wise that I ever made.

The job as Field First was a snap, just a lot of coordination and making sure that everybody and everything was at the right place at the right time. I didn't appreciate CPT Danner's method of handling the troops. He felt that the final test was the only thing of importance.

I knew the test was important to the cadre as well as the trainees, but not that important to try and use underhanded and illegal methods to attain a good score at the expense of the trainees. One system was that the cadre was supposed to encourage three trainees to purchase flatware or china from members of the committee. I had a run-in with CPT Danner over this. I refused and he asked why. I told him that the trainees needed every penny they had and none of them needed to purchase these items, especially from a group that'd be testing them. Another time he encouraged a young Sergeant and a PFC to break into a reserve forces building and steal various items. They stole some cots and bedding. They were subsequently investigated and managed to get out of the mess, but things like that were not a part of the Army that I was used to.

I remember the day President Kennedy was shot I was conducting a class in dismounted drill. I gave the trainees a break, went to the orderly room and got a radio. I went back to the training area and we listened to the radio for the remainder of the afternoon. This was a great shock to both Marian and me. We watched the TV all weekend including the report of Oswald being shot and killed.

We had a Lieutenant who had a girl friend in Atlanta. One payday, he picked up the payroll from the finance office and came back to the company.

I was eating breakfast when he walked over to me, set his brief case on the table, and said, "I have to go to Atlanta, so you pay the troops."

I said, "I'm not the pay officer and can't take the responsibility for that much money."

He said, "I trust you," and walked out.

I didn't break it down into envelopes or even count it. I felt if it was short, he'd have to make it up. I got the company clerk and one of the NCOs to assist me and I paid off directly from the stack, just counting out the money and handing it to each man. I came out on the money, but both of us could've been in big trouble had there been a shortage.

General Salet was a well-liked General who had good working relations with the City of Augusta and especially the people who ran the Masters Golf Tournament. He provided billeting on Post for visitors and work details for the golf course prior and during the Masters. Company D received a call from Regiment to provide one NCO in white shirt and slacks to drive during the Masters Parade. 1SGT Penwell came to me and I told him all our NCOs are tied up, but to get him off the hook, I'd go on the detail.

I reported in white shirt and slacks as instructed and was assigned to drive some Beauty Queen in the parade and to the Clubhouse for a reception. After the reception, I was given a series ticket to the Masters, thanked, and then drove the young lady back to her hotel. I was elated because that afternoon detail gave me a pass to the Masters for the week. I went back to the Company and asked 1SGT Penwell for a five-day leave starting on Monday.

For the next five years, I just about lived at the Masters. I was there for the first tee shot Monday morning during practice and for the last putt on Sunday evening at the eighteenth green. The following year, I went in uniform because any military person in uniform could get a day pass for $2.50. During those two years, I got on the list and received a season badge. I stayed on the list until 1970 when I was notified that I was being taken off the list because of overcrowding of the course. They didn't say so, but because I was living in Augusta, I wasn't bringing any money into the city, so the ticket could be more profitable by being sold out of the Augusta area. I had enough friends there and I 'was able to pick up a complementary ticket, if I desired to go. The crowd got so large that unless you were a crowd watcher, you could get more golf from the TV than from being on the course.

Marian had never worked since we were married except for a couple of months while waiting to join me overseas. The children were in school and Glenda could look after Kevin after school until one of us got home. She looked into being a waitress and in sales, but didn't think she would enjoy that type of work. She had worked as a secretary before we were married so I asked her why she didn't go back to school. She in turn asked, "Can we afford it?"

She checked all the business schools and colleges in the Augusta area. We discussed prices and finally decided on the Augusta Business College because they gave a course for Executive Secretary. She enrolled and I helped her in the evenings when I could. Most of the time, I just called out words for her to practice her spelling, but mainly I cleaned the kitchen while she studied.

One of the Cooks from D Company lived in the same park and one evening he came along the street and we talked as I washed the dishes. The next day during lunch I was in the dayroom shooting pool when he came in.

I was ready to shoot when he said in a loud voice, "I saw Sergeant Towe washing dishes last night."

Without looking up, I replied, "They are my damned dishes and I'll wash them anytime I want." I went ahead and made my shot and he left the dayroom without another word.

Promotions were opening up and I heard they were going to conduct a Promotion Board at Post. I was looking forward to the Board because Post had published a point system to be used for promotions. Points for each of the following categories were listed: time in service, time in grade, decorations, service schools, certificates of achievement, and letters of commendation. I knew with my record, I'd be close to the top of the list and I was eagerly waiting to go before any Board.

I was in the mess hall when one of the Sergeants came in and asked me how I did before the Board. I asked him what he meant and he said they had a Post Board the day before. I escorted two men to Battalion Headquarters that afternoon and while talking with the Sergeant Major, I asked him about the Board and he said CPT Danner didn't recommend me.

A few days later, as I was eating lunch with two other Sergeants, CPT Danner came over and said, "Towe, get ready. I'm sending you before the next Post Promotion Board."

I thanked him and said I'd be ready. When the next Board convened, I still wasn't on the list. This time I went straight to the Sergeant Major and he said let's go in and see the Colonel. There had been a change of command and this was a new Commander since my arrival in the battalion. The Colonel said, "Towe, CPT Danner refused to recommend you for promotion and his only explanation was you weren't ready. I couldn't go over his head with a recommendation for you."

When I heard that, I started boiling and immediately went back to the Company. The 1SGT was gone, so I walked into CPT Danner's office and closed the door.

He looked up and asked, "What do you want?"

"I would like to know why I wasn't recommended for promotion," I said.

He said, "I don't know what you're talking about. They haven't had a Board."

That was when I completely lost it.

"You're lying through your damned teeth and you know it. You told me in the mess hall while I was eating with two Sergeants to get ready for the Board. And now when the Colonel asked you about my recommendation, you told him I wasn't ready."

He started to get up and said, "You can't talk to me like this. I'm an Officer."

I said, "Sit down, Captain, and listen and you'd better listen damned good. You say one word or try to block my going before a Board again and I'll go directly to the IG. I will expose every rotten thing you have done in this Company, and that will include making the cadre sell dishes for the committee, having two men break into the reserve storage building, lying to the investigator about that crime, taking carloads of expendables home and a number of other wonderful things. When I get through talking, you'll probably get your sorry ass kicked out of the Army or go to the stockade. I'm going to Battalion and get out of this Company and away from you and I wouldn't advise you to try and stop me."

I turned and left, slamming the door so hard it almost came off the hinges.

As I left the Company area, I met the Sergeant Major. He was looking for me because the Battalion Commander wanted to talk to me. We returned to Battalion Headquarters and on into the CO's office.

The CO said, "Towe, how would you like to work for me for a while. I have a couple of projects that I want done."

I said, "Yes, Sir."

The first project was a testing area with a dozen stations. I drew a plan for the area and he approved it. Then I took a detail and cut a path through small scrub oak and cleared an area for each testing station.

I had worked for him for about three weeks when the Sergeant Major told me I was going before the Promotion Board in a couple of weeks. When the Board met, I was the first to go before them. The President of the Board commented, "You must've had to be unlucky over the years to have not been promoted, especially with a record like yours."

I answered all their questions to the best of my ability and left the room feeling good. Later, I learned that each board member had me as number one on their check sheet. On May 11, 1964, I was promoted to 1SGT E8 and transferred to Company B of the 6th Battalion, 2nd Training Brigade. The 4th Battalion Sergeant Major told me that CPT Danner came to see the Battalion CO about my promotion, saying that he hadn't recommended me and the Colonel told him that since Towe was working for him, he didn't need Danner's approval.

The Promotion Ceremony took place at the Officers' Club and Major General Salet and Marian pinned on my First Sergeant E8 chevrons. This was the second time that Marian had been through this drill. She had helped Major Hughey pin First-Sergeant chevrons on me eight years ago when I was in the 4th Armored Division at Fort Hood, Texas.

I knew most of the 1SGTs and SGMs in the Regiment so the 6th Battalion was no stranger to me. I had told all the 1SGTs that if they wanted to make Sergeant Major before I did, they'd better do it before I had time in grade to get a waiver. They only had one Board before I became eligible and no one in my MOS appeared before it. I appeared before an E9 Board in June or July of 1965 and again came out number one in my MOS and was placed at the top of the waiting list for Sergeant Major.

After living in an apartment in Germany for over two years, we decided that we needed a larger place, so we began looking for a rental house. It seemed that everything we liked was out of our price range, so we started to look into buying a house. Again, the ones we wanted were priced beyond our means. After awhile, Marian got disgusted with our looking and finally refused to go with me. She said when you find something you like and we can afford, then I'll go look at it with you.

In June, I saw an ad in the paper and went to talk with the owner. It was a three-bedroom, bath and a half, ranch-style brick. The owner wanted a small equity and someone to take over the payments. I asked him to hold it until the next afternoon, when Marian and I'd come out and look at it together. We decided that this was something we could live with so I paid the equity, signed the mortgage papers, and I was the proud owner of a home that we would keep for the next twenty years. We sold the trailer and moved into the house all in one month. On June 16, 1964 we moved into the house at 1826 Cypress Street, Augusta, GA.

The only problem I had in B Company was there wasn't enough cadre. At one time, we were running the company of two hundred and fifty trainees with one officer and eight enlisted cadre. This was during the major buildup for the Vietnam War and all Officers and NCOs were being sent there. To increase the number of trainees in each cycle of training, the Post Engineers erected tents for the expansion. I had about a hundred trainees sleeping in tents and using port-o-lets.

The cadre consisted of one 2nd Lieutenant, 1SGT, one Supply Sergeant, one Mess Sergeant, two cooks, a Field First Sergeant, and two Drill Sergeants. Each of the Drill Sergeants had two Platoons and the Field First had one Platoon. We used holdovers (trainees waiting for shipment or for the next cycle to start) in many positions. I had one as company clerk and one was Company Armor who was in charge of the arms room. The Supply Sergeant was also mail clerk and had a trainee as an assistant. The mess hall had four as assistant cooks. Every Platoon Sergeant and Squad Leader was a trainee.

We still had to perform our normal duty-roster duties, such as Company Charge of Quarters, Battalion Duty NCO, Regimental Duty NCO, and Guard Duty. I put every NCO in the company on CQ except the two cooks and this caused a problem. The Mess Sergeant informed me that he didn't have to pull CQ, so I looked through all the regulations I could find and found nothing that prohibited the Mess Sergeant from performing any roster duty. I informed him of this and put him on duty as CQ. He was an alcoholic with twenty years of service and wasn't any good to the unit or the US Army.

He came to work about eight or nine each morning and left about two or three in the afternoon. My thought was if I, as 1SGT, could pull CQ, so could he. His first duty came up on Sunday and about 8:00 AM. I received a call from the CQ that Sergeant Sheridan had not showed up to relieve him. I told him I'd be out in a few minutes. I went out to the Company and let the other Sergeant go home and pulled CQ myself. Monday morning I reported to LT Faulk that Sergeant Sheridan had failed to show up for duty. He said, "Top, you handle it the way you think best."

Sergeant Sheridan came in about nine and I called him into the orderly room and asked him why he had missed duty. I also asked him if he had seen his name on the duty roster.

He said, "Yes, and I told you I didn't have to pull any company details being a Mess Sergeant."

I told him that I was tired of his drag-assing around and he had two choices. One, he could go to personnel today and put in for retirement, or two, he could go before the Battalion CO for unit punishment. I warned him I'd request that the Colonel bust his ass a stripe. He again informed me that he didn't have to pull any Company duty and wanted to talk with the Battalion Commander to get me straightened out and off his back. I picked up the phone and called Sergeant Major Garretson He told us to come on over.

We went to Battalion and SGM Garretson escorted us into the CO's office.

The Colonel asked, "What's the trouble, Sergeant Towe?"

I explained that SFC Sheridan had failed to report for duty and I'd like to initiate field-grade unit punishment.

He turned to SFC Sheridan and wanted to know what his story was. SFC Sheridan explained that as Mess Sergeant, he didn't have to perform Company roster duty and I was picking on him. The Colonel turned to the Sergeant Major and asked whether that was true. SGM Garretson replied, "Towe is right. No one is excused from roster duties, but normally certain NCOs are exempt from duties and the First Sergeant is the first one to be exempt. Towe has been pulling CQ due to the shortage of NCOs for a couple of weeks now."

The Colonel turned to SFC Sheridan and said, "I'm going to give you the same choices as your First Sergeant gave you. Either put your retirement papers in today or report to me tomorrow for unit punishment. Do you understand that?"

We were dismissed and SFC Sheridan went immediately to the IG complaining we were railroading him out of the Army. I received a call from the IG and explained the situation regarding the shortage of cadre and that I was pulling CQ. He said SFC Sheridan was lucky. Most units would have reduced him first, then made him retire. According to information I received from other NCOs in the regiment, he never did understand why he had to retire.

The trainee that I was using as company clerk was shipped out so I decided that I'd go to an on-duty typing class, since I was doing all the work that a clerk would normally do. I went to the Education Center and enrolled. At our first class, the lady who was doing the teaching gave us a typing test. I typed about thirty-seven words per minute on the test.

After she checked the papers, she said, "First Sergeant, I feel that you are wasting your time here. You typed thirty-seven words per minute with your hunt and peck system. After you break all your bad habits and learn the touch system, it's doubtful if you will improve over a couple of words per minute. It's up to you, you can stay or go."

I decided to go so I am still using my hunt and peck system thirty-nine years later.

I lost one of my two cooks to Vietnam and got another cook who had just returned from Korea. This one was a problem from the word go. He reported in about two in the afternoon and said he had to go to Finance for a partial pay so that they could find a place for his family to stay. I directed him to Finance and about thirty minutes later I received a call from our pay clerk. He said, "Top, I can't give this Sergeant a partial pay. Let me come up and talk with you about this."

Finance was only a couple of blocks from my orderly room so he was there in a few minutes. We're talking about an NCO with over twenty years in the Army, not some recruit that doesn't know what he's doing. The Finance clerk gave me the story. This Sergeant had made out an allotment for all but fifty dollars per month to his wife before leaving the States. During the seventeen months he spent in Korea, he drew full pay and his wife still received the full allotment. Prior to leaving Korea he drew a maximum partial pay and while he was on a delay en route from Fort Lewis Washington, to Fort Gordon, he'd gone to three Air Force Bases and drew partial payments from them.

To accomplish this, he removed the partial pay slips from his record before going to the Air Force Finance Office. All of these slips were waiting for him when he arrived at Fort Gordon. He came back to the orderly room mad as hell because they wouldn't pay him. I sent him to the Red Cross and when he showed up the next day, we went to see 2nd LT Paulk, the Company Commander. I had told LT Paulk about his troubles the evening before so he sat and listened while I talked with the new cook. I welcomed him to the Company and explained the shortage of personnel.

Then I told him about my talk with Finance. He said it was all a mistake and when I asked about the allotment and full pay while he was in Korea, he said that he drew the money, but it was the Army's mistake, not his. Then I explained that he'd be in trouble if he started getting letters of indebtedness.

He had been in the Company about three weeks when he came in and wanted me to look at his new car. I asked him how he expected to pay for it and he informed me that he and a friend had opened a fish and seafood restaurant up on the lake. I wished him luck, but reminded him that his mess hall duties came first. He told me not to worry, that he understood.

During the next month, I started checking the mess hall before leaving in the evening to see who was cleaning up. About three different times, I found a trainee supervising the cleanup. When I called the cook in, he had a dozen excuses; the other man at the restaurant was sick so he had to leave early to cook; a sick kid; he had to go pay on a debt. I told him that he was pushing his luck with me and he should retire. He said he wasn't financially able to retire. The Army was taking his money to pay for that mistake they made. Each time I wrote a report on him, I put it in a special folder because I knew he was a loser and sooner or later he'd cross the line.

I usually went in at 5:30 AM each morning. That gave me time to check the activities of the night and set up the details and appointments with MSGT Crosby. LT Paulk and I arrived at the same time and MSGT Crosby informed us that the cook wasn't in.

LT Paulk asked, "What are we going to do?"

I asked him if he ever fried a egg and he said yes. I then said you're going to fry eggs by the hundreds this morning. Crosby rounded up the cadre and we headed for the mess. I sent MSGT Crosby out to hold reveille and police call. When the troops arrived for breakfast, we served them eggs to order with bacon, toast, and hash browns. We had set out the milk, coffee, and dry cereal. We had prepared the full meal and had come close to following the master menu for the day.

Lt Paulk asked me what I intended to do with the cook. I said I was going to force him to retire. When he came in about nine that morning, I asked him what happened. He said they had a large party that came in late so he had stayed there until three in the morning cooking for them. He got to bed at four and was too tired to come in and pull his shift. I asked him who he thought was going to feed the troops. He said that he never thought of that. I said let's go see the Company Commander. He wanted to know why and I said you'll find out when we get there.

When we arrived, LT Paulk let me do the talking. I looked the cook straight in the eyes and said, "When I have to do your job, then I don't need you. I have a stack of letters of indebtedness two inches thick on my desk already. On numerous occasions you have left a trainee in charge of the mess hall at night. I have counseled you about your responsibilities and still you haven't changed. I think it's time for you to retire before anything else happens."

Again he said he couldn't retire because he had too many debts.

Then I looked at LT Paulk and asked, "What should we do about his failure to report and being absent this morning?"

LT Paulk said, "Those are serious charges and I don't think Company punishment is sufficient. I will recommend a Field Grade Article 15 by the Battalion Commander."

The cook asked what will happen there?

LT Paulk continued, "Both the 1SGT and I have tolerated you for too long. I will suggest that the Battalion Commander reduce you one grade."

The cook said, "Let me think about it."

LT Paulk said, "You either go to personnel this afternoon or I will send the Article 15 paper work to Battalion the first thing in the morning."

When the cook got off shift, he went to personnel and put in the paper work for his retirement. Finance Center later informed me that it would be about four years and seven months before he'd receive his first retirement check.

SGM Garretson was a good Sergeant Major and I enjoyed working with him. He was a fuddy-duddy type person who got excited over little things. One day I was out checking the police in our tent area when SGM Garretson called me over to Battalion. I trotted over and he told me he had checked one of my barracks and one man had been issued two left boots. I want you to get that man up to the Clothing Issue Point this afternoon and get this matter taken care of immediately. I said okay and went on with my inspection.

When I got to the second floor of the second Platoon barracks I remembered the left shoes. I immediately found the left shoes and checked a couple of bunks down and found two right boots. I checked the names and placed the boots under the correct bunks and forgot about them. About two days later, SGM Garretson caught me out back of the supply room and called me. I met him halfway and he reminded me that I had not reported back to him after I had taken that trainee to the Issue Point and changed the boots.

I looked at SGM Garretson with the most innocent face I could muster and said, "I didn't report back because I didn't see any need to take Jones to the Issue Point."

He said, "You mean to say there was no need to take him over there like I told you to?"

I looked him in the eye and said, "Sergeant Major, the man had two left feet."

I turned and walked about ten paces when he shouted, "Towe, come back here."

Then I explained that the trainees had mixed up the boots and I straightened them out.

He said, "Towe, I'm going to nail your ass to the wall one of these days," and started laughing.

Grovetown, GA, was a small town at the back of Fort Gordon and was known as a bad place for a GI to get caught driving. I always let my cadre off anytime I found a few hours when I didn't need them. We worked many long hours and a couple of hours break was a big relief. One afternoon I let one of the Sergeants off and he stopped in the Hay Loft for a beer on the way home. He called me and said the Grovetown police were watching his car and could I send out someone to drive him home. I told him not to move and especially not to drink anymore beer and I'd take care of him. I had the company clerk drive the Supply Sergeant out to the Hay Loft, then follow them home and drive the Supply Sergeant back to the Company. They drove out and the Supply Sergeant went in and got the other Sergeant and thy left the Hay loft with the Supply Sergeant driving. They were stopped by the police and the Supply Sergeant explained that he hadn't had a drink. They gave him a field sobriety test, which he passed with flying colors. Then they arrested the other Sergeant and charged him for riding drunk. I went over to the police station and paid the Sergeant's fine and the charge was listed as, "Riding while drunk." In one month this small town wrote more traffic tickets than the City of Augusta.

General Salet retired and we got a new Commanding General, Major General Walter B. Richardson and an Assistant Post Commander, Brigadier General Pepke. General Richardson was hell on wheels. He had been a Combat Commander in Europe during WWII and had been an armored division CG in Germany sometime during the fifties. Sergeant Major Cliffe, our Regimental Sergeant Major, had been in the same division with him. He told this story about one cold morning when General Richardson was going up a tank trail in his jeep and it quit running. He stopped a tank and got a track bar from the tanker. He ordered his jeep driver to go with the tank commander and get another jeep. While the jeep driver was gone, the General beat the jeep with the track bar until the windshield, hood, lights, steering wheel, and all four fenders had to be replaced. You really had to stay on your toes at all times. He always carried a big stick with him and everyone referred to him as Father Moses. He'd suddenly appear in your reveille formation and if you made a mistake, he'd go into a rage.

He inspected C Company mess one Saturday. Everything was going smoothly until the entourage went out the back door. All at once he started cussing and threatening to bust the Mess Sergeant, relieve the CO and 1SGT, and to this day no one from C Company knows what set him off.

He'd get into his sedan on Sunday afternoon or in the evening and ride around the Post with a duce and a half truck following him until he had a truckload of trainees who didn't salute his Two-Star Standard mounted on the military sedan. I remember getting a call from our CQ one Sunday afternoon telling me General Richardson had picked up one of our trainees.

The trainee's Company chain of command was required to go to Post Headquarters and retrieve the errant culprit. They couldn't reach the CO or Platoon Sergeant, so I went and picked him up from the Post Duty Office. He was instructed to write a three-hundred-word essay on the importance of military courtesy in the US Army. The trainee was scared to death and was sure he'd be punished and sent to the stockade. I drove him back to the Company and he told me at least three times that he was standing on the corner looking the other way when the General passed.

I told him that I'd assist him with his essay and that calmed him down. We went to the orderly room and I got out a copy of FM 22-5 and typed an essay for him. I instructed him to copy it in his own hand writing and bring it back to me no later than Wednesday morning so that I could send it through channels to the General. The trainee was a sixth-grade dropout from school who had been drafted for the Vietnam War.

He came to me Tuesday evening before I left for home with the copied essay. You could tell that his penmanship must have been very slow and laborious and he apologized for the poor writing. I told him that was all right and that he had done a good job and the General would be happy with it. I doubt he'd have ever been able to write an essay, but most likely would have made a good "grunt."

We finally got a new PX and the first thing General Richardson did was to put out the word that all vehicles, military and civilian, would be combat parked. This meant you'd always back your vehicle in and pull forward when leaving. Can you imagine the havoc caused by these instructions? There was a Regimental-size MP school plus the Post MP Company stationed at Fort Gordon and there were still not enough Military Police to investigate all the fender benders on the first day of combat parking. After one day that order was rescinded.

You had every problem imaginable when dealing with basic trainees. One morning a Platoon Sergeant came in and said Top, I have a new one for you. I said let me have it. He had chewed out one of the trainees for not shaving and the trainee ran over to a port-o-let and lowered himself into it feet first. I thought he was kidding, but he said he pulled him out and had a couple of the trainee squad leaders take him to the shower.

I told him to get him over here and I'd send him on sick call. I didn't know if the chemicals would harm him or not. The dispensary called later in the morning and said he was okay. About a week later the same Platoon Sergeant came into the orderly room and threw a Polaroid photo on my desk.

"Well," the Sergeant said, "he did it again and this time I brought you proof."

The photo showed a trainee down to the shoulders in a port-o-let. The trainee was eventually separated from the Army as a 208 (mentally disturbed).

The Supply Sergeant was also the mail clerk, so I had the CO appoint me assistant mail clerk. The Supply Sergeant, SSG DeLahousa, came into the orderly room with a mail bag and said it had been dropped off the mail truck by mistake. It should have gone to B Company, 5th Battalion. I told him to leave it here with me since I was going to Regiment and would drop it off at the Regimental mail room. I went up to the mail room window and a Sp5 asked me where I got that mail bag in a tone that was displeasing to my ear. I told him that his people dropped it off by mistake. Before I could finish, he informed me they didn't make mistakes like that. I responded by telling him in my best First-Sergeant voice that the only people in the Army who didn't make mistakes were people who sat on their dead asses and did nothing.

The Regimental Adjutant heard us and came out in defense of his people and demanded to know why I didn't give them the mail bag and leave. SGM Cliffe heard us and came out to join the fray and see what the commotion was all about.

The Lieutenant said, "Sergeant Towe came in here accusing our people of making mistakes. If anyone made a mistake, it was the First Sergeant."

SGM Cliffe gave the Lieutenant a hard look and asked, "If someone in the mail room didn't make a mistake, why in hell is Towe standing here with a mail bag belonging to the 5th Battalion?"

Then he added, "Towe, give them the mail bag."

He then turned to them and said, "Next time get your 'ducks in a row' before you start accusing one of my First Sergeants of anything."

Again I got hit with an undesirable NCO. There was a Master Sergeant Charles Crosby from Mississippi who had a run-in with General Richardson. MSGT Crosby was a Range NCO (an NCO who rode around and made sure range guards were posted at the proper points and that ranges were properly policed, etc.). One afternoon he was lying across the hood of his jeep when General Richardson came up. He continued to lie on the jeep and saluted.

General Richardson went into orbit. He said, "Send that Sergeant to one of the training regiments and I never want to see him again."

I got a call from SGM Cliffe that SGM Chesser, the Post Sergeant Major, wanted to see me immediately and SGM Cliffe didn't know why. Cliffe and Chesser were good friends who went back to WWII. On the drive to Post Head-quarters, I tried to think what kind of trouble I or one of my men might have caused and how serious it might be. I had met SGM Chesser through SGM Cliffe and had a beer with them on a couple of occasions and they both had sat on my E8 board and were present when I was promoted.

When I arrived, SGM Chesser told me to have a seat. He then said, "I have a big problem, so I called Cliffe and he said you could probably help me out. I have a MSGT who is an alcoholic with almost twenty-years of service. Some-how he got in the General's sights and I want to keep them as far apart as possible. If you can, take him and give him a job and he'll give you a good day's work."

I said okay and he called MSGT Crosby in and introduced us.

MSGT Crosby was the nearest thing to a grizzly bear I'd ever seen. He stood about six-two and weighed about three hundred pounds and it all looked like solid muscle. He told Crosby to stay out of the General's way and if I had any trouble to let him know. On the drive back to the Company, Crosby told me that the range patrol job was the most boring thing he'd ever done so he started drinking on duty. This was something he'd never done before.

I told him I had a job for him that wouldn't be boring and would definitely keep him on his toes and I hope out of trouble. He said "Good, that's all I need." I told him he was going to be my Field First Sergeant. I asked him if he'd ever done that before. He said he had done everything except 1SGT and he didn't have the education for that.

MSGT Crosby worked for me for about six months before he retired. He proved to be an exemplary soldier. Not one trainee ever missed an appointment and the Company was on time for all classes and formations. He came in at 5:00 AM each morning and was always the last NCO to leave in the evening. I never knew of him having a drink during duty hours even when the trainees went to the range for a week. He was a workhorse and I thanked SGM Chesser for sending him to me. With our shortage of NCOs, he was a real lifesaver.

He invited me to drop by his room one Saturday afternoon after we had taken care of the Company for the weekend. He had stopped by Class VI and picked up a couple of fifths of Jim Beam and a bottle of coke. He got some ice and a couple of glasses and I mixed a light one. He said he usually started with a couple of fingers straight. He wrapped that bear paw of his around the bottle and his hand covered just about all of it. He turned it up and guzzled almost half of the bottle in one gulp. Then he said, "Now I'll have a bourbon and coke." He put two ice cubes in the glass, filled it almost to the brim with Jim Beam and poured less than a tablespoon of coke in and mixed it. He stayed in his room and drank for the entire weekend and showed up Monday morning ready for another week.

He put in his retirement papers and bought a new car. He promptly went out and wrecked it and was charged with DUI and thrown into jail in Augusta. I got a call and went down and bailed him out and SGM Chesser held his traffic ticket until he was retired.

For some reason, General Richardson moved General Pepke and his office to the back of the Post. They even erected a flagpole in front of the office. This gave us two flagpoles on the same Post. If they had moved him another block back, he'd have been out in the boondocks. I liked General Pepke. He was a very quiet-spoken individual, but with a voice of authority. His office was less than a block from my orderly room, so I saw him frequently. On a few occasions, he saw me outside and stopped and we went to the mess hall for a cup of coffee.

He was interested in my family and asked about Marian, Glenda, and Kevin. He had a tremendous knack for remembering names and always called everyone by name. He also wanted to know about the welfare and training of the trainees because they were scheduled to be in Vietnam shortly. He often commented on how young they looked to be sent into combat. I agreed with him because I was older than he was. He was President of my E9 board and I had the pleasure of serving under him again later.

When the Department of the Army decided to have "Drill Sergeants," they decided to call it the Ailes concept after Secretary Ailes. The School was to be located at Fort Jackson, so they sent the first instructors to study under the Marines at Paris Island. When they were fully trained, a Company from Fort Gordon was sent to Fort Jackson for training. Mr. Ailes spent just about the entire training cycle with them. I knew the 1SGT and all the cadre who went to Fort Jackson. After the first Company finished their training cycle, we then were detailed to send our field cadre to the Drill-Sergeant School.

When these NCOs started coming back and teaching the new concept, I wanted to know what they were being taught. I went to see SGMs Garretson and Cliffe and asked to be sent to Fort Jackson to observe a class. Orders were cut for three 1SGTs to go for two weeks. We went over and they gave us the run of the school. We were cleared to go and observe any classes we wished. They gave us lesson plans for all classes and it was a two-week period well spent. I was pleased to know as much about what was supposed to be taught as my Drill Sergeants. A couple of times I was able to make corrective criticism of classes due to the expert knowledge I had gleaned from Fort Jackson.

I created quite a stir over a short suspense date when I was accused of going over the heads of a lot of individuals in a case that I still feel I was right. I got a call about 4:30 PM one Friday evening from Regimental S3 to come up and get a suspense item with a short fuse. I picked it up just as they were closing the office for the night. I got back to the Company and looked at the stack of papers

I had picked up. It was a trainee report requested by CONARC (Continental Army Command located in VA).

When the request left CONARC, they had a ninety-day suspense date, meaning that they required the information to be back to them within ninety days. It had sat in Third Army Headquarters for thirty days and then sent to Fort Gordon with a thirty-day suspense date. It stayed in Post Headquarters for twenty days and Regimental Headquarters for five days before it was forwarded to Company B, 6th Battalion.

This was usual procedure for a lot of paper work. Everybody wanted to sit on it to the last minute, so that other people would think they'd done a lot of work. When I looked at the request, I blew my top. They wanted a report on all trainees who had graduated from Company B during the previous year to include: number of troops received into the Company; the number that graduated from basic training on schedule; the number AWOL; and the number on emergency leave, hospitalized, or injured in training. They also wanted the number recycled into the Company and the number recycled out.

All this information had to be located, assembled into a given format, typed, and sent back to Regimental Headquarters before 8:00 AM Monday morning. I showed it to LT Paulk and he tried to get someone from Battalion and Regiment, but everyone had gone for the night. On Saturday morning the battalion CO was off and SGM Garretson couldn't help me, so I went to Regiment and found that SGM Cliffe was also out. A lonely 2nd LT was all I could find in the S3 Section. The only advice he could offer was to say just go ahead and do it. No one offered to call Post G3 about an extension on the suspense date.

I went to Post Headquarters and was talking to the Operations Sergeant about it when the Post G3, a full Bird Colonel, came over and asked me what I wanted. I had met him a couple of times before when he'd been inspecting training and also at the NCO Club on Bosses Night. I showed him the time the report had stayed in various headquarters and the amount of work required from LT Paulk and me to meet the Monday morning deadline.

He looked at the report and said, "This is insane." He turned to the Operations Sergeant and told him to change the report to give me a fourteen-day extension. Monday morning all hell broke loose. Both Battalion and Regiment wanted to see me at the same time. I went through the chain of command getting my ass chewed at every stop, but still felt good because by getting the fourteen-day extension, I proved my point. I worked on that report every spare moment that I had and finally completed it nine days later. When it got back to Post Headquarters, the G3 himself gave me a call and said I'd done a good job.

One afternoon, I sent a trainee to Regiment with a report for the Adjutant. A few minutes later, I received a call to come and get him. Apparently, he had gone into the Regimental Commander's office while there was a conference going on. When I got to the Adjutants office, the trainee was sitting there so frightened he was trembling. Every one from the lowest clerk in the Adjutant's Office to the Regimental CO had chewed him out, but it seems no one asked him why he went into the CO's office. I asked him why he had done so.

He answered, "First Sergeant, I came up here looking for a sign outside saying Adjutants Office, I went all around the building looking at signs. I found Regimental Headquarters, S1, S2, S3, and Mail Room. Then I came to a sign that said 'private' and thought that my being a private, this surely was the door I should enter."

The Commander's Office was on the side of the building facing a side street. This was the door that the Commander entered and left by and he decided it should have a sign saying it was his office so he came up with the word "PRIVATE." The next day the sign was gone.

One of the Sergeants in the Company came to me one payday and said he had been overpaid by $1500.00 and wanted to know what to do to keep from getting his pay screwed up. I said let's go to the Finance Office and get it straightened out now. I drove him to the Finance office and went to the desk where a Sp5 was seated. I explained what had happened and he informed me that he didn't have time to take care of the Sergeant and we'd have to come back later in the afternoon or on Monday. I asked him if we were interrupting his reading of Playboy. That was what he was doing when we entered. He turned his back on us and I demanded that he turn around so I could see his name tag. He turned with a scowl on his face and I wrote down his name.

When we left the office the Sergeant wanted to know what he should do now. I asked him if he'd like to make a few bucks and he said yes. I told him we'd go to the Post Bank and open a savings account and then when the Army wanted their money back, he'd have it with interest. But under no circumstances was he to touch that money.

We went to the Post Bank and opened the account. About three months later, I received a call from a Warrant Officer in the Finance Section who said he had the name of a Sergeant who had been overpaid and he wanted to see him immediately so that he could make arrangements to have the Army repaid. I told him I'd bring the Sergeant up. So once again we went to the Finance Office.

The same Sp5 was at the front desk and when I told him I was there, he started to get pale, but pointed to the Warrant Officer's Office. We went in and reported and he started to chew out the Sergeant. I interrupted him and asked him if this was about the $1500.00 dollars he had been over paid, and he said yes. I asked him how he'd like to get the money back, in cash or a bank check. He said, "What do you mean, does he have the money?" I said yes and pulled my trusty note book out of my pocket and referred to my notes. I told the WO that he came to me about the over payment and we came here that afternoon to return the money, but the Specialist sitting out there said he didn't have time to fool with us and we'd have to come back the following week. I told the Sergeant to put the money in the bank until someone here decided they wanted it.

The Warrant Officer called for the Specialist in a loud voice you could hear all over the building. At that moment, the Specialist knew that he had messed his nest. He had paled considerably since we first came in. He started to deny that he'd talked with us and the WO told him to shut up, because the 1SGT has notes showing date, time and your name, now get out of here. I'll talk to you later.

The Warrant Officer said a check would be fine. We went to the bank, got a bank check for $1500.00 and the interest in cash. When we came back, the WO apologized for the inconvenience and said he was going to recommend unit punishment for the Specialist.

I always felt that the further down the line in the chain of command, the harder it was to lose a man. The Platoon Leader, Platoon Sergeant, and Squad Leaders worked and lived with the soldiers of the Platoon. They knew the men and became closer than anyone else to them. They were the ones that had the foxhole bond with each other. When one of them was killed in action, they lost the most important man in their lives at that time. He was the man their lives depended on day and night. The further up the chain of command, the losses became mere numbers instead of men. It had hurt me deeply when I lost a man in combat in Korea and equally as bad when I lost the first man, even if not in combat.

One afternoon, one of our trainees fell out on a march from the field. He was a robust, good-looking soldier about six feet tall and an excellent trainee. He said he was having headaches and dizzy spells. I sent him to the dispensary and they immediately sent him to the hospital. Before leaving for the night, I received a call from the hospital advising me that he had been admitted. I'd just gotten to the orderly room about 5:15 AM the next morning when I received a call that he had died. It hit me hard. Why should this young trainee die here while on a march from the field with all that we were losing in Vietnam. I walked out of the orderly room and across the street and had a good cry. It still hurts to lose a man.

On December 27, 1965, the 16th Battalion, 2nd Training Regiment was activated and I reported for duty as the Battalion Sergeant Major. Major Rex Shelton was assigned as Battalion Commander. Our Battalion Headquarters was a building in what was known as "The Tile Area." It consisted of a group of tile buildings that were erected during the closing months of World War II to be used as a Separation Center for mustering out WWII US Army veterans. For the past twenty years, the area was used occasionally by reserve units for summer camp. The buildings all had broken windows, no locks on the doors, and no electricity or water. The Post Engineers supplied all the materials and a little labor to get the area ready for trainees. The cadre refurbished the buildings with the help of details from other battalions, but also rolled up their sleeves and did a lot of the work themselves. MSGT Wisda reported as Operations Sergeant so he, Major Shelton's driver, and I did the work in the Battalion Headquarters Building. We erected walls and doors so that the CO and XO had decent offices. The clerk and I shared the front of the building and MSGT Wisda had the back for S3 (operations section).

In early January, 1966 we received a levy for a twenty-hour course to be conducted by members of the hospital staff. The course was Emergency Medical Treatment for non-Medical Personnel. I told Major Shelton that everyone was tied up, so I'd attend the class. I completed the course on 24 January, 1966.

During the next thirteen months, we ran five cycles through the 16th Battalion. We could train two hundred men for each of our five companies at one time. During the existence of the Battalion, we trained approximately five thousand men. The Battalion was deactivated on February 21, 1967. Major Shelton had been promoted to Lieutenant Colonel and General Richardson and Marian pinned on my SGM chevrons on January 26, 1966. I was promoted to Sergeant Major. There had been only one person on Post promoted to SGM since I made 1SGT and he was in a different MOS.

As for retiring, I was locked in; first, when I made 1SGT E8, I'd have to serve two years before I could retire as an E8; then after twenty months and promoted to E9, I was locked in again for another two years. That would give me twenty-five years. The next longevity raise was at twenty-six years and it was a good one, so I decided that I would stay until then before considering retirement. Marian was now working as an executive secretary for the Red Cross Director of the Fort Gordon Hospital. The kids were both in school within walking distance of the house. We had a maid that worked about five or six hours a day. She cleaned house, did the washing and laundry, and cooked the evening meal. Things were going really well with us and we were enjoying our life, she her work and me, the Army. Any time I could get a pass or leave, we either went to Savannah to the beach or up home to Walhalla, SC, which was a three-hour drive. The war in Vietnam had heated up over the past two years, but I decided that I wouldn't volunteer for this one. When they needed me, they'd send me orders.

In his way, Major General Richardson had been good for Fort Gordon. When I first arrived there, the Post had run down badly, the streets had just about washed away, and all the buildings were dilapidated old WWII wooden barracks. When driving, you had to watch where you pulled off the street because the ditches might be four or five feet deep. There were no curbs anywhere on Post. During the Vietnam buildup, General Richardson had gotten the Post a modern Post Exchange (PX) and all the streets had curbs. Grass was mowed regularly and you'd better have a good police call at least once a day and most times twice because it was utter hell to get caught with a candy wrapper or cigarette butt in your company area. I was the keeper of the Battalion coffee pot. I washed the big thirty-cup pot and filled it with fresh water and the correct amount of coffee before leaving the office every evening. The first person to arrive in the morning plugged in the pot and we had fresh coffee for the morning. I was usually the first one in, so I plugged in the pot and went out to check the night activities. I hit all orderly rooms and usually a Company for breakfast. If I remember correctly, breakfast was about thirty-five cents. That was less expensive than I could eat at home and I didn't have to cook.

One morning I stopped to check Company A. 1SGT Knowles, a grizzly old First Sergeant was at his desk just inside the front door. The trainees had been threatened with their lives if they came through that door. They had to enter through the side door and the supply room. While I was standing there, a timid knock came on the front door. 1SGT Knowles never looked up. The knock came again and was a little louder this time.

Knowles growled, "If that's a trainee, I'll kill him." The knock was repeated, but much louder.

Knowles, in his best Top-Sergeant voice hollered, "Come in."

A trainee peeped into the orderly room and Knowles roared, "What the hell do you want?"

The poor trainee stuttered a couple of times and in a frightened voice answered, "First Sergeant, I just wanted to tell you that your car is on fire." We rushed outside and put the fire out. It was caused by an electrical short. I told Knowles that if I'd been that trainee, I would've stood there and watched his car burn before I knocked on that door the second time. We'd just gotten the buildings livable and the latrines cleaned up and operating, but they didn't have an adequate heating system when we had our first major freeze. On Friday night the temperature dropped to about twenty degrees and only got up to the low thirties by Saturday.

Col Shelton called a meeting of the COs and 1SGTs and ordered them to have extra men on fire detail because they were predicting even lower temperatures for Saturday night. The temperature dropped even lower that they predicted, down to about zero. I got a call Sunday morning and every- thing on Post was frozen solid. Pipes were busted all over and the commodes had frozen and cracked. We called Post Engineers, but the only ones they were able to reach were all working at the main Post. We did manage to get the company that supplied port-o-lets to the tent areas in the Regiment and they made a Sunday delivery to us. The mess halls had cooking pots full of water, so they were able to serve breakfast.

We got through the day and Sunday night without any frostbite cases and only a few cold butts from the outside toilets. COL Shelton had finally got a couple of people from Post Engineers out to the Battalion area about 9:00 AM and they were still standing around at ten when General Richardson appeared on the scene. He walked through one latrine and practically went into orbit, but fortunately, it was all directed at the Engineers. They got on their radios and in about thirty minutes a convoy came over the hill and into our area. They had pipe, plumbing equipment, new commodes, electrical heaters, and an army of workers. Since General Richardson was still pacing the area, not one word was spoken; they just went right to work. They knew that any hesitation would cause them to be fired on the spot, to hell with the consequences. I'll say one thing for the General, that was the first and only time I ever saw the Post Engineers really work.

By night, they had all our plumbing restored, but they planned to be in our area for a week finishing up some of the things they had failed to do when we first moved into the tile area. Marian reported that the hallways in the hospital were like skating rinks. For all WWII and Korean era vets, you'll remember the old wood-constructed hospitals with the long hallway across the entire front of the hospital and the wards off this hall. They were heated by steam and the steam pipes ran overhead in the halls.

All these pipes had burst and the water froze in the hallways.

Each year we went through the drill of giving all trainees who desired a leave, one for Christmas. This sounds simple until you think about the number of trainees we had at Fort Gordon at any given time. We had two regiments of basic training, a regiment of advanced infantry training, and a regiment of military police. Then there were the students of the Signal and Civilian Affairs Schools. All of these soldiers were released on Christmas leave at one time, so Post Transportation had to have numbers for bus and air transportation to all destinations.

The Adjutant was CPT Sterling. He was the brother of SSGT Bobby Sterling, who was my Platoon Sergeant at one time while I was in Company I, 5th RCT in Hawaii. I informed CPT Sterling at a staff meeting that he needed to send a letter of instructions to the First Sergeants so they could start planning for the Christmas Exodus. This was about a month before the trainees were to depart. This letter was to include the number not going on leave so the First Sergeants and I could make up a duty roster to cover all details over the Christmas Holiday. Also, Post would need the number traveling by air and by bus and their destinations. The Companies were operating with about 220 trainees each, so this was one big job to get it all coordinated.

I reminded the Adjutant once about the letter and he said he would do it when he got around to it. All the First Sergeants were after me for the instructions, so on Friday morning, one week before the trainees were to start on leave, I sat down and wrote the letter and told the clerk to cut a stencil of it for me. MSGT Wisda and I ran the stencil and I hand carried copies to the First Sergeants and set up a meeting for Saturday morning to discuss who would keep their mess hall open and what cadre would be present over the holiday.

I gave COL Shelton a copy and explained that personnel involved needed to know what was going on and the Adjutant hadn't started on the letter. I placed a copy on the Adjutant's desk and when he came in about 2:00 PM, he came out of his office with the letter in hand. He proceeded to tell me that I couldn't send the letter out and pointed out the format that I had used, a misspelled word, and a couple of commas missing or in the wrong place. I said, Captain, I waited for you to write that letter for three weeks, so this morning I wrote it in the simplest language that the dumbest First Sergeant or Field First could understand. It's too late for you to correct it now.

COL Shelton was standing in the background and said, Sergeant Major, I'm going to the range and left. The COL finally returned at the end of the day. His driver came in and asked about what had taken place inside just before he and the COL left. He said the COL got in the jeep and laughed all the way to the range.

On February 22, 1967, the 16th Battalion, 2nd Training Regiment was discontinued and I was transferred to the 5th Battalion, 2nd Training Regiment and relieved SGM Gordon who was retiring. I knew that SGM Gordon and the Battalion Commander remained in the Battalion until about nine or ten each night waiting to see if anything significant had occurred.

About 5:15 PM the first evening in the 5th Battalion, I packed up and was ready to leave. The Battalion CO asked me where I was going and I said, home to have dinner with my family. He said we usually stick around a while and I asked him why. After hesitating a moment, he said, just in case something might come up. I said, Colonel, that's why we have a Battalion Duty Officer and each Company has an NCO as Charge of Quarters and a Duty Officer on call. You live about six or seven minutes driving time from here. You can drive here as quickly as you can walk to a couple of the companies. You should go home and have dinner with your wife and family for a change. Should anything significant happen, both of us would be here in fifteen minutes. Sitting here in Battalion Headquarters is not going to prevent something from happening. He said, I never looked at it that way. After that, we were there if we were needed and put some of the responsibility on the junior officers and the NCOs. The Colonel started spending more evenings with his family.

In October, 1967 I went to Washington for the Association of the U. S. Army meeting. While waiting for the Sergeant Major's Luncheon, there were about four or five of us talking to the Department of the Army Personnel Sergeant Major. He asked us if we had any problems that he might help us with. I presented one of my pet peeves, and that was NCOs with over twenty years of service who were alerted by Department of the Army for transfer to Vietnam or other overseas areas would trot down to the Personnel Office and put in papers for retirement. At that time, the DA would rescind the overseas orders and after this action, the NCO would cancel his retirement papers. After seeing some

NCOs pull this a couple of times, it was disgusting and a morale issue for the NCOs with less than twenty years service because one of them would have to file the rescinded orders.

The DA Personnel Sergeant Major said he would look into the policy. He saw this the same way I did. Sometime in early 1968, we received word that if you came out on orders, you must go to the new assignment and serve one year. You could put in your retirement papers, but you had to serve that year before the effective date of the retirement. When those instructions came down, you couldn't find a parking space within two hundred yards of the Personnel Office because they were all filled with "old farts" putting in their retirement papers before they came out on orders. I was glad to see this regulation because it sure got rid of a lot of deadwood, including some who had dodged an overseas assignment for four or five years.

That evening after Marian, Glenda, Kevin, and I finished dinner, I told them that we had to make a decision immediately and each of them should express an opinion since Glenda was sixteen and Kevin was twelve years old. I explained what the new regulation meant for us. I had been back in the states for almost five years and should be near the top of the list for another overseas assignment. Both Glenda and Kevin said that the decision was up to me. Marian said, you do what you want to but remember that if you don't go to Vietnam, you'll always regret it. That settled any thoughts of retirement at that time. The Army had given me seventeen good years since Korea and I didn't feel that I should leave it now when my experience was most needed. I just sat back and again said to myself, I'll serve where ever they desire to send me.

On February 1, 1968, the Regimental Sergeant Major retired and I was assigned to Regimental Headquarters as the Regimental Sergeant Major. In a period of four and a half years, I'd gone from Sergeant First Class E7 and Field First Sergeant to Regimental Sergeant Major, E9. Patience and persistence had finally paid off along with a little luck and a lot of hard work.

In early 1968, The Department of Defense decided to separate the E9 into Command and Staff positions. In the Army each Sergeant Major was given the choice of being a Staff Sergeant Major and working in a staff position or becoming a Command Sergeant Major and working directly for a Commander. The first increment of CSMs applied to Post, Division, or higher positions occupied by a Sergeant Major. There were 191 appointed on the first increment orders published in early February, 1968.

VIETNAM

I chose to go with the CSM program and was appointed in the second increment on May 1, 1968. I received orders for Vietnam three days before I was appointed to be Command Sergeant Major. I had orders for the 3rd Brigade, 4th Infantry Division, Pleiku, Vietnam. This was in the highlands which I preferred to being down in the delta. When I received orders, SGM Raymond Upp, who had replaced me as the 5th Battalion SGM, again replaced me as the Regimental SGM.

I cleared Post and this time there was no family displacement. Marian, Glenda, and Kevin would remain in Augusta for the year that I would be gone. The kids would continue in the same schools and Marian would continue to work for the Red Cross. On 10 May 1968, I departed Fort Gordon for a thirty-day delay en route before reporting to Travis Air Force Base. This base had been renamed from Fairfield Susan where I went and came through going to Hawaii in 1949 and returning from Korea in 1950.

Two days before my leave was over, my father died and I called for an extension and received a new reporting date of June 22, 1968. My brother Andy was a SSGT in the U. S. Air Force with twelve years service. He was stationed in Tuy Hao, Vietnam and had been in Nam for about six months. He came home on emergency leave for our father's funeral.

At that time, there was a rule that no more than one family member would serve in Vietnam except when the family members signed a waiver. He liked his assignment and said that if he didn't sign a waiver, they'd send him somewhere in the Far East for the year that I would be in Vietnam, then send him to Vietnam again to complete the other six months of his tour. I wanted the assignment to the Highlands so I didn't wish to wait for six months before receiving another assignment. We decided to both sign waivers and serve there at the same time. When his leave was up he returned to Tuy Hoa and on June 22 I reported to Travis Air Force Base for transportation to my third war.

When I was ready to leave, my mother said, you have come back from two wars already, be careful and come back to me again. I have often thought about the pain and anxiety I must have caused my mother over the years. First, when I left home as a seventeen-year-old kid who felt that he was ready to take on the world and then when I left from Hawaii for Korea in 1950 and now going to Vietnam. I now realize that she must have felt that three is the lucky charm, or three strikes and you're out. She had kept her star in the window during WWII and Korea and my sister said that she proudly placed the two stars in the window for my brother and me in Vietnam.

It was hard to leave Marian and the kids, but I tried to put on a strong front. I knew it was easier on me to be leaving them, than it was for them to stay behind not knowing if I'd survive or not. Marian's job with the Hospital Red Cross brought her in contact with the war wounded every day since Fort Gordon was designated a rehabilitation hospital.

Marian drove me to the airport on the morning of June 22, 1968, and I said a teary good-by and departed Augusta, GA for San Francisco at 5:00 A.M. and arrived in San Francisco at about 8:00 AM. SGM Legg met me at the airport and I spent the day with him and Marta. He drove around and showed me how San Francisco had changed since I was there in 1947. We drove through Haight Ashberry and saw all the hippies and flower children. He was stationed at The Presidio of San Francisco with the Sixth US Army Headquarters. Marta fixed lunch and we talked for the rest of the afternoon. I had to report to Travis Air Force Base at 8:00 PM so they drove me to the airport and remained with me until it was time to board for my upcoming flight.

I arrived in Hawaii in the morning and had a two-hour stop over. I called the Bodies who Marian and I were good friends with in Bamberg, Germany. They were Hawaiians and Howard was a baseball player with the 5th RCT. They had retired and gone back to their home in Hawaii.

Our next stop was Wake Island to refuel, then to Clark Field in the Philippines. I remembered I had been in the Philippines twenty-three years before just a few hundred miles south. It seems I'm always going back to places that have memories for me, some good and some bad. I had time to brush my teeth and shave and it was on to Bein Hoa, Vietnam.

Everyone was still up tight after the Tet Offensive, so I didn't move around too much and I needed some sleep. I had my records checked the next morning and flew on to Pleiku that night. Nothing around Pleiku moved at night except the Viet Cong, therefore I was stuck in a shack at the Pleiku airport until 8:00 AM the next morning before there was any transportation to Camp Enari, Headquarters, 4th Infantry Division.

The jeep carried me to the 3rd Brigade Headquarters where I was briefed by the Adjutant and the Personnel NCO. I was issued standard equipment and a weapon with ammunition. The PS NCO arranged an appointment with the Division CSM and I had lunch with him. We discussed the Division and compared backgrounds. At this time I had three days in country with three hundred and sixty-two days left. I never kept a short-timers calendar, one on which you marked off each day of your tour.

On June 27th, the PS NCO arranged a flight for me on a CH 47 Chincok helicopter to Kontun where the 3rd Brigade was located at Fire Base Mary Lou. The previous CSM had departed Vietnam while I was on emergency leave so I had to learn the ropes by myself as I went along. I asked a lot of questions and received some good and not so good advice.

I reported to COL Eugene Forrester and he explained that I was to go with him each time he flew out of the fire base. When we landed, he'd look up the officers and I would check on the enlisted men. I usually looked for the 1SGT or the Platoon Sergeants. I also talked with as many enlisted men as time permitted. COL Forrester did the same and when we were back on the chopper, I reported my findings to him. I checked on supplies, water, mail, cokes, and ice cream, all the little things that helped maintain the morale of the troops.

I knew the importance of mail call because I went for three months without a letter from home back in 1944. I left Bainbridge, MD in May and didn't receive a letter until the last of July or first of August when we arrived at Kwajalain, in the Marshall Islands. After three months without a letter my hopes were not high at mail call but I still went. It shocked me when they called Towe and I had a packet of about ten recent letters. My mother wrote you haven't mentioned your new sister in any of your letters and I know that I've told you about the baby. The next mail call I received over a hundred and fifty letters. I placed them in order of date and from whom and started reading them. I was walking on air for all of the following week.

On July 18th we had a change of command ceremony for COL Forrester and COL Stan McClellan. COL McClellan was to be the Brigade Commander for the next six months. At that time all Commanders were in a command slot for six months and a staff position for six months. The ones who were going to be promoted to general went to the Pentagon and the others went out to graze in the back forty.

COL McClellan was on his second tour in Vietnam. He'd been Commander of an Infantry Battalion as a LTC, then back to the Pentagon and back to Vietnam to get his ticket punched for Brigadier General. He was an enlisted Sergeant and went to OCS (Officers Candidate School) and was elected to the OCS Hall of Fame, Fort Benning, GA while serving as the Brigade Commander. This was a major highlight in his military career. He was a chip off the General Patton block. If there was a shot fired in our AO (area of operation), he wanted to be there. I enjoyed serving under him, but was scared to death half the time.

August 2nd we moved to the Oasis, a large Brigade-sized Base Camp located about forty miles west of Pleiku. Here I had my own private tent and a sandbagged conex for a bunker. I used the S1 shower or at times the Colonel's shower and had maid service through support funds issued to the S1 to hire Vietnamese labor. The maid kept my water can full, swept the dirt floor of my tent, and made my cot.

We had a Platoon run into the enemy and we went to the area, but couldn't land nearby. We landed about a click (1 kilometer) from the action. Colonel McClellan, his radio operator, and I dismounted from the CC (command and control) chopper and made our way through the jungle to where the Platoon was. The action was over by the time we arrived, so we received an action report and the Platoon Leader gave us an escort back to where we left the chopper.

We operated with the Vietnamese Army at Plei Mrong, and set up a CP (Command Post) about 800 meters outside their fence, but not in sight of the camp. COL McCellan named this the "Stump CP" due to a large stump located in the area. We had moved the CP, but were expecting visitors to come there for a briefing.

A small contact was made in the area, so the Colonel left me at the closed CP alone. It is frightening being alone in the jungle and having no idea where the enemy might be. I knew that the VC checked all closed camps for ammo and food, or anything else they might be able to use. They came back for me before the visitors arrived.

Our motor pool was a mess with over 75% of the vehicles on deadline, so the Colonel sent me to the rear to get it cleaned up and get the vehicles off deadline. He said if anyone questions your authority, tell them to call Hunter 6 (Hunter 6 was his call sign) and he would quickly set them straight.

I went to Camp Enari that evening and went to the motor pool about 7:30 AM the next morning. I was the first man to arrive. The motor pool crew finally showed up around 8:00 AM and I asked the Motor Sergeant when the Motor Officer came to work. He said usually before nine. I asked him to get me the work orders and requisitions for all the vehicles on deadline. We were working with those papers when the Motor Officer, a young Captain, showed up.

He yelled, "What the hell are you doing in my motor pool? Nobody asked you to come in here and start ordering my people around."

I didn't appreciate his tone of voice so I said, "COL McClellan sent me here to clean up this damned mess you have and get these vehicles off deadline. If you don't like it, get on that radio and call Hunter 6 and I'm sure he'll let you know why I'm here."

He turned red and bit his tongue to keep from letting his big mouth overload his little ass. I was using the XO's jeep, so when we got the paperwork together, I headed to the Division S & T (Support and Transportation) and the Sergeant Majors Office. He looked at the paperwork and then we went to see the Chief Warrant Officer.

He also looked at the paperwork and checked the records, then looked at me and said, "Hell, Towe, most of that stuff has been sitting here for days and weeks waiting to be picked up. You'll need at least a 2 and a half ton to haul it all." I got on the phone to the motor pool and had the Supply Sergeant send a truck to the 4th S & T.

When the truck arrived, they loaded engines, transmissions, wheels, tires, batteries, spark plugs, trays, and bags of miscellaneous items, and just about anything else that'd fit on a vehicle. The Warrant Officer told me that anything they didn't have today, it would be ready for pickup either tomorrow or the next day. I thanked him and went to lunch with the S & T Sergeant Major.

I returned to the motor pool and found every one sitting around doing nothing and all the parts still on the truck. I called them all together and informed them that all those parts were to be installed prior to the end of the day. One Sp4 informed me that it was only three hours to quitting time. I informed him the US Army day is twenty-four hours long and we were going to work until the last part is on a deadlined vehicle, so let's get started.

I organized teams with the best mechanics starting on the major repairs such as changing engines and transmissions and the other mechanics and drivers handling small repairs like batteries, tires, and alternators. I wasn't a mechanic, but I got my hands greasy along with everyone else. Less than an hour passed before the Captain was just like the rest of us and asking the Motor Sergeant what he wanted him to do.

We had the deadline report down to less than 50% by 5:00 PM when the Motor Officer made his report to Brigade Headquarters. We knocked off for dinner at 5:00 PM, ate and returned to work and continued working until around eleven. The morale had gone up 100% among the motor pool crew when they had materials to work with. The griping and complaints had stopped completely long before we called it a day. All the work had been accomplished except for a couple of engines and a transmission. I told them that they had done a great job and to let the rest of it go till morning.

When we left the motor pool everybody was happy. The next morning I picked up the Motor Sergeant and a truck before heading to the 4th S & T. I introduced the Motor Sergeant to the Sergeant Major and the Chief Warrant Officer and they assured him that if he had any trouble getting a requisition filled to come and see them immediately. We received a lot more parts and the Sergeant was instructed to return the next day for everything on back order.

I took the afternoon off and went to the PX on a shopping trip. While I was there, I bought a 208 piece set of Noritika China for both Marian and Glenda and had the package shipped home. That evening our deadline report was around 10%, so I met the Division Sergeant Major for a good steak and a couple of beers. The next morning I caught a chopper back to the Oasis and gave the Colonel my report.

On September 27, one of our four-man LRRP (Long Range Reconnaissance Patrol) was attacked by a VC (Viet Cong) enemy Platoon and one member was hit in the chest. We went to the area of contact to see if we could be of assistance. They had called in a medical (Dust Off) mission and gun ships had arrived on the scene. The Dust Off tried two runs but was unable to land due to heavy automatic weapons fire and had to back off. The medical helicopters were not armed and had no protection and couldn't fire on the enemy positions.

CSM Glenn H. Towe [Ret'd]

The wounded man was bleeding profusely from his chest wound and COL McClellan knew that he was in serious trouble.

He came up on the intercom and said, "Towe, we are going to go in low and slow enough for you to go off the skid. Get that soldier stabilized the best you can. Then call and we'll come in and pick both of you up."

I gave him a Roger and we headed in. We started receiving fire before we got close to my dismount point. I was standing on the skid as the pilot made his run. He came in fast, slowed to about ten miles per hour and I bailed out. I hit the ground trying to run, but the momentum sent me ass over tea kettle on the ground. This was fortunate because I started to receive fire now.

I made my way about forty yards to where the wounded man was. One look and I began to hope that all my medical training might pay off. He had a sucking chest wound. This indicated that one or both lungs had been punctured, but the round hadn't gone all the way through. There wasn't an exit wound on his back. I talked to him while I examined him. He was alert and wanted to help. I had him place his left hand over the wound and apply all the pressure he could exert.

I had the LRRP Leader call the Colonel and tell him I was ready to be picked up and to have the machine gunner fire at the edge of the woods as they came in. I also instructed the LRRP team to give me covering fire. I had the wounded man put his right arm over my shoulder, keeping his left hand on the wound. Then I picked him up in my arms and ran the forty yards to the pickup point. I arrived at the same moment as the chopper and as I stepped on the skid, we lifted off.

They pulled the wounded soldier and me into the chopper as we gained altitude. We were still receiving enemy fire during the entire operation. Aboard the chopper, I took my knife and cut a patch for the wound out of a poncho and taped it over the wound with duck tape. COL McClellan had gotten the hospital at Pleiku on the radio and handed me the headset. I was connected to a surgeon and he asked me if the patient was still alert and I said yes. Then he asked what medical attention he had received and I told him about the patch that I had applied.

Is it holding, he asked? I said yes. I told him we had an ETA of about twenty minutes and he said he would stay on the line with me until we landed and to keep the patient awake and alert.

When we landed, the surgeon and a medical team were there waiting. The surgeon talked to the patient as they wheeled him straight to the operating room and started performing their medical miracles. A few days later, I was making my usual weekly check on our troops in the hospital when I met the surgeon I had talked with on the radio. The patient had made good progress and had been shipped out. He also told me that if I hadn't applied that airtight patch, the soldier would've most likely died. With all the men that we lost and when you feel that you had a hand in saving one, it makes you feel absolutely great.

One month later, we had about the same situation occur, another wounded man on a hot LZ (landing zone). COL McClellan asked me if I'd like to try the same method of recovery we used a month earlier to save the man with the sucking chest wound and I replied, let's go for it. I'd feel as safe on the ground as I did at the height we were circling the LZ. Again I bailed out, but this time I didn't fall. I located the wounded man in a small wooded area and found, after bandaging his wound that he was able to hop along on one foot. I called back that we were ready to be extracted. We made a run for it and the man hit one foot on the ground for about three of my steps, but it wasn't like having to carry him. The chopper came in and we got aboard without getting hit although we did draw a lot of fire. I don't know why they were trying to wipe us out instead of the chopper. The door gunner was able to suppress the fire until the chopper got back in the air.

We made an interesting trip out to the Tea Plantation on the highway between Pleiku and the Oasis. The Plantation was run by a Frenchman who had been in Vietnam since the French ruled. He had a beautiful villa located in the center of the Plantation. It was furnished in old colonial and very dark and cool inside. He had servants who served us tea and small sandwiches and cookies. We had all this before he and the Colonel could start to talk business.

There was an agreement between the US Forces and the Viet Cong that they wouldn't use the tea plantation as a secure area for their troops and we wouldn't shell, bomb, or maneuver our troops in the area. It was surprising that both sides honored this agreement. There were outbuildings where the workers lived and the entire plantation was very well maintained and clean. I was always leery about going through there in convoy because there were some good ambush sites along the highway. I tried to visualize what living would've been like there during the French Colonial Days.

In late November, a Special Forces Camp located on the Cambodian border came under attack from a flat trajectory artillery piece and ground forces were noted in the area and planning an attack on the camp. The majority of the infantry battalions and artillery were attached to the 3rd Brigade. The artillery was zeroed in on the landing pad.

When the Colonel asked the pilot to land, he told us that the only way he could do that would be for him to come in low and for us to hit the ground running. The Colonel said, let's go for it. We went in fast and then slowed over the pad and the Colonel and I bailed out. I hit the ground running straight for a bunker. When I looked back to see where the Colonel was, I saw him walking leisurely across the field. They really had that field piece zeroed in on the landing pad and must have fired just as we came in because the shell hit dead center of the pad where the chopper would have been had we sat down. COL McClellen came in the bunker and asked for a medic. He had a small piece of shrapnel in

CSM Glenn H. Towe [Ret'd]

his arm from the shell. Then he said, "Another purple heart."

This weapon was firing from about 6 kilometers inside Cambodia and the camp was four kilometers from the border. That would give it at least a ten kilometer range. At that time, we weren't allowed to fire into or fly over Cambodia.

I only got into trouble with COL McClellan once. His call sign was Hunter 6 and we had a Battalion CO whose call sign was Tiger 6 and mine was Zebra 10. One of the Companies of the Battalion was in an attack and the Battalion CO had landed because he was airsick. COL McClellan came on the internet and told me to tell Tiger 6 to get his airsick ass in that helicopter and get up here where he could see what was going on.

I came up on the net with Tiger 6, "This is Zebra 10 with a message from Hunter 6. He wants you back here where you can have better control, out."

Hunter 6 came over the internet and said, "Sergeant Major, that wasn't the message I told you to send, now send it again properly."

This time I sent, "Tiger 6, this is Zebra 10. Correction on message from Hunter 6, get your airsick ass up in the air so you can see what's going on, out."

The next time I saw the Battalion CO, he told me that one day I'll be under his command and I replied, "It'll be my pleasure to be your Sergeant Major, Sir."

Another duty that I undertook during this period was the coordination of the travels of the Donut Dollies. They were the young ladies who worked for the American Red Cross. They worked in teams of two or three girls each and visited with the troops at the various firebases. They carried their bags of goodies and games with them and were an excellent morale builder for the young troops. They would normally go out to one firebase and stay for the day. They had no means of transportation of their own and no priority over anybody else.

A lot of people resented them and wouldn't try to assist them in getting a ride to a firebase. In such a case, they'd stay at the Oasis for the day. COL McClellan said at a briefing one evening that he was assigning the Sergeant Major the duty of coordinating transportation for the Donut Dollies and he expected them to get out to the firebases on the first available chopper going that way including his. I had a little trouble the first couple of days, but when the companies and staff saw that I meant to follow the Colonel's orders and get the girls out, they started cooperating.

Then the job got easy as they began calling me when they had a bird going out to see if they were getting the Dollies for the day. They even went to firebases where it wasn't safe, but they insisted they wanted to go to the troops and therefore they were sent. Two of them were on a

firebase when it received mortar fire and one of the girls got hit in the arm with a piece of hot shrapnel. The wound was not serious and was treated by the unit medic. We were in the area, so COL McClellan went in and picked them up on our way back to the Oasis. I continued this duty for the remainder of my tour.

I didn't usually have any sympathy for prisoners, but one of the companies had captured one and brought him into our aid station for treatment late one evening. The next morning, COL McClellan told me to get a chopper and take him to the Division POW Compound (prisoner of war) in Camp Eneria. I went to the Medic tent for the prisoner and found a thirteen-year-old boy and I asked to see the Interrogation Report. He had been picked up one night in his village during a Viet Cong raid about a month ago. He had been shown how to load and fire a rifle and throw a hand grenade and that was the extent of his military training except for being given classes on the Communist Doctrine.

I looked at him and thought except for the Grace of God, that could be my son, Kevin, and my heart went out to him. I went over to the cot where he was lying and you could see the fear in his face and eyes as he lay there trembling. I attempted to get him up to walk and the medic told me he wasn't able to walk because of the gunshot wound through the calf of his leg. From looking at his skinny body, I estimated he'd weigh only about fifty or sixty pounds. I picked him up in my arms and carried him to the Loch (light observation helicopter) and placed him on a seat and fastened his belt. I sat in the seat beside him. As we took off, I placed my arm around his shoulder and talked to him in the softest voice I could manage and that he could hear. The sound of my voice calmed him down and he stopped trembling. I think he was afraid I was going to throw him out of the chopper. We arrived at the POW Compound landing pad and I again picked him up and carried him over to the compound gate. Once there, I was met by a big six-foot-plus MP. I asked him to get a wheelchair for the prisoner.

He said, "Put the little son-of-a-bitch down and let him walk. We don't baby prisoners in here."

He said the wrong thing in the wrong voice to the wrong person. I said, "Look Sergeant, I asked you to get me a wheelchair for this kid. Now I'm telling you as a CSM. Get a damned wheelchair out here on the double and don't say another word."

He managed to get out two words, "You can't..." before I stopped him by saying, "Stop right there before you let your big mouth overload your little ass. Now get that chair before I really get mad."

A Captain came up during my last tirade and asked, "What's wrong, Sergeant Major?"

I reported to him and explained that I had asked the Sergeant to get a wheelchair for this boy and all I got was a song and dance from him. He turned to the Sergeant and told him to get a wheelchair out here immediately.

I asked the Captain if this was the way the compound was run and he answered, "No. That Sergeant has been in trouble before and he'll be taken care of."

CSM Glenn H. Towe [Ret'd]

The Brigade Adjutant, PS NCO and CSM Towe in front of the 3rd Brigade TOC in Camp Eneira, Pleiku, VN, May1969.

MG Pepke, CG 4th Infantry Division, visits the Oasis.
Front row, left to right, MG Pepke, COL McClellan and CSM Towe, Fall 1968.

Army Medics conducting Med Cap. Medics go into a Vietnamese village and treat the sick, give shots and pass out food and candy to the kids.
Central Highlands, VN, August 1968.

CSM Towe and CSM Pullie getting some sage advice from MG Stone.
NCO Club, Camp Eneira, Pleiku, VN, August 1968.

The wheelchair arrived and the Captain escorted me to the dispensary where I said good-bye to the little kid. I informed the Captain that COL McClellan had an interest in any additional information the kid might give and would be by tomorrow to check on it and the kid.

We went by the next afternoon and I was informed that the SFC who had given me a hard time was now on convoy duty from Pleiku to Dat To. I realized the enemy had caused me a lot of grief, but I try to rationalize he was doing a job the same as I was. I can forgive the soldiers who tried to kill me and came close on a few occasions, and did kill many of my friends.

The things I could never forget were the atrocities committed on our troops after they became prisoners. I also feel that same way toward our troops who committed the same acts on enemy POWs. When he becomes a POW, usually he isn't able to cause you any further harm so why abuse him.

I went on a five-day leave to Kuala Lumpur, Malaysia. I found that I could take a five-day leave, but had to find an R & R tour with an empty seat, so the first one that came up was Kuala Lumpur. It was a very short flight from Vietnam, which made it more enjoyable. There was one other CSM on the flight.

We landed and cleared customs and were waiting outside the terminal when a military sedan drove up. The driver came over and said he was there to drive us to our hotel. A Major came over to the driver and said, "I'm ready to go, what are you waiting for?" The driver replied that he was here for the Command Sergeant Majors. The Major told him that he was an officer and we were just enlisted men. The driver told him he knew that, but his instructions were to pickup the two CSMs and not Officers. Then he added, if the Sergeant Majors don't mind, I can drop you off at your hotel. We said that would be okay with us. When the Major started to get into the rear seat, the driver told him he'd have to ride in the front seat, the rear seats were reserved for us. The Major didn't say a word except the name of his hotel. He didn't even say thanks or give a tip to the driver. As rude as he was to the driver, I hoped the trip into the city spoiled his R & R. The first thing I did after checking in at the hotel was call Marian. It was nice to be in a safe place where I could relax and talk with her. I always had good food when I was there. About five of us went to the Chinese Restaurant in the hotel the first night for dinner. I ordered shrimp and ended up with a seven-course dinner. We ate and drank beer or wine for about four hours. I finally asked the waiter where my shrimp were and he replied that would be the next course. When we finished the meal and realized what a long time we had spent eating, I decided it was time for bed. It had been a long day after having an afternoon flight from Vietnam.

Shopping there was a new experience for me. All the shopkeepers wanted you to come in and have tea, coffee, or a beer before talking business. I went to one of the better pewter companies there and spent the entire afternoon touring the factory, all the show rooms, and even the company sales offices. I ended up buying pewter Christmas presents there for Marian and having them shipped home. I also spent the better part of the day going through the flea market. It was supposed to me one of the largest in the world. Everyone wanted to bargain with you. Even if you saw something you liked and agreed to pay their price, they still wanted to bargain. That was a way of life with the tradesmen and it also helped to pass the time. If you so desired, you could get roaring drunk without spending a penny. Everybody offered you beer or wine just to talk with you or to reveal his skill at bargaining.

I took a couple of tours and found the area to be beautiful and the people friendly and all were eager to talk with an American, even if he was a GI. Then it was over so quickly and back to Vietnam and the war. I had an early-morning flight back to Saigon and was lucky to catch a flight back to Pleiku that afternoon and then on to the Oasis all in one day.

In early December, we ran an operation south along the Cambodian border to Ban Me Thuot. There had been a sighting of North Vietnamese Regulars, so everything in the area moved south. I was sent by COL McClellen to the Special Forces Post in Ban Me Thuot to keep tabs on any enemy intelligence they might develop. I stayed with them for three days and they were just like us. Nothing new had developed, so we were getting ready to go back north to the Oasis.

COL McClellen called me in and said we had patients in the hospital in Tuy Hoa, so while we were this far south I might as well go over and check on them. I'd also be able to see my brother while I was there. He was a Staff Sergeant in the US Air Force and was close to finishing his tour in Vietnam. I caught a ride over to Tuy Hoa and spent two days with Andy and also visited our wounded troops. We had both been home at the same time for our father's funeral. Andy was leaving at that time and I had another six months to go. We had a few beers and talked about family and people we knew. It was a nice visit and I thoroughly enjoyed it. I made my way back to Camp Enari and on to the Oasis just in time to head out again.

COL McClellan called and asked me to meet him in the briefing tent. When I arrived, the Assistant Adjutant 2nd LT and the Chaplain 1st LT were with COL McClellen. He was sending us to the Long Bien Stockade near Saigon to visit the prisoners for Christmas. The Adjutant had our tickets for a flight the next morning to Saigon along with hotel reservations. I packed my bag and went to Brigade Rear in Camp Enari where I had a room that I stayed in whenever I was in that area. I kept a suit of clean fatigues, underwear, and toilet articles there, just in case I came in from the field without my travel bag.

We had a decent flight from Camp Enari to Saigon. Since we arrived late in the evening, the Chaplain and I after checking into the hotel, went to the lounge for a drink and then to the dining room for dinner. After a good steak and fries we headed to the lounge again and the Chaplain continued to drink. I decided that I didn't want a hangover the next day, so I didn't try to keep up with him. Finally I left him there and went to my room and to bed. After breakfast the next morning, we caught a bus and headed for Long Bein Stockade.

When we arrived, a Sergeant came out and I told him we'd like to meet with our men. He told us to wait a couple of minutes and went back inside. While he was gone, both the Lieutenants were bitching that we'd probably be there all day and not get to see all our troops and COL McClellen would chew them out for not doing a good job. They sounded just like two privates on a ditch-digging detail. I had looked at the Stockade Commander's sign and it said Commanding Officer: COL Ivan Miller. When the Sergeant came back, I asked him if that was the same Colonel they called 'Ivan the Terrible' and he said yes. He asked me if I knew him and would I like to talk to him.

I said yes and he went back into the office. I had known him in Fort Gordon where he was Provost Marshall and attended all the Bosses Nights at the NCO Club. This was a gathering that I had arranged to get the NCOs and their bosses together to improve working relations between the different units on Post. We met on the last Friday of each month.

A couple of minutes later, COL Miller came out. He was a big bear of a man and dwarfed me. He was smiling and said, "Towe, what the hell are you doing here?" I told him I was with the 3rd Brigade, 4th Infantry Division and introduced him to the Chaplain and the Adjutant and told him we came to see our troops for Christmas. He turned to the Sergeant and said, "Take care of them and show them whatever they want to see. Then come with me, Towe."

He threw one of his huge arms over my shoulder and we walked off. They'd had a stockade riot a short time before and he was called in to clean up the mess. He had cut two-inch slots into CONEX boxes (steel shipping containers) making them into isolation cells for the ring leaders and had the other prisoners in a fenced area away from them. It had been a big mess and made all the papers, but he did a good job of cleaning it up in record time. We went back to the office and had coffee and talked for a couple of hours. He wanted to know about Marian and the kids and about the combat units. The Sergeant came in a while later and said the Lieutenants had finished, so COL Miller and I said our goodbyes. The Lieutenants had a chance to sit down with each of our prisoners and chat with them. We caught a bus back to Saigon and toured the city until dark, then went back to the hotel dining room and lounge for the evening. The next morning we caught a flight back to Camp Enari and on to the Oasis. We reported to COL McClellan and the Lieutenants told him about our reception with COL Miller. COL McClellen looked at them and said, "Now you know why I sent the Sergeant Major with you."

Christmas and New Years were very quiet all over our AO (area of operation), but also very lonely being away from Marian, Kevin, and Glenda. I don't remember what they got for Christmas for each other. I had sent Marian and

Glenda the china service and pewter for Marian. I sent Kevin a tiger suit and Marian got him a bicycle with a steering wheel instead of handlebars. Christmas was always a big day with the family and I missed it.

We had a Platoon-size patrol get ambushed on a mountainside just east of Plei Djereng. It occurred on the afternoon before COL McClellan was to go to Hawaii on R & R and meet his wife. The Platoon consisted of about 20 men and was hit hard. There were about eight or nine KIA and a couple of walking-wounded. We got artillery fire on the area and evidently drove the enemy off because they never mounted a second attack.

Movie star Pat O'Brien visited the Artillery Fire Base late in the evening and was able to pull the lanyard on one artillery piece as it was being fired in support of the Platoon in contact. I managed to talk with him briefly before they rushed him off to another stop on his agenda.

The Platoon was trying to climb a mountain with as many KIAs as they had able-bodied men. They were dragging the body bags up a steep mountainside which would've been extremely difficult to climb even without their packs and weapons. When we left the area, they'd put out security and settled in for the night.

The next morning, the XO who'd been left in charge of the brigade while COL McClellan was on R & R, and I departed the Oasis about 8:30 AM and flew out to Plei DJerang and started circling at about 4000 feet. I asked if we were going to land and was informed that we might get in the way. We monitored the radio as the Platoon struggled to move up the mountain. They had moved about 100 yards in the steep terrain all morning. We returned to the Oasis for lunch and then returned to our position over Plei DJereng and circled for the entire afternoon, continuing to monitor their call signs. At the evening briefing nobody had a suggestion on how to relieve the situation. The next morning, the XO told the pilot to go back to Plei DJereng as he had the previous day. I asked him if he was planning to land and the XO told me no.

I told the pilot to take me down to where there was a Company CP and drop me off and the XO could stay on the ground with me or go back up. The pilot landed and I checked in with the Company Commander, Lt Jackson. (I'm not sure of the name.) He informed me that the Platoon estimated that it'd be late the following evening or the morning after that before they'd reach the CP.

The Major from the helicopter company was listening to this conversation and I asked him if he could use a penetrator and pierce the triple canopy jungle with a cargo net. That was when Lt Jackson broke in and said I had no respect for his dead troops and none of them would be moved in a cargo net. I tried to explain to Lt Jackson that I had all the respect for the dead soldiers that anybody could have, but he was killing the other members of the Platoon who were trying to bring them out. I also felt that if the dead had a 'say so' in it, they'd prefer to ride a cargo net out than be dragged over the rocks and dead trees for another two days. He still said no way would he use a cargo net.

I knew the Platoon was getting into bad shape and should they hit another ambush, the remainder of the platoon would most likely be wiped out. I talked to the Major and the Company Commander and they told me I'd be placed on report before going off by himself.

I was informed the Aviation Company could have a chopper with cable and penetrator in the area in thirty minutes. I told him to get it and also to have helicopters ready to transport the deceased to the morgue.

I called the Platoon Leader and informed him what the plan was and to be ready to pop smoke and inform the pilot when he was hovering directly over him. The penetrator worked and we lifted the bodies out two at a time and laid them out side by side on the ground where each was positively identified before he was moved to the morgue. We completed the operation before 11:00 AM and the Platoon was moving up the mountain. Food, water, and ammunition were also carried in by the cargo nets to supply the Platoon for the rest of the move out.

The XO had stayed for the whole operation, but never spoke or asked what I was doing. The Major from the Aviation Company and I ran the whole show. We went back in for lunch and were informed at the 6:00 PM briefing that the Platoon had made it up the mountain and had been picked up and flown back to the base camp.

When COL McClellan arrived back at the Oasis from his R & R, he called me to his quarters. He said, "Towe, I've heard two stories of what happened out by Plei DJereng and I'd like to know the truth." I told him how the XO and I circled around all the first day and how I had the pilot finally land on the second day. There I found no organization and a Platoon really hurting from trying to bring the body bags up that mountain. I also informed him about LT Jackson's remarks about not using body bags and how the Aviation Major and I worked to extract the deceased. He asked if the XO had contributed to or suggested any solutions. I answered no. Then he said, "Thanks, Towe. That's all." He then added as an afterthought, "I'd have done the same thing."

That evening the XO was gone. He'd been relieved from duty as the XO of the 3rd Brigade, 4th Infantry Division. I've often thought about that operation and the XO's failure to act. Was it that he didn't know what to do or was he just afraid to act, fearing that he might make the wrong decision. As for myself, I don't really know if I made the right decisions, but I knew that something had to be done and nobody else was trying to solve the problem. I have always lived by one rule: in an emergency, do something even if it may turn out to be wrong.

On January 18, 1969 we had another change of command ceremony, COL Grunthier relieved COL McClellan who had completed his six-months command time. This made my third Commander in about seven months and all three were different with different ideas on how to command the Brigade. That proves that to be Sergeant Major you have to be flexible. COL Grunthier was a staff and intelligence-oriented person, while COL McClellan was a combat and soldier-oriented Commander.

An example of this was once we had a Company in the attack with the S3 (operations officer) coordinating the attack while we went forty miles in the opposite direction to look at a cave that had probably been an enemy hospital. The cave was located at the base of a mountain about a half mile down from where we had to land. The nearer we got to the cave, the more pronounced the path was. The path showed plenty of use and in the cave were found a lot of used bandages, as if they had treated wounded soldiers there recently.

I felt a lot safer working with COL Grunthier than with COL McClellan, but it wasn't near as exciting. The remainder of my tour was spent chasing shadows. We checked every footprint in the AO. Another time we walked about a mile into the jungle to see where the VC had fired two rockets at Pleiku.

We had two men at a listening post southwest of the Oasis at night when one of them was killed by a tiger. He was sitting where he could observe the trail while the other man was asleep about ten yards back in the bushes. The tiger attacked and killed the man, then dragged him about ten or fifteen yards before dropping him, yet the other man never woke up. When he couldn't find his partner, he called in and reported the man missing. A cavalry team was sent in and they located the mutilated body.

On January 29, 1969 I notified the Command Sergeant Major's Section in the Pentagon that I desired to return to Fort Gordon, GA, when my Vietnam tour of duty was over. On March 23, 1969 I received orders to report to the US Army Return Detachment, Long Binh on June 17th for transportation back to the US and assignment back to Fort Gordon, GA.

In April I went on R & R to Sydney, Australia, along with CSM Johnson, Division Artillery CSM and a First Sergeant from the artillery. Early in the year one of our Brigade CSMs, CSM Gilbert, was killed while he and the Brigade Commander were attempting to land on a hot LZ to pick up a wounded soldier. He was engaged to an Australian woman, so the Division CSM asked us to carry some letters of condolence and other items to her while we were on R & R in Sydney.

I arranged to attend all the briefings along the way about conduct in a foreign country and especially regarding drugs. I was excused from these briefings, but wanted to know what information the younger troops were receiving. Drugs were the main subject at each of these briefings from Battalion Headquarters until we loaded on the plane.

I flew from Pleiku to Saigon and reported to the R & R Section for transportation to Sydney. We departed Vietnam at 3:00 PM for Sydney in a chartered commercial plane. We landed at Darwin, Australia, at 10:00 PM and stayed in a warehouse for approximately four hours because we couldn't land in Sydney until after 7:00 AM. We finally landed at about 7:30 AM and as I was going through customs, I noticed that the customs officials had four young soldiers in custody. I asked why they were holding them and I was told they had tried to bring drugs into the country. They were to be held in a stockade until our flight back to Vietnam departed. At that time, they'd be loaded on the plane for the flight back. I didn't feel sorry for them because they should've had at least five briefings covering carrying drugs into the host country.

We were bussed to our hotel and then we were on our own for five days. We had breakfast and immediately set out to discover Sydney. We found that the bars opened from noon until 2:00 PM and then closed again until six. Lunch was a sandwich in a stand-up bar in a basement. There were no tables, just some circular tables built around the metal support poles used to support the building. The Australians were very friendly and they all wanted to know about America, but were also interested in telling you how great Australia was. It was interesting that not one of them wanted to go to America.

We were standing at a table with a couple a few years younger than we were when suddenly they invited us to a party that night at their apartment. It was a BYOB (bring your own bottle) affair. That evening we picked up a bottle and went to the party. It was very interesting to see how they partied. The thing that impressed me most was the amount of alcohol they consumed. We nursed one or two drinks all evening, but had plenty of help in consuming our bottle. We left the party early because CSM Johnson and I had an early meeting the next morning with CSM Gilbert's fiancée.

She picked us up the next morning at 9:00 AM in her car and we went for coffee. There we gave her the letters and other items and explained the condolences from the Division Commanding General, Officers, Noncommissioned Officers and Enlisted Men who had known him. After some tears and many thanks to us, she composed herself and she said that she would like to show us around Sydney.

She drove out to an animal park where they had just about all the native animal species of Australia. We had lunch at a very nice café there and we encouraged her to order a native lunch for us. After lunch, she drove back into town and we went on a tour of the famous Sydney Opera House and other local historical places. We asked her to have dinner with us and she suggested The Sky Walk near the Opera House. She called and made reservations at seven.

She dropped us off at our hotel for a nap and shower before she picked us up again a little after six. We went directly to The Sky Walk. It was a restaurant located on the 47th floor of a 48 story building. The restaurant was delightful and it made one complete rotation every hour. While you were seated, you couldn't feel it moving. We had a window seat and as we ate and talked, we got a panoramic view of the entire city. My heart was in my throat as we came down in the elevator at a speed of 1250 feet per minute. It felt as if the floor had dropped out from under us. We made arrangements to meet again for coffee on our last day in Sydney. She told us over and over how much it meant to her to see us, because we had both known CSM Gilbert. I often think about her and what her life has been like for the past thirty-five years. That was to have been his last tour in Vietnam. He was planning to retire, get married, and live happily ever after in Australia.

We went on a tour of Sydney which was very interesting. The guide was well versed on the history of Australia and especially Sydney. Sydney was settled as a penal colony of England and now is one of the best known harbors in the world. We rode the hydrofoil out to the beaches and looked over the Australian beauties in their skimpy swimming suits. I also took a hydrofoil tour of the harbor that included the shipping industry. April was the fall of the year there, but it was still rather warm. The trees were just beginning to get their autumn colors.

I did a lot of walking around town and spent some time shopping for Marian, Glenda, and Kevin. Australia is noted for its opals, so I bought jewelry for Marian and Glenda and a boomerang for Kevin. All of this I had shipped home from Australia rather than trying to carry it with me.

We went to some of the nightclubs, but most of them were crowded with very young people that looked like they were too young to be out at night, much less drinking. The music was so loud you couldn't hear yourself think much less carry on a conversation.

Since I missed Australia during WWII, I was elated at the chance to get there while I was in Vietnam. Marian and I had discussed meeting in Hawaii for my R & R, but we couldn't afford transportation for her and the kids so it was decided that we wouldn't meet and I'd go to Australia. It was another magnificent stop in my travels and one that I'll never forget.

When I arrived back at the airport, the customs officials were there with the four young soldiers they had picked up on entry for drug violations. On the flight back I went to where two of them were seated and asked them why they had tried to get through customs with drugs. Their answer was they had heard from their buddies that all you did in Australia was walk right through customs, so they had their shaving kits full of pot. What a hell of a way to spend five days R & R in Australia.

I stayed overnight in Saigon and flew back to Pleiku the next day and on to the Oasis to finish my tour of duty in Vietnam.

Marian is one of the few military dependents that have heard a B40 Rocket in actual flight. Our communications people had a connection with a MARS Station in the state of Washington where they'd patch through a call to your dependents. You arranged the time by mail and they'd try and connect you. I received a call in my hooch about nine one night that they were able to reach Marian. The phone was passed out through a small hole in the sand bags around the communications bunker to where you could have a little privacy during your call.

When I got on the phone, I said, "This is Glenn, over," and she answered, "Honey, this is Marian, over." At that time a B40 rocket came through the Oasis and missed the corner of the communications bunker where I was standing by about ten feet. Marian came back on and said, "My God! What was that? Over." I replied, "Incoming. Out." That was the extent of my phone call to her from in country. I want back to my hooch and wrote her a letter to let her know I was alright.

On June 16, they had a going away luncheon and awards ceremony at the Oasis prior to my departure. I was expecting to get an Army Commendation Medal, but received a Legion of Merit, a Bronze Star w/V device for valor, and the Army Commendation Medal w/V device for valor. These all came as a shock to me.

I left the Oasis after lunch and flew to Camp Enari. I picked up my orders and flew over to Pleiku Air Force Base early that evening. I left Pleiku at 10:30 PM and arrived at Cam Rahn Bay a little after midnight. I stayed in the transit billets over night and boarded a charter flight for the US at 1:30 PM on June 18, 1969.

We flew to Cadena Air Force Base on Okinawa and had a four-hour stop-over. I had a good steak dinner with a Japanese beer at the NCO Club before heading on to Honolulu where we had a two-hour stop before flying on to Fort Lewis, WA. While in Honolulu I called the Bolties and let them know that I had survived my Vietnam tour. We arrived in Tacoma at 8:00 PM and I was issued an army green uniform and given a briefing prior to going to Seattle for a flight to Augusta, GA, and home.

At the briefing, a Major advised us to wear civilian clothing while traveling home because someone might spit on us at the airport. I wore the same civilian clothing that I had on R & R. I sure didn't want to spend time in jail somewhere for knocking some stupid peacenik on his ass. I arrived at Seattle too late to get a flight out and slept in the waiting room until morning. I got an early flight out, changed planes in Chicago and flew on to Atlanta.

There I boarded two planes in succession. They each returned to the loading dock because of low oil pressure.

I got my ticket back and changed air lines before finally getting a safe flight to Augusta and my sweet darling, Marian. I arrived in Augusta about three hours late but it was still a wonderful homecoming.

I came home from three wars and the reception I received was very different with each. After WWII, I came back aboard an aircraft carrier to bands on the dock, movie stars, big hugs, coffee, coke, donuts, big welcoming smiles that meant a job well done. I came home from Korea early in the war aboard a hospital plane and a big welcome at the Fairfield Susan Base Hospital with movie stars and Red Cross Volunteers with coffee, cokes and donuts. They assisted in making phone calls home for the men whose families had a phone. They also sent wires and wrote letters. Then came the Vietnam Homecoming and a briefing at Fort Lewis, WA where I was told that I might be spit upon if I wore a uniform home.

It was good to get home again and be with Marian, Glenda, and Kevin after being away for a year. This was our longest separation since we were married. The previous long period was for six months when I went to Germany the first of October, 1952, and Marian and Glenda joined me in April of 1953.

We drove to my mother's home in South Carolina after a couple of days. As usual she was overjoyed to see me and to have me home safe again. This was the third war she had seen me come home from and I'm sure she was hoping that it would be the last one. My mother seemed to be grieving herself to death. She had been active all her life and always had at least one or more people to care for. After my father's death, she was home alone and one of my sisters had moved away taking the grand children that she had practically raised. There was nothing left for her to do but sit all day. She lasted until December when she passed away in her sleep. This affected me a lot more than my father's death because I was much closer to her. Also, I left for the Vietnam War shortly after he was buried.

After visiting with all the relatives, I reported for duty with the 3rd AIT (Advanced Infantry Training) Brigade, Fort Gordon, GA on June 28, 1969. COL Kyle W. Bowie was the Commander and a Miss Bridges was his secretary. COL Bowie was a fine officer and I enjoyed serving as his Command Sergeant Major. He said that his door was open to me at any time and that I was to report any problems pertaining to the enlisted personnel directly to him.

This caused a run-in with the executive officer, a LTC. He called me into his office one afternoon and said, "Sergeant Major, I noticed you going into COL Bowie's office without reporting to me first. From here on, you'll report to me on all matters prior to talking with the Colonel, do you understand?"

The tone of his voice pissed me off plus knowing that the Colonel told me that his door was open and for me to report all enlisted problems directly to him. I told the XO that I was instructed by COL Bowie to report directly to him.

He replied, "That has been changed. You'll report to me first."

I said, "Colonel, I think now is the time to get this matter straightened out between us. COL Bowie is in his office so let's go in and just see what he has to say about this."

He said, "There's no need to disturb the Colonel, I'm telling you to report to me."

I looked him straight in the eye and said, "I'm a Command Sergeant Major and I work directly for the Commander. Until he informs me otherwise, I'll continue to report directly to him. You can take my word for it or let's go see him right now. I'm sure you already know if we go in there, the Colonel is going to agree with me. I'll work with you, but until you are a Commander, I won't work for you. Let's go in now or forget that you ever called me in here, it's your choice."

His face was lit up like a pickled beet and he said, "You are dismissed."

We were training men who had just completed basic training and were to be assigned to infantry units either in Vietnam or Germany. This training involved unit tactics, and training on all infantry weapons. This wasn't new to me because I was assigned to AIT Companies at Fort Hood, Texas in 1955-56.

On October 12, 1969 I along with the Fort Gordon contingent of the Association of the US Army flew to Washington, DC to attend the annual Association meeting. I'd been there a few times before, but I always enjoyed the trip. It gave me a chance to renew friendships with some of my old Army buddies. The trip lasted from Wednesday until Sunday afternoon. We flew up and back on a National Guard plane. On October 20, 1969 we received word that all basic and advanced infantry training would cease at Fort Gordon with the current cycles. The 3rd AIT Regiment was to be the closing facility.

We had a change of command ceremony for COL Bowie. He was departing to be a Brigade Commander in the 1st Infantry Division in Vietnam. LTC Billy C. Durant assumed Command of the Regiment while we phased out all infantry-type training on Post.

As each Company in the 1st and 2nd Regiments completed the current training cycle, they'd ship the trainees to their new units. The cadre and holdovers would turn in all weapons and equipment and the remaining cadre and trainees would be transferred to a Company in one of our Battalions to await further transfer. We went from an Advanced Infantry Training Regiment to a Holding Company. One day we might have fifty NCOs and a hundred trainee holdovers and the next day we wouldn't have enough holdovers to pull KP duty.

As always, Marian and the children ate the Thanksgiving Dinner with me at one of the mess halls on Post. This was one of the Military Traditions we always followed. Thanksgiving Dinner in a mess hall, with the troops, and Christmas Dinner at home or with relatives. The Battalion and Regimental Staff split up so as to cover all the messes in the Regiment or Battalion. I always went on Post on Christmas Morning if I wasn't on leave. I visited each mess hall and wished the cooks and KPs a Merry Christmas and checked to see that every thing looked good and the food was properly prepared.

My mother died on December 8, 1968, just eighteen months after my father's death. This hit me hard because I always felt closer to her than to my father as I mentioned before. We went from Augusta, GA, to Westminster, SC for the funeral. My brother Andy came home, too, and this was the first time I had seen him since I last saw him in Vietnam.

During the month of March we closed the First and Second Training Regiments, shipped all the cadre and trainees, and closed all the buildings. In one month it went from a thriving section of Fort Gordon to a ghost town. I'd spent almost six years of my career at Fort Gordon training some of the finest young soldiers America has ever produced. The majority of these soldiers went on to fight in Vietnam and I'm sure a lot of them became casualties with many being killed in action. I never felt I was sending a young soldier to his death because I felt I had given him the best training that I was capable of. This also applied to the troops I trained for the Korean War.

On March 19, 1970 I was assigned to the Southeastern Signal School, Fort Gordon, with duty at the School Brigade. CSM Jack Pitts, the Training Brigade CSM, who was a friend of mine, told me that for the time being, he didn't have a job for me. I became very proficient in the skills of carrying a clip board around all day and looking busy.

During this time, I attended a two-week orientation of the Signal School. I was with a group of Officers and NCOs who toured every class the school had to offer. We sat through a lot of class presentations from the computer to pole climbing and wire splicing. The computer consisted of large reels of tape with all kinds of information on them. The instructor asked my name, typed it in, and the reel started spinning and when it stopped, he hit a couple of keys and it printed out my entire military record. This amazed me to no end that he could locate my entire history in a few seconds.

For three months I spent more time playing golf than I spent soldiering and in the process, knocked about five strokes off my handicap.

On July 1st I was transferred to the 8th Battalion, School Brigade, as the CSM. The Battalion was not involved in any training. We were providing living quarters and supply and mess facilities for school troops. I also had to provide all details requested by Brigade or Post. This was the problem area. We had to pull support troops from the various classes to perform these details. I met with the Chiefs of each Section and explained my situation and that I would treat each of them equally as to the number of men needed each day. Should a problem arise, all they had to do was to let me know and I'd do every thing in my power to help them solve it.

I had trouble with only one SGM over the details I requested. He was a cry baby from the start. I tried working with him but soon found out he didn't wish to furnish any men from his section for details. He informed me that I could get them from other sections. I called him for details one day and he put the Major on the phone who was the Officer in Charge of the Section. He started chewing my ass out royally about giving his SGM a hard time.

I listened to him for about five minutes and he finally hung up. COL Diaz, my CO, was sitting by my desk and asked me what the call was all about. I told him the complete story. He told me if the Major got on the line again to complain, to put him on the phone immediately. A couple of days later, I called the

SGM for a detail and the Major got on the line again. COL Diaz was sitting across the room at the clerk's desk.

I nodded to him to pick up the phone and by then the Major was getting warmed up. He let me know that he wasn't going to furnish any details and for me to stop harassing his SGM for such details. After about three minutes of this, COL Diaz interrupted him and said, "Major, do you know who you're talking to?" There was a gasp on the other end and the Colonel continued, "This is COL Diaz. I am the Battalion Commander here and Sergeant Major Towe works for me. He does a fine job of carrying out my orders and I'm the only one here who's going to chew him out for anything. He is dealing with about twenty other sections for details and he gives me a report each morning as to our responsibilities. He informed me that your section is the only one that tries to give him a hard time. Major, if you'd like to continue this discussion in my office, my door is open and I'll be waiting for you."

After a long pause, the Major got his voice back and said, "No Sir, that won't be necessary." Then Col Diaz dropped the hammer on him. "Major, it's time for you to learn that an officer has no place getting involved in the Sergeant Major's business. You'll get your ass burned every time." Then he hung up.

I was in the club a couple of evenings later and the SGM came over and informed me that I had caused him to get chewed out by his Major. I told him, you put that Major on the phone because you figured that would get you off the hook for a couple of men for detail. You opened the can of worms and now you're going to live with that problem. I was informed by COL Diaz that if you gave me any more trouble about a detail, to let him know and he'd call your Major and have him personally march the detail over to our headquarters.

In August they changed the School Brigade CSM to a young Sergeant Major and his branch was Signal Corps. They didn't even bother asking me if I'd like the job. I decided that I had done enough housekeeping for Signal School and I was ready to rejoin the "Grunt Army." I called the Sergeant Major Section at the Pentagon to see what they had open. I was told the only position open overseas was Germany.

I went home and talked it over with Marian and we agreed that the Signal School would drive me crazy or out of the Army and I wasn't ready for either at that time. The next day, I called the Pentagon and accepted the assignment. It was 2nd Battalion, (mechanized) 13th Infantry, 8th Infantry Division, Coleman Barracks, Sandhofen, Germany. It was just a few miles from Mannheim where all quarters and support facilities were located. I was instructed to start clearing Post for September travel. I got concurrent air travel for Marian, Kevin, and me. Glenda was starting Clemson University in September. I arranged for an agent to rent our house for the three years we'd be gone.

I sent a letter to the CSM of the 13th Infantry informing him of my assignment and in turn I received a reply from the CSM of the 3rd Brigade, 8th Infantry Division stating that they needed a more experienced CSM in the Cavalry Squadron and they wanted me to go there. It was the same post and all family support facilities were the same. I had received my port call so I sent him this information along with my acceptance of the change of duties.

We made our final visits with the family, dropped Glenda off at Clemson and checked into a guest house at Fort Gordon. Mary Lou and her children came down to see us off. Teary good-byes were said and we were on our way. This was my fourth trip to Europe and Marian's third. We were looking forward to the new experience.

Marian, Kevin, and I were to report to McGuire Air Force Base, Wrightsville, NJ for air travel to Rhine Main Air Base, Frankfort, Germany on September 12, 1970 for departure on the 13th. That was Kevin's thirteenth birthday and a sad one because we'd taken him away from his girlfriend. We departed McGuire at 1:00 AM and flew to England where we sat on the end of the runway out in a pasture for over four hours waiting for the British customs to clear the passengers we let off. They finally shut down the engines and let everyone off. We sat around the plane, smoked, and ate sandwiches and soft drinks until at last, the British cleared us for departure.

We arrived in Frankfort at about 5:30 PM and were met by two Sergeants from the 3rd Brigade, MSG Tippen from the 13th Infantry Battalion that I had known from Fort Jackson in 1952 and SFC Saunders from the 3rd Squadron, 8th Cavalry.

They secured our luggage and drove us to Mannheim to the apartment of the CSM of the Cavalry Squadron where his wife had cooked a delicious dinner for us. After introductions we had a couple of cocktails and ate dinner. SFC Saunders then drove us to our quarters.

Sergeant Sanders had signed quarters for us at 34 A Lincoln, Benjamin Franklin Village, Mannheimm, Germany. It was a two-bedroom apartment and he had checked out linen and all the beds were made. This was a far cry from the reception I had received on my last arrival in Germany when I reported to the 1st Battle Group, 15th Infantry in September 1960, when the Staff Duty NCO got drunk and forgot to pass on the instructions from the CSM of my arrival.

SFC Saunders was at my disposal for the next few days while I was getting settled in. When I went to Frankfort Air Base to pick up my cats, I found out that one had been lost in shipment and that was very upsetting to the three of us.

I went to 8th Division Headquarters and had lunch with the Division CSM and met all the Section Chiefs that I needed to know. The Squadron was in Grafenwoehr for weapons training. I went up and spent a day with the CO and met all the First Sergeants and Company Commanders. I was then ready to replace the existing CSM who had already started packing and clearing to go back to CA for retirement.

COL McClellan and CSM Towe talk with CPT Bao Commander of ARVN Forces, Plei Mrong, VN, 1968

I began to notice the changes immediately in the Seventh Army, 7th Corps and the Army in general from what I had left in 1963. The Seventh Army and 7th Corps had been the finest in the world. The discipline, training, morale and esprit de corps had gone out the window. I attribute this to the Army system of ticket punching where the best went to Vietnam then back to the pentagon and back again to Vietnam with promotions in between. The others were sent to Europe. The units were under strength, had poor morale, and the maintenance of equipment was very poor. Drugs and alcohol use by the enlisted ranks were prevalent and this resulted in the NCO Corps leadership not being strong enough to lead and guide the lower NCOs and enlisted troops.

My first experience with the above observation was when the Squadron returned from the major training area.. Our A Troop had been taken off Air Bourn status shortly before I arrived and they were still peeved over it. I told the CO that I was going to observe reveille in a different Company each morning. I went to A Troop for my first observation and nobody was out for the formation. I went in and checked with the CQ (charge of quarters). He said he went through each barrack and woke the men. I asked him about the 1SG and was told he came in about 7:00 AM and the CO usually came in around 8:00 AM. He didn't know who the duty officer was.

I decided that this had gone far enough and I'd hold reveille myself. I went through the barracks and the ones who didn't get up, I used my past training with the 169th Infantry in 1952 on dumping cots. I could catch a cot with a man in it and flip it upside down before he could get his feet on the floor. It took me about thirty minutes, but I held the first reveille in A Troop in months.

I returned to squadron headquarters and reported to the CO what I'd done. About 9:30 AM the CO and 1SG from A troop came in to see the CO. He asked me to come in with them. The CO told the COL what I had done turning over cots in his Company area and he didn't appreciate it. My CO asked him and the 1SG the date that either of them had conducted reveille the last time. They both said that the duty officer usually conducted reveille, but neither knew why he didn't this morning.

The Col said, "I'm going to follow the example set by the Sergeant Major this morning and start checking reveille myself and I expect to see either the 1SG or CO or both in front of the formation. Do you have any questions?" That was the last time I held reveille during my army career.

On 19 October I reported to Gibbs Kasern to participate in Carousel IV, a Command Post Exercise (map and black board war) for five days. It was interesting to see how a higher headquarters operated.

We received Mr. Shue, a CWO Supply Officer, and after about three days he called me and asked about having lunch with him. We went to a small German Gasthaus where we could talk privately. He asked about the unit and my initial impressions. He told me the supplies were in bad shape and he couldn't find the property book. We were short over 100,000 rounds of small arms ammo and one case of hand grenades. The hand grenades worried me because at that time "fragging" was poplar with some of the disgruntled young troops. This came from Vietnam where they threw grenades into the quarters of the Platoon Leaders and Company Commanders. We discussed the problems of the squadron and how determined he was to develop it into a respectable US Army unit.

After talking with Mr. Shue, I knew it wasn't my imagination running away with me and there wasn't any question about the unit being in extremely bad shape. Mr. Shue finally found the property book. As for the missing ammo, the unit was told for the past two years that when you went to the range, fire your basic load and it'll be replaced. About a month later, he told me that he'd found three five-ton ammo trucks on blocks in the ammo dump. All of them had been cannibalized.

I started checking the squadron area in the evenings. I'd go to the orderly rooms, troop dayrooms, and barracks asking how things were going. The one answer I received most was, there's nothing to do around here except sit in the barracks, drink beer, and use pot. I went to the CO and told him that Id like to conduct a class on travel in Western Europe and see if we could get some of our troops interested in spending some of their off-duty hours touring instead of sitting around bitching. He told me to go with it and informed operations to schedule my classes any time I desired.

I set up the classes for 3:00 PM once each month and all new enlisted men were to attend. I started them at three o'clock so that if I ran over the hour, I could continue as long as the troops wished. I went to the travel agent on post and drove to the Frankfort Railroad Depot picking up travel brochures and railroad schedules. In Germany, the trains always ran on schedule and you could set your watch by their arrival and departure times. I explained that because of our location, they had ample time for travel all over Western Europe because we didn't have any training scheduled for Saturdays. They were free from 5:00 PM Friday until 6:00 AM Monday In that time frame, they could travel anywhere in Western Germany, south to Vienna, Austria, Switzerland, France and north to Amsterdam, Belgium, and Luxembourg. This was an opportunity of a lifetime, I told them. You are here and this may be your last trip to Europe, so make the most of it.

This being my fourth trip and Marian's third, we had visited just about every place from Venice to the Netherlands. If you are interested in partying, go to Munich, Amsterdam, Paris, or The Hague. You can leave Frankfort after 5:00 PM on Friday and get to any of those places before they start rocking. Anywhere you go, there are museums, castles, cathedrals, and battle grounds; something for each person's taste. After the first couple of classes, the CO recommended that officers and dependents who hadn't been in Germany before, attend one of the briefings. It wasn't a cure for the situation, but it did get a lot of the troops out of the barracks on the weekends and on leave.

One morning the CO asked me to check on the squadron motor pool and find out why our deadline was so high. I went over about 9:30 AM and nobody was working. I asked the Motor Sergeant where everyone was and he said they were at the snack bar having breakfast. I walked over to the snack bar and chased all of our men out and sent them back to the motor pool. I held a formation there and asked them why they were in the snack bar. They informed me that the motor pool section didn't have to stand reveille. They slept in until 7:45 AM, barely made the 8:00 AM work formation, and then went to breakfast at the snake bar. I informed them from now on, the snack bar was off-limits until the 10:00 AM break-period.

I found out that this was a "no-no" according to the Division IG, Major Welsh. I explained the deadline problem to him, but he still said no. After talking with him, I went back to the motor pool and held another formation. Major Welsh later became the Squadron Executive Officer. He was a good officer and I enjoyed working with him. I explained to the men that I couldn't put the snack bar off-limits. This got me a big cheer, but then I explained my other alternative. I, or the Motor Sergeant could hold a formation, take roll call, and anyone missing would be recommended for a field grade Article 15. This was punishment by the Squadron Commander.

The next morning, I checked the snack bar and found five of the motor pool personnel eating breakfast. I went to the motor pool and held a formation and those five men were missing. I waited for them to report back to the motor pool and then marched them to Squadron Headquarters for a Field Grade Article 15. The CO fined each of them $50.00 dollars and sent them back to the motor pool. I became the Supreme Bastard of Headquarters, but our deadline improved.

At one time, I would have agreed with the troops and eaten at a snack bar instead of the mess hall, but not at this time. The Army messes had improved from what we veterans of WWII and Korea knew. There were milk machines on the chow lines with all the milk you wanted and coke machines in all messes. The average breakfast meal was cereal, eggs to order, hot cakes, French toast, and SOS. Lunch was the normal Army menu plus hot dogs, hamburgers, a salad and soup bar, pasta, and desert bar. The evening meal was about the same as lunch.

The US Army Europe decided to have beer available for consumption along with your meal, if you so desired. We had a squadron meeting and all the enlisted men wanted beer in the mess. The mess Sergeant came in and asked me how much beer he should have available. I told him to have an eight-rack soft drink dispensing machine and to put in six racks of beer and two of soft drinks. I checked on the consumption daily and after the first couple of days, we replaced two racks of beer with soft drinks. In less than a month, we were down to one rack of beer and seven racks of soft drinks. The only men drinking beer were usually a few of the older NCOs.

Glenda came to visit us for Christmas. It was good to see her after a four-month absence. It was nice having her home for the holidays and we hated to see her return to Clemson in January.

In February, we moved to a three-bedroom apartment at 25 F Columbus, Benjamin Franklin Village. This was the unit designated for my family and my rank. SFC Saunders took a detail and moved me.

Marian had learned to ski while we were in Bamberg in the early sixties, so she went with a friend of ours to chaperone a school class down in the Black Forrest for a week. I went down on Friday afternoon with the kids that were in school during the week. I sat in the chalet drinking hot wine and watching them ski. I decided then that I'd learn to ski, although I was over forty-five- years-old at that time. I bought a pair of skis and boots and the next time we went down, Marian showed me how to snowplow and I was on my way. I enjoyed skiing and over the next few years, I developed into a fair intermediate and could get down most any slope without breaking my neck.

An example of discipline occurred at a Community Meeting of the Mannheim Sub-Post. The CO went to a meeting and upon his return, he called me in and said, "Sergeant Major, you're going to attend the next meeting and I want you to listen to the comments carefully." At the next meeting, I reported to the community center. There were MPs at the doors, so I went in and took a seat.

The panel consisted of Field Grade Officers, all Colonels, Lieutenant Colonels, and Majors, who were seated on a stage. The Chaplain was there and other staff officers from the area and each of them discussed their areas of expertise. Afterwards, a Colonel asked if there were any questions or comments from the audience. One black soldier stood up and said angrily, "It's the sorry sons-of-bitches like you that are the cause of all our problems. If you just let us alone, then you wouldn't have any troubles."

At that, I got up and headed for the door. The young MP asked me as I walked by, "What's wrong, Sergeant Major?"

I told him I wasn't raised that way and I didn't have to listen to that kind of crap.

The CO wanted to know how the meeting went and I told him what happened. He said, "You're lucky. As a CSM, no one's going to question your leaving, but as an officer, I had to sit through over an hour of that crap."

We received a new Brigade CO, COL Slavish, and he wasn't at all happy with anything that was going on. First, he wanted the Cavalry Squadron to be under his control at all times. We were assigned to him for support and housekeeping, but when we went on alert, we became OPCON (operational control) to Division. The Brigade CSM returned to the US for retirement and the Division CSM recommended that I go to Brigade as the CSM. COL Slavish said that he wanted an airborne CSM who'd shape up the Brigade and added he'd already called friends in the CSM Section to send him an airborne CSM.

His friends at the Pentagon must've felt the same way towards him as we did. The CSM they sent was black, five-foot-seven, and weighed all of 250 pounds. The Division CSM told me later that COL Slavish came to Division practically on fire with anger and stated he wanted that CSM moved immediately. He told COL Slavish that was a DA assignment and there was nothing he could do about it.

They went in to see the Division Commanding General, who told COL Slavish, "You have exactly what you asked for. You didn't want any Battalion CSM in the Division, so now you're going to have to live with what you have." Actually, I liked the new CSM and he was easy to work with.

In May, Glenda returned from college and informed us that her grades were bad and she wasn't returning to school in September. She went to work in the bank section of the American Express. Marian was disappointed that she had dropped out of school, but was happy to have her home. Kevin was also giving us a lot of trouble at that time and that continued for a number of years.

In March I received orders to report to Hawkins Barracks, Oberammergau, Germany to attend a Senior Noncommissioned Officers Management Seminar in April, 1972. The Seminar lasted for two weeks and was very informative. As you can see, I was still going to school every chance I got and I liked it.

In April, 1973 I returned to Oberammergau to be a monitor for the next class. Oberammergau was located just a few miles up in the mountains from Garmish. I was familiar with the area having gone to Combat Intelligence School there in 1954.

While I was at Oberammergau, I received a call from Marian that her sister's husband had been killed in an accident at work. He was working in a nuclear reactor when a piece of steel fell on him. Marian and Mary Lou had always been very close as sisters, so Marian informed me that she was flying out the next morning to SC for the funeral. She asked me to stay until the course was over and that Glenda and Kevin would be okay until I got back. I arrived back in Coleman Barracks to face a hectic three weeks. Glenda was born in the 8th Infantry Division and was now getting married in it.

Glenda had become engaged to a Lieutenant from the Squadron and was to be married on May 6 in the Benjamin Franklin Village Chapel, Mannheim, Germany with the reception to follow in the NCO Club. Marian had left right in the middle of the planning stage, but one of our dear friends, Annaliesa Schaffer, from Fort Gordon took over and continued the planning while Marian was in SC. Rachel Land, Mary Lou's daughter, flew back to Germany with Marian for the wedding.

The wedding was one that only a Cavalry Squadron could have performed. After the ceremony, the Squadron Officers in Dress Blues, spurs, and sabers formed the "Arch of Sabers" for the bride and groom to pass through as they left the Benjamin Franklin Village Chapel. Just as they came out of the chapel and entered the arch, six skydivers jumped from a helicopter with their smoke streamers. They landed across the street in a minor-league ball park.

Later at the reception, somebody at the wedding party commented, "Boy, that Sergeant Major must have a lot of pull to get jumpers for his daughter's wedding." I didn't tell them that the jump was for the opening day ceremonies for the Little-League Baseball season.

In July I went to the range for the annual weapons qualification and proved that I still had a good eye and steady hand as I qualified as Expert with the Caliber .45 pistol.

In August the Brigade CSM set up an orientation tour with the Berlin Brigade for Sergeant Majors. The six of us went by train through the Russian Section of East Germany to Berlin, where we were guests of the Brigade for four days. We had to travel through East Germany at night, which reminded me of traveling through the Russian Zone of Austria to Vienna twenty-four years ago. We were given the VIP treatment with an elaborate reception and lunch with the Berlin Brigade CSM and had the run of Berlin for four days and nights. The tours covered all of the American sectors of Berlin, including the Wall, the airport where we conducted the Berlin Air Lift, the city, and the residential areas.

We were asked if we'd like to accompany one of the US Army Patrols through East Berlin. All the others declined, but since this would probably be my last chance to go into the area, I accepted. The Patrol Leader/driver picked me up and we proceeded to Check Point Charlie, the only entrance available into the East by Americans. We spent two full hours driving around in East Berlin.

The first impression was the damage from WWII that was evident everywhere we went. The store fronts were practically bare and had just a name and there were very few cars on the streets. The people all wore old clothing and they never looked you in the eye. The Patrol Leader/driver was well informed on East Berlin and was a wonderful tour guide. He went down embassy row, pointing out the rubble piles that had once been the Embassy show places of the world. We went to the bunker where Hitler and Eva Braun committed suicide. It had been twenty-seven years since the end of WWII, but the drive back through Check Point Charlie was like leaving a war zone shortly after a battle and stepping into a modern American City. To me, that was the high- light of the four days spent in Berlin. We traveled back through East Germany at night with all the windows covered.

I was designated as a delegate of the Pathfinder Chapter of the Association of the US Army to attend the Association meeting in October in Washington, DC. The delegates from Germany flew on a Chartered Flight from Frankfort to New York. We changed planes and flew on to Dulles International Airport on October 8th and checked into the Sheraton Park Hotel for five days. I attended all the meetings, luncheons, receptions, and dinners at the expense of the Association.

Here I ran into an abuse case between a senior officer and female NCO. In visiting the hospitality rooms of various units and while looking for friends and past acquaintances, I met a SFC WAC from Fort Gordon. She remembered me from a luncheon that she and her husband and I had attended in Fort Gordon. She asked me if she could discuss a problem that had arisen since her arrival in Washington that morning. I said sure and we moved over to a quiet corner away from the other guests.

She spoke softly and said, "That Colonel you were just talking to told me that he's coming to my room tonight and I don't know what to do."

I knew the Colonel was an alcoholic from past meetings with him and after seeing him here, I could tell that he was well on the way now. I asked her to tell me how all this happened. He'd told her that he was coming to her room and when she objected, he said, "Why the hell do you think I brought you along on this trip?"

He was in charge of room assignments and issued the keys, so he had a key to her room. I told her I could help her, but she'd have to trust me and do just as I say.

I said, "I have a room with two beds. You can sleep there but first, you must call your husband and tell him what has happened and explain to him who I am. And if the Colonel asks who I am, just tell him that I am a family friend protecting you while you are away from your husband. I'm sure he'll let your husband know as soon as both of you return. Tell your husband to tell him that he knew you had to stay in my room to get away from him and you were lucky that a friend of the family was available when needed and he will provide an affidavit stating that you were being harassed by him." She spent four nights there and was always in bed when I came in and gone when I awoke in the morning. I saw the Colonel a couple of times, but he just gave me a dirty look and didn't speak.

After I returned to Fort Gordon waiting for retirement, I called the SFC and had lunch with her and her husband. He said that when the Colonel returned from Washington, he called him in and said, "I have some bad news for you. Your wife slept with a Sergeant Major while she was in Washington."

He said he looked the Colonel in the eye and said, "Yes, I know. He's a friend of the family who was keeping you from attacking her."

The Colonel started turning red. He then told the Colonel that if he ever made any further abusive remarks to his wife again, he was going to his CO and press charges. He also told the Colonel that the Sergeant Major has agreed to testify at his court-martial. By then, the Colonel looked pale green and dismissed him in a very weak voice. After that, I felt like saying "chalk up another good deed for the Sergeant Major Corps."

After the meeting, I had a seven-day leave, so I flew to SC and visited both our families. Since my mother and father died, coming home had lost a lot of its excitement. I flew back to Washington to spend a couple of days with one of Marian's nephews, Louis Rimrodt, who lived in Arlington, VA and worked at the Patent Office in Washington. When he went to work, I caught a cab to the Smithsonian and spent two full days there and still didn't manage to cover it all. We'd meet after he got off work and he'd show me around Washington. He was not only a good tour guide, but a wonderful host. I thoroughly enjoyed my time with him and my stay in Washington.

In December I forwarded a request to the CSM Branch at the Pentagon requesting a month curtailment of my overseas tour. That would get me back in August instead of the middle of September and would allow Kevin to start his senior year of high school with the rest of his class.

As usual, we were still attempting to improve troop morale, so the Mess Sergeant, Motor Sergeant, and First Sergeants decided to have a Christmas party for all the dependents and any of the soldiers who wished to attend. Every family was invited to have lunch in the mess hall with the troops. We had a large, decorated Christmas tree that reached to the ceiling and the mess hall was also beautifully decorated. All the NCOs and Officers had chipped in to buy presents for each child attending and fruit baskets for the families. It started snowing as we were finishing lunch and that added to the holiday spirits.

The party started after lunch with recorded Christmas Music and a sing along with some of the "all-time Christmas favorites." Santa Claus arrived riding on a WWII armored car along with snow flakes about the size of silver dollars. The party was a great success, especially due to the efforts of MSG Hernden, the Motor Sergeant who played Santa Clause and provided the armored car, and SFC Hass and his cooks for their tireless efforts.

COL Slavish pressed us to put a Bar to Enlistment on NCOs who failed to perform their duties properly. We had a SFC report to B Troop for duty as a Squad Leader. I met him when he arrived and gave him an orientation of the Squadron and local area as I did for each newly assigned enlisted man. I also had a quarterly welcoming dinner for new NCOs.

I unfortunately seated him and his spouse next to me. I sat through two hours of her telling me that he could walk on water, how he would make CSM and that she wanted me to move him to Squadron Headquarters as my assistant. I told her that Sergeant Majors didn't have assistants. 1SG Harris had informed me early on that the new SFC was, in fact, a real dud. When they went to the field, he went on sick call. He had many letters of indebtedness and always had other things to do instead of running his Squad. Once he went to Heidelberg on sick call, so 1SG Harris asked him to visit a member of his Squad who was hospitalized there. Upon being discharged from the hospital, the man returned to his troop, where the unit had received a letter of indebtedness on him. 1SG Harris called him in and found that he had sent money with his Squad Leader to pay the debt. The SFC was called in and asked about the money. Apparently, he had paid one of his own debts with the money instead of paying the private's debt. His explanation was that a letter on the private would not look as bad for the private as one on a NCO and he had intended to pay the private's debt on payday.

1SG Harris and I decided this would be a good time to see if Brigade would fully support a letter on an NCO. 1SG Harris submitted the forms and letter to me with times of counseling attached on Friday morning. I wrote the Squadron endorsement and had the personnel NCO get it typed. I hand carried it to Brigade at noon.

1SG Harris informed me the next morning at reveille that he was in the Coleman Barracks Senior NCO Club Annex on Friday night. This particular NCO was on duty and his wife came into the club alone. A few minutes later the Brigade CO came in. They talked for a few minutes and left the club together. After about two hours, they returned to the club for a couple of minutes before leaving in their separate cars.

We weren't sure exactly what was happening, but we found out about 9:00 AM. The Brigade CSM called us to report to him immediately. When we arrived, he told us not to ask any questions and handed us each a copy of orders dated March 13, 1973. I was to report to the 5th Battalion, 68th Armor as CSM, and 1SG Harris was to report to the 3rd Battalion, 68th Armor as a 1SG. We were to report to our new units prior to noon that day and were also informed by CSM Anderson that we could clear Post the following week.

After I had been in the Battalion for about a week and had poked my nose into all the barracks and cubby holes, I told the CO that we had a serious drug problem. He wanted to know how I could tell. I asked him to accompany me through one of the barracks. The barracks consisted of two- and four-men rooms. Due to the high incidence of theft, the men were allowed to keep the doors to their rooms locked. We went to the front entrance of a barracks and I stopped and told the CO to take a deep breath and tell me what he smelled. He said it was a kind of sweet smokey smell. He didn't recognize it as pot. When I told him what it was he seemed surprised.

We went back to his office and discussed what should be done about it. I recommended that we conduct a surprise shakedown of one barracks in each company selected at random. The Company CO was informed and he had a formation of one Platoon and escorted the men from one room at a time into their rooms. We found drugs and drug paraphernalia in every room. After that, we had a shake down of the entire Battalion at one time.

Since the First Platoon shakedown, most of the men had gotten rid of their drug supplies in their rooms. Drugs at that time were as bad if not worse than in Vietnam and this contributed greatly to the low morale and created severe disciplinary problems.

CSM Glenn H. Towe [Ret'd]

CSM Towe directing air traffic in the Central Highlands, VN. We had three operations going at once with a lotb of confusion as to what helicopter went where. I was traffic controller for two days. November1968.

My replacement came aboard the end of March, so I was killing time waiting for a port call. In April, I received an assignment to the 101st Airborne Division, Camp Campbell, KY as a Battalion CSM. I knew that I wasn't going airborne this late in my career and especially putting up with the crap of being a leg in a jump battalion. I would have completed thirty years in November, so I decided this would be a good time to hang it up. I called the personnel SGM in Heidelberg and requested that I be retired in November instead of proceeding to the 101st Airborne. He told me to put in my retirement papers and he'd recommend approval and forward them to Washington with assignment to Fort Gordon where I would serve until my retirement on November 30, 1973.

In May I was again chosen as a delegate for the Pathfinders Chapter of the Association of the US Army. This trip was with the Division CSM to Garmish, Germany for five days. I always enjoyed going to Garmish ever since I visited there while going to school in Oberammergau in 1954.

On June 13 I received orders to report to Fort Gordon, GA for retirement and on the 20th, I received a port call for 3 July. I cleared Post and we packed our bags and proceeded to Frankfort. Upon arrival there on 2 July, we checked into the Rhine Main Motel. We flew from Frankfort with a two-hour stop in Shannon, Ireland and arrived in Charleston, SC at 8:30 AM on the 4th of July. I rented a car, picked up our luggage and drove to Mary Lou's in Seneca, SC arriving at approximately 5:00 PM.

We visited all the relatives for a few days and then Marian and I drove down to Augusta to check on the house. Upon arrival, we found the house was not rented and was in a deplorable condition with broken windows, stained carpets, holes in the wall, and doors kicked off the hinges. All the faucets were leaking and the bathtub looked as if it hadn't been cleaned since we moved out three years ago.

On leaving three years before, I had gone to Post Housing and gotten the name of an agent who handled rental properties. I agreed with him that he was to make the monthly payments and keep up the maintenance on the house and he could keep the remainder of the rent for his services. I knew that I had to pay a couple of months rent while I was gone.

When we got to his office, he told me the house wasn't rented and I found out that he had set the rent too high to keep it rented. He reported that the last renters had moved out without paying and he hadn't had time to clean it up before I arrived. He also told me that he didn't think I was returning until September. I asked him what the hell he'd been doing for the last three years to let the house get in this condition. His face turned red and I answered the question for him, evidently, not a damned thing.

I had talked with my next door neighbor prior to calling him and she had told me the type of people he had rented to and the rent he was charging. The house payment was supposed to be $90.00 a month and he was renting for $250.00 to $350.00 per month. He started telling me all he planned to do and I stopped him cold and told him that he had already done enough for me and with the mess he made I didn't want any additional help from him.

Then I told him what I planned to do. I said I'm going to the Post Housing Office and file a report on you and recommend that you be barred from doing business on Post. I don't want another GI to go through this mess. He started begging me not to do that and said he'd fix up my house. I told him he should have thought of that earlier.

I went to the Post Housing Office and filed a report requesting that they bar him from the Post. They informed me that this was not the first report on him and they'd take the necessary action to bar him. I found out a few days later that they had removed his Post privileges.

On August 6th, I reported to The US Army Garrison, Fort Gordon for duty while waiting for my retirement. I asked the 1SG what he had for me and he told me that all the Company did was keep me on the morning report and I belonged to the Post CSM. The Post CSM was CSM Buford Brown. He and I made CSM on the same orders in May 1968. I hadn't seen him since I departed for Vietnam in June 1968. We had coffee and caught up on our travels and families since we had seen each other. He said that I could get ready for my retirement because he didn't have a job for me.

He had received a call that morning that another CSM was being assigned to the Post and he didn't even have a slot for him. This was good news for me as it would give me time to finish the repair work I had started on the house while on leave. He got my phone number and said he would call if he needed me and to stop by for a cup of coffee if I came on Post.

I ended my service in the US Army on 30 November with a total of thirty years service and was placed on the retired list and transferred to the Retired Reserve on December 1, 1973. After retiring, I reflected back over my years of service and gave a lot of thought to my many accomplishments, the awards, and promotion to the highest enlisted rank. The two events that I remember with the most personal satisfaction and gratification were number one: training my Platoon in I Company, 5th Regimental Combat Team, Hawaii for our eventual combat mission during the Korean War and the manner in which the Platoon performed as a well-trained combat rifle Platoon with high morale, strict discipline, and esprit de corps. The next accomplishment on my list was taking an alcoholic NCO, an NCO who rode the sick book, and one who was overweight along with castoffs, Section 8s, and 208s from other Platoons and Companies in the 1st Battle Group, 3rd Infantry Division, and competing against all the other rifle Platoons in the Battle Group. We came in second place in the overall scoring. Both of the above events were accomplished without the benefit of a Platoon Leader. It was my sole responsibility and I completed it with a sense of great satisfaction and pride.

I knew that I needed something to keep me busy after I retired so I started to look for a job. I thought I wanted to work in an auto supply room so I went out to see a friend of mine. He said that it was a good job and I asked him about time off. When he said they got one Saturday a month off and two weeks vacation and each of those depended on how busy the dealership was, I told him thanks, but I'd be better off staying in the Army.

Then I started looking for part-time work and found an ad that stated part-time worker needed, good with tools, preferably some one who is retired. I called and went to see Olie Redd who was just getting started in the "Handyman Service." I liked Olie and enjoyed working for him except for one thing, he always did everything on the double, never slowing down and couldn't tolerate staying on a job over two or three hours. This was okay except when he got paint jobs. I hated to paint and told him so. He wanted me to buy 49% of the business and then he planned to expand the operation. I told him no, that I didn't want to be tied down all the time. Besides, he never took any time off and if I owned half of the business, I'd feel obligated to work as many hours as he did. That would halt my golf and ski trips and I'd be back in the same situation as I was when I retired.

I was approached by a friend of mine from the Georgia Railroad Bank. He was a vice president and wanted me to work as a public-relations officer with Fort Gordon in the Augusta area. I explained that my drinking the past several years had gotten to the point where I'd be rather reticent to do that kind of work. I just might have one too many when the urge hit me and end up embarrassing both of us. Also I didn't want to get tied down to where I had to stay on a schedule.

As for the drinking, when I returned to Augusta for retirement, I never went back to the NCO Club. That was when I broke my beer-drinking habit. I still have an occasional beer or a glass of wine with dinner, but it's been twenty-five years since my last hangover. I can truthfully say I went to work with a hangover occasionally, but during my entire service I never had a drink in the morning before going to work.

CSM Towe near Bametuet, VN, on the way to Tuy Hoa to visit 3rd Brigade patients in the Air Base Hospital. Also to visit my brother, Andy, who is stationed there in the Air Force. December 13, 1968.

CSM Glenn H. Towe [Ret'd]

In December I joined the Fort Gordon Retired Golf Association and the Augusta Chapter of the Crescent Ski Council and held offices in both. I was the Tournament Chairmen of the Golf Association and Vice President of the Ski Club. I was an active participant in both sports for a number of years. During the next eight years, I was between a ten and fourteen handicap golfer. I haven't played now in about three years, but I shot a seventy-nine next to my last round. In June of 1977, I played thirty-one rounds of golf in a five-state area.

I skied all the major resorts in Colorado, but most of my time was spent on the slopes in NC, VA, WV, GA, and TN. One winter I skied over forty days and didn't go out west once.

In 1974 Mr. Redd found a partner for his business and I started my own Handyman Service. I never advertised and all my business came by word of mouth. In just a few months, I had more work than I could handle. I tried to hire some help, but the part-time workers I got were more trouble than they were worth. I decided that if I couldn't do the job by myself, I turned it down. I did the small jobs that nobody else wanted. They all wanted to build an addition or a major repair. I refurbished bathrooms from a new sub-floor, tile work, and installed new fixtures for lighting and did the same for kitchens. The only painting I did was what I built, other than spray-painting a couple of houses for friends. I hung drapes, curtains, blinds, and repaired windows and rotted woodwork, children's swings, and most anything else that could go wrong in a house.

During this ten-year period I made enough money from my business and golf to pay for my vices. We lived on my retirement pay and banked Marian's salary. She worked not only as an Executive Secretary for a Civic Center Manager, but also for the headman of a stove manufacturing company and both paid well.

I was only called a "sandbagger" once and that was while I was in Bamberg, Germany. Jim Legg and I played the course at Montieth Barracks in Nuremberg when we had time. The 1SG of Headquarters Company had played with us a few times. He had a new putter and driver he wanted to try out so we invited him to come along. We had always played nickel and dime, but this time he wanted to play a quarter a hole with double for birds and triple for an eagle. Jim was a better golfer than I was and I was shooting to an eleven or twelve handicap. He explained to the 1SG that he was better than either one of us and that I'd normally beat him.

The 1SG still insisted the new clubs would make up the difference. Jim and I were both as hot as firecrackers on the 4th of July on the front nine. Jim had two birds and an eagle and I had three birds with all of ours coming on different holes and we halved the other three holes shutting him out. We went on to the club house for a drink and waited for him to join us. He came over to the table and threw our money down and said, "You two are nothing but sandbaggers and I'll never play with you again."

Glenda moved to Panama City, FL and Kevin went to Murfreesboro, TN to live so that left Marian and me alone. We spent about half of our time with them along with a lot of time with our folks in SC. I'd go on a golfing or ski trip and she'd travel around with Marie Scott, a friend of hers in Augusta. Between all of this activity, I continued to run my business. Some weeks I worked sixty or eighty hours and others none. That was the reason I didn't get tied down on a regular job.

In 1982 Marian and I began talking about going back to SC to live. All of our families were getting older and in relatively bad health. For us it was no trouble to travel back and forth the one hundred and thirty-five miles between Augusta and Walhalla, but for any of them to come to Augusta, they had to plan for months ahead where we could be on the road in less than an hour.

In January 1983 we started looking for a house in or near Walhalla. By March we bought an old stone house and I started remodeling it. We moved the last of our possessions from Augusta in October. The house in Augusta finally sold in February 1984. The house we bought was a two-story stone house with an attic, a basement, and a detached garage. Marian started having breathing problems and difficulty with the stairs, so we decided to build a house. We finally settled on a lot about two hundred yards from the house where we were married in 1951.

I went into a hundred-fifty-plus-year-old forest with an axe and chain saw to clear a housing site. I cut one oak there that I measured out and it could be sawed into an oak beam 12 X 12 inches and forty feet long. I hated to cut it, but it was in the middle of the bedroom so it had to go. I built a 20X36-foot shop before starting the house. I contracted the house, but did a lot of the work myself involving the wiring, lighting, and drainage systems. We moved into the new house on Labor Day, 1990 and continued to improve on the yard and area for the next ten years when we were home. In 1997 Marian got to the point that she could no longer work in the yard due to her breathing difficulties.

In 1996 I joined the Combat Infantrymen's Association and in September, Howard R. Head from Walhalla became the National Commander and asked me if I'd help him get it organized. I said I'd give it a good try for ninety days and see what I could do with it. I was appointed National Adjutant seven years ago and I'm still with it as National Chief of Staff.

Yesterday I was seventy-eight years old and as I look back I have no regrets about my life. I enjoyed my military service immensely. It gave a poor boy from the Great Depression the opportunity to travel and see a lot of places and be involved in three wars that I could never have done in any other profession. I was blessed in finding a wonderful wife who agreed to travel with me wherever I was assigned. We have two wonderful children whom we love dearly and who love us in return.

This past December, I finally reached a major milestone. After thirty years of active duty, I'd been retired from the military service for the same number of years. I am still active in the community and in most of the veterans' organizations. I am a Charter Member of the local Purple Heart Chapter, the Oconee County Veterans' Council, and an active member of the local American Legion Post.

I organized or helped conduct the past five Veterans' Day Parades and was the keynote speaker for Veterans' Day and Memorial Day Ceremonies and many other occasions. My firm belief is that you should give something back to your community and staying active will keep you healthy and young. I believe in that simple rule with all my heart.